Acknowledgments

We gratefully recognize the ideas and concepts drawn from Michael J. Croasdaile, whose own practical bent gave us the original inspiration to develop this approach.

We owe special thanks to our co-worker, Scott Seely, an author in his own right, for coding and testing the Visual C++ 6.0 case study. Be sure to check out Scott's book, *Windows Shell Programming For C++ and MFC Developers*.

We thank our employer, Stratagem, Inc., for providing us opportunities of education, research, and practical experience in this arena.

We thank our spouses and children for allowing us the time away to create this book.

Last, but not least, we thank each other for the tolerance to explore ideas, the absolutely inspired collaboration, and the commitment to make this book happen.

Contents

Preface xi
Introduction xv

Part I: A No-Fluff Approach to Getting It Done 1

Chapter 1   Object-Oriented Development 3
   Overview 3
   The Need for Object-Oriented Solutions 3
   The Basics of Object-Oriented Theory 7
      Class 8
      Abstraction 8
      Encapsulation 8
      Inheritance 9
      Aggregation 9
      Polymorphism 9
      Object Types 10
   Introducing the Unified Modeling Language 11
      Stereotypes, Comments, and Constraints 13
      Use Case Diagram 13
      Class Diagram 15
      Sequence Diagram 17
      Statechart Diagram 19
      Collaboration Diagram 20
      Activity Diagram 22
      Component Diagram 24
      Deployment Diagram 25
      Package Diagram 26
   Chapter Summary 27

Chapter 2   Introduction to Our Approach 29
   Overview 29
   Focus on Deliverables 34
   The Iterative Style 35
   General Techniques 42

v

Contents

    Facilitation. 42
    Project Management. 44
    Change Control Management 46
    Issue Management. 47
    Training 47
    Documentation 48
    Infrastructure 48
    Testing 49
Evolving Roles That Champion Business Change 51
    Role Definitions 52
        Business Area Expert 53
        Database Architect. 54
        Document Architect 54
        Infrastructure Architect 54
        Object Architect 55
        Object Developer 55
        Project Manager 55
        Project Sponsor 55
        Trainer 55
        User 56
Chapter Summary 56

Part II: The Approach. 57
Overview. 58
Depth of Object Modeling at Various Levels of Development 58
Demonstration of the Approach with a Case Study 60

Chapter 3   Chart Solution. 61
Overview. 61
Activities. 62
    Establish Project Scope 62
        Define Problem Assessment 62
        Create Initial Use Case Diagram 66
        Create Initial Class Diagram 72
        Establish Documentation Approach 74
        Establish Training Approach 75
        Explore Infrastructure Architecture Options 76
        Establish Project Standards 78
    Plan Solution Packaging and Delivery. 78
        Develop Solution Area Scope Statement 79
        Tailor Approach 84
        Estimate Tasks in Project Plan 85
        Apply Resources to Project Plan 86

	Prepare the Cost/Benefit Analysis	88
	Confirm Solution Strategy	90
	Obtain Solution Strategy Confirmation	91
	Assess Risk	91
	Chapter Summary	94
Chapter 4	**Structure Solution**	95
	Overview	95
	Activities	96
	Structure Use Cases and Classes	96
	Refine Use Case Descriptions	97
	Structure Class Diagram	100
	Select Reusable Classes from Class Library	108
	Structure Documentation	109
	Structure User Instructions Guide Framework	110
	Structure Information Reference Guide Framework	110
	Structure Training	111
	Structure Training Curriculum	111
	Specify Training Delivery Mechanism	112
	Structure Infrastructure Architecture	113
	Specify Infrastructure Requirements	115
	Develop Conceptual Deployment Diagrams	118
	Evaluate Third-Party Software	122
	Establish Infrastructure Acquisition Timeline	125
	Establish Software Distribution Procedure	126
	Specify Security Restrictions for Solution	127
	Implement Deployment Diagram for Development	128
	Train Project Team	129
	Plan Iteration Refinement Strategy	129
	Specify Iteration Refinement and Duration	129
	Confirm Solution Structure	131
	Obtain Solution Structure Confirmation	131
	Assess Risk	132
	Chapter Summary	133
Chapter 5	**Build Solution**	135
	Overview	135
	Activities	136
	Model the Solution	136
	Build Use Case Scenarios	137
	Build Sequence Diagrams from Use Case Scenarios	142
	Leverage Reusable Classes from the Class Library	145
	Prototype User Interface Applications	146
	Build Statechart Diagrams from Sequence Diagrams	153

Build Collaboration Diagrams 156
Build Activity Diagrams 158
Assess Class Diagram 160
Build Component Diagram 168
Create Use Case Test Plan 169
Refine Database Structure 171
Create Logical Data Model 173
Create Solution Area Database Structure 175
Build Application 180
Create Collaboration Test Plan 181
Create Collaboration Test Beds 182
Build Methods 183
Execute Collaboration Test Plan 195
Build Documentation 195
Build Documentation Components 195
Build Training Material 198
Refine Training Curriculum 198
Confirm Solution Build 200
Create Use Case Test Beds 200
Validate Use Case Scenarios 200
Confirm Usability of the Documentation Components 201
Confirm Content of the Training Curriculum 201
Prepare Build Solution Change Requests 201
Obtain Solution Build Confirmation 203
Assess Risk 204
Build Solution Iterations 204
Second Iteration 205
Third Iteration 214
Second Increment 216
Chapter Summary 221

Chapter 6   **Integrate Solution** 223
Overview 223
Activities 225
Integrate Solution Areas 225
Integrate Class Diagrams 225
Integrate Database Structures 230
Modify Application for Integration 231
Refine Implementation Diagrams 232
Enhance Component Diagram 232
Create and Integrate Deployment Diagram 233
Build Operations Guide 240
Integrate Documentation 241

Contents

    Standardize User Instructions Guide 242
    Standardize Information Reference Guide 242
    Standardize Documentation Distribution Procedure 242
  Integrate Training 242
    Modify Training for Integration. 242
    Transform Training Curriculum into Training Support Materials . . 243
  Integration Test the Solution 243
    Create Integration Test Plan 243
    Build Integration Test Beds 245
    Prepare Integration Environment for Testing 245
    Integration Test the Application 246
  Confirm Solution Integration 246
    Obtain Solution Integration Confirmation 246
    Assess Risk 246
 Chapter Summary 247

Chapter 7   **Implement Solution**. 249
 Overview. 249
 Activities 250
  Prepare Implementation Environment 250
    Plan Implementation Schedule 250
  Implement Infrastructure Architecture. 252
    Implement Supporting Architecture 252
  Train Users 253
    Schedule Training Participants 253
    Implement Deployment Diagram for Training 254
    Prepare for Training Sessions 255
    Train Users 255
  Implement Application 256
    Back Up Implementation Database 256
    Implement Database and Application Components 257
    Back Up Converted Database 257
  Confirm Solution Implementation 258
    Support Implementation 258
    Obtain Feedback for the Post-Implementation Document 259
    Obtain Solution Implementation Confirmation 261
    Assess Risk 261
 Chapter Summary 262

Conclusion 263
 Highlights of This Approach 263
 Selling This Approach to Your Enterprise 264

Contents

Deliverables Glossary. 265
Bibliography 275
Index 277

Preface

When we first endeavored to understand object-oriented development, we read the usual books, subscribed to the typical newsgroups on the Internet, and read many publications. We found great volumes of information inapplicable for the average, chaotic pace of software development. Mostly, it was too theoretical for our taste. Each author had a different slant on what constituted object modeling, often with differing diagrams and definitions representing the same concept. We decided what this industry needed was a good five-cent guide (well, OK, inflation ruined a perfectly good cliché) that applied the sound principles of object-oriented thinking to the development of business solutions.

This book provides a systematic approach to object-oriented development using an iterative style. Additionally, we include how other vocations involved with the object-oriented development process (such as project management, documentation, testing, training, and infrastructure) interact during a development project.

We believe an approach should be flexible enough to allow customizing it for a specific use. If the level of formality is stifling, it manifests itself in the delivered system. The great architect Louis Henry Sullivan once said, "Form ever follows function." This also applies to developing systems. If the approach is too rigid, the final product will also be too rigid. The greatest need in any depiction of a business is flexibility. This is true whether we are referring to the analysis, the design, or the "programmed" solution. Businesses must remain responsive to the ever-changing influences of day-to-day operation. We feel our approach is complete. It covers many areas not typically included in an approach. However, please feel free to customize and adapt it to your own culture. We prefer that you use some of our approach, rather than none at all—oatmeal is better than no meal.

Preface

Renowned object methodologists Ivar Jacobson, James Rumbaugh, and Grady Booch have significantly contributed to the harmonious integration of the varying object-oriented notations and semantics with their submission of the Unified Modeling Language (UML) to the Object Management Group (OMG). The Unified Modeling Language is a best practices model specification that defines the notations and semantics for object-oriented development. With its submission and subsequent approval in September 1997, many of the conflicting modeling styles merged and enhanced to provide common understanding. "The most recent updates on the Unified Modeling Language are available via the World Wide Web, www.rational.com/uml."[i] As of this writing, the OMG is updating the UML document set to a new release level, tentatively scheduled for mid-1999 and still pending.

The focus of the UML was not to necessarily standardize a process.[ii] We investigated the level of UML understanding in our field and found that most people do not have the time to sift through the semantics in order to produce an approach. You, like many others, may be asking yourself "How do I use this information?" and "How do these diagrams relate?" This book answers these and other commonly asked questions. Many books are simply prose about the UML notation set, for example, describing the model elements for a specific diagram. These books lack a practical direction on how to actually make the UML work. Most information technology professionals want to apply their years of experience to an approach that works best with a new technology. They need to understand both the basic concepts and the nuances inherent in the approach. To avoid this shortfall, we have included a clear, business-based case study that uses a single example from start to end.

Why is this book different? It is easy to understand, covers the full life cycle of development, and specifies the deliverables, roles, and techniques. We did not set out to create yet another modeling style. Rather, we leverage the modeling conventions found in the UML. We, like the UML authors, will continue to "promote a development process that is use-case driven, architecture-centric, and iterative and incremental."[iii]

Some object-oriented books omit the full life cycle of project development. With other books, business people may find they do not have the time to get past the jargon. This book is for you if you do not have the time to read those tomes of knowledge without falling asleep. Our hope is to reach the folks out in the trenches, those who are trying to deliver a system in a reasonable amount of time, while still fighting for quality and pride in their work. We show you what steps to go through when object modeling, how detailed to get during the life cycle of development, and what skills you need at each step.

This book assumes that you have a general, but not detailed, knowledge of object-oriented theory. The intended audience for this book is all information technology professionals—for people responsible for managing projects using object-oriented technology and for people responsible for structuring projects based on system uses and constraints. In other words, it covers project management, analysis, design, and implementation strategy. It will not teach you everything about the UML, nor will it teach you how to program in the language of the case study. Nevertheless, we do tie the two concepts together in an innovative approach to show you how to execute a project successfully.

Building upon our research and experience in the industry and charged with the attitude of "if not us, who?", this is the result. We sincerely hope that it is of benefit to you.

See you on the next iteration!

---

i Rational Software Corporation, et al. *UML Summary version 1.1*. N.p. September 1, 1997, pp. ii.
ii Ibid., 5.
ii Ibid.

Introduction

We have split this book into two parts. Part I is for those unfamiliar with object-oriented concepts or the iterative style. We do not cover detailed object theory, but rather distill the absolute minimum to get started. Part II is our approach for surviving an object-oriented project, complete with a case study illustrating a fictitious project from beginning to end. We represent project deliverables throughout the case study.

Part I: A No-Fluff Approach to Getting It Done

These chapters provide grounding in the basics of object-oriented concepts and discuss our slant on applying the iterative style to the object development process.

Chapter 1: Object-Oriented Development

This chapter discusses the need for using an object-oriented approach and presents a brief overview of object-oriented concepts and terminology. We examine why an object-oriented approach enables the current competitive impact of deploying on the Internet. The chapter also includes an introduction to the Unified Modeling Language (UML), explaining the need for its creation and its role in all future object-oriented development. We describe the traceability inherent between the diagrams, as well as illustrate and define the notation specific to each diagram.

Chapter 2: Introduction to Our Approach

We present an overview of our approach to object-oriented development applying the iterative style of development and its benefits in today's project life cycle. We differentiate our approach with a focus on deliverables, rather than tasks. The goal of completing the deliverables defines the essential process. We discuss how deliverables produced by typically disparate vocations (project management, documentation, testing, training, and infrastructure) not only coexist and support each other, but also are naturally intertwined to develop a complete solution. We define iteration and increments, and their natural fit with object-oriented development. We summarize general techniques used throughout the approach.

This chapter also examines the types of skills required to make the project succeed and groups those skills into the roles that people assume during solution development. It provides the purpose of each role needed to employ the techniques and produce the deliverables. We promote integrated teams with vocation-related responsibilities that interact to develop a complete business solution. Although each has its unique characteristics, each depends on the others for the team to attain success.

Part II: The Approach

These chapters show how to fulfill an entire project life cycle illustrated with a case study. We describe each task with the roles, responsibilities, and the techniques to apply it. We group tasks by activity and group activities by iterative phases. Within each phase, we explain the depth of modeling required before moving on to the next. We separate each of the five phases of the approach into its own chapter. The general structure of each task begins with the roles and their participation, followed by relevant technique-oriented discussion. Additionally, we provide a case study component to illustrate each technique.

Chapter 3: Chart Solution

The Chart Solution chapter describes how to assess the business problem, set the project scope using object modeling, identify requirements, and plan the project strategy. We present how to frame the business situation with modeling to lay groundwork for the solution.

Chapter 4: Structure Solution

The Structure Solution chapter describes how to refine object models to understand the work required for building a solution. We suggest ways to segment the solution to produce subsystems in parallel and build from the core outward. We describe how to detail the project plan for iterative and incremental development.

Chapter 5: Build Solution

The Build Solution chapter describes how to finalize object models for application creation through iteration. We discuss steps for building the various solution deliverables including the application, the database, the documentation, and the training materials.

Chapter 6: Integrate Solution

The Integrate Solution chapter describes how to merge multiple subsystems developed in parallel with the current released version of the solution.

Chapter 7: Implement Solution

The Implement Solution chapter describes how to deploy the solution for version release and obtain confirmation of a completed solution.

Conclusion

The Conclusion summarizes the topics presented in the book and suggests ways to adopt the approach in your enterprise.

Deliverables Glossary

The Deliverables Glossary provides descriptions of all the deliverables identified in the approach.

Part 1

A No-Fluff Approach to Getting It Done

Included in This Part:

Chapter 1: Object-Oriented Development
Chapter 2: Introduction to Our Approach

Overview

Part I is comprised of two chapters. Both chapters set the backdrop for presenting the approach in Part II. We introduce object-oriented concepts and present our view of what successful iterative development entails. We propose why object-oriented techniques are important and how the iterative style adapts to the object development process.

If unfamiliar with object-oriented (OO) concepts, we recommend reading Chapter 1 before proceeding to the other chapters! Topics in this chapter include: brief descriptions of the more common terms used in OO, introduction to the Unified Modeling Language (UML), reasons to use the object-oriented style, and the trend towards Internet solutions underscoring the need for OO.

Chapter 2 succinctly defines incremental and iterative development and explains how we applied these concepts in developing our approach. We highlight the need to concentrate on delivery of project components, the "deliverables," and not as much on the process itself. After all, the ultimate goal is to produce a solution and not be tangled up in the journey. We also present general techniques used throughout the approach.

Finally, we examine skill qualifications necessary for project success and define the specific roles used throughout the approach. A complete project team encompasses skills beyond just object developers and architects. The roles we present include the vocations of project management, documentation, testing, training, and infrastructure. We also incorporate the business view roles of the Project Sponsor, Business Area Experts, and Users.

Chapter 1
Object-Oriented Development

Overview

This chapter discusses the need for applying object-oriented concepts when building business solutions. We discuss object-oriented basics and terminology to provide grounding for the concepts presented in this book. This includes class abstraction, encapsulation, scalability, reuse, inheritance, and polymorphism. We introduce the Unified Modeling Language (UML), explaining the need for its creation and its role in all future object-oriented development.

No current book on information technology would be complete without reference to the Internet. The impact of the Internet on application development is the single-most important change in business systems of the last decade. We explain why the Internet underscores the need to create solutions using an object-oriented approach. We highlight the special considerations required for applying the object-oriented style to Internet development.

The Need for Object-Oriented Solutions

Yesterday, the primary focus for information management was on centralized, operational systems. Today, focus switches to decentralized client/server systems. Tomorrow, the focus moves to decentralized, integrated systems that align fully with the strategic business model.

Early implementations of client/server systems relied on a two-tier architecture, that is, one server and at least one client. With two-tier, the client issues a message and waits for the server to return a message. Transactional processing in two-tier architectures is thus synchronous. This led to contention as the number of concurrent users increased. With two-tier architectures, either the client or the server must retain the synchronous information about the object the client is working with. This is known as maintaining object state. Maintaining object state affects performance and manageability. Putting too much object state management on the database server tends to build bottlenecks. Putting object state management on the client often requires upgrades to many machines.

One resolution to the bottleneck was to move more processing from the client into the database server using triggers and stored procedures, known as thin client/fat server. The typical problems of just applying stored procedures and triggers in a two-tier style drove system performance to an unacceptable level. The next response was further partitioning into a three-tier view, which separates out much of the application (non-database) functionality and places it on its own processing platform—the application server. It allows asynchronous implementation (i.e., no constant connection).

The purpose of three-tier partitioning is to ensure scalability, achieve stability, and localize change. This requires a flexible object approach that allows moving components around to optimize performance.

Today, the Internet provides an opportunity for global business relationships that are rapidly becoming an important means of business communications. It has evolved from merely publishing to conducting a considerable number of interactive business transactions.

Forecasts for information technology tell us that we need to be able to adapt quickly to business changes, something that IT professionals have been unable to accomplish historically. Enterprises must take advantage of the technology revolution, which is agile, virtual, global, and fast-evolving. They must react to events moving rapidly in new directions. "The best corporations reinvent themselves to put new ideas to work; the worst are left to fester in their disorganized mess."[1] Enterprises must minimize the time from originating the idea of a solution to enabling the actualization of that solution. There is a critical business need to adapt to the increasingly rapid change in technology trends and strategic business positioning.

It is no surprise that Internet-based applications are driving technology to a whole new level. The potentials of e-commerce as a major business trend make distributed deployment a necessity. This need must be addressed while architecting applications that will remain durable well into the next millennium. Internet applications must be self-contained

---

1 James Martin. "Cybercorp: A Business Revolution." In *DCI's Database & Client/Server World Conference Proceedings*, Vol. III, Chicago, IL, December 12, 1996, D35-3.

on the client machine and able to communicate with a diversity of data, behaviors, and sources. Because the Internet opens opportunities for communicating between enterprises, it also compounds the ways that information technology solutions must interact. The Internet requires multi-platform integration, high performance, high reliability, and scalability. Information technologists that do not make the paradigm shift to object-oriented modeling will not be able to respond to the rapidly changing needs of the business.

Internet solutions tend towards a customer focus and require greater reliability. If a customer is unable to connect to your web site and receive results in a reasonable amount of time, that customer will go elsewhere. Unlike an in-house solution, enterprises cannot reliably guess how many users will initially access their web site. Thus, designs must be able to scale with improved technologies to respond to an increasing user base.

The Internet gave birth to n-tier architecture. N-tier architecture typically adds a web server and a "thinner" client, the browser front end. This introduces a whole new tier strategy. Now, n-tier design must include the addition of the web server as a specific tier.

As with three-tier systems, objects are an obvious choice for the Internet because they are simple, natural, changeable, manageable, and leverageable. Using an object-oriented style allows you to deploy components efficiently to the appropriate processor based on proximity and operational requirements. A legacy application, users, or other related objects may determine proximity. Operational requirements include security considerations, platform configurations, or the need to operate in parallel with other components. Well-defined components can request information freely between processors because they are self-contained.

Older designs slow change because they cannot rapidly respond. A two- or three-tier architecture is unacceptable for Internet access. We must now design for flexible component deployment and use of multiple processors creating adaptable, scalable systems. This begs for an object approach to partitioning components and easily distributing them to appropriate processors.

The type of service an object provides makes transitioning to components simple. Classifying each object as interface, control, and entity isolates change to a "local" level roughly following the tier. This is called partitioning by style of service. Service styles may overlap within any one object, but the object should be most inclined to only one style. Interface objects typically reside on the client machine and are mostly concerned with the behavior of the graphical user interface (GUI). Control objects define the business domain and contain the bulk of the business rules. Entity objects only have the responsibility of shuttling data between the control objects and the database, thereby providing persistent storage and retrieval of objects. We discuss object types later in this chapter.

Three-tier partitioning can also minimize the number of simultaneous connections to the database. While the application server manages client use of the data, the database server coordinates the database connections for each subset of objects. All connections to the database reside in the database server.

The direction of the Internet is heading towards transactional processing. Similar to the challenges faced with the two-tier move to database servers, putting transaction-processing ability on the web server makes it a bottleneck, too. You must also consider a rollback strategy for undoing change when an error occurs. The Internet's infrastructure does not allow a typical rollback strategy, a two-phase commit, to exist naturally. This does not obviate or minimize the business need to deploy applications on the Internet. Technology overcomes these difficulties as it evolves. However, until the underlying architecture fundamentally changes, if ever, this remains another facet to incorporate in object deployment on the Internet.

In addition, the design of the Internet infrastructure forces an asynchronous connection; that is, there is no constant connection between any of the services, GUI, and application services. This is where maintaining state becomes critical. Strategies for maintaining state abound, but all try to fit a round peg in a square hole.

The answer to these challenges is to design flexible solutions using object modeling. What is object-oriented development all about and why should you make the paradigm shift? An object modeling approach acts as a communication vehicle for succinctly capturing business meaning and translating it into a technical solution. By using standard object-oriented notation, you significantly reduce the ambiguity between an object model and its supporting application code. You then have a higher probability that the resulting system naturally aligns with the business solution. Object modeling is the integral technique for creating robust designs of business domains, adaptable architectures, and reusable components. By adhering to these principles (regardless of the number of tiers), you have a better chance of success when creating user interface, database, and application components. Employing an object-oriented style fulfills this need by packaging together data and behavior for a specific aspect of the business. Those of you who in the past saw the merits of a well-structured data model that stood the test of time, can now imagine how to additionally structure data access and manipulation with object modeling. A well-modeled business domain provides the specifications for components that you can move around to appropriate processors, obtaining optimal performance without serious recoding. Major benefits of object modeling include that it:

- Provides a means to manage complexity,
- Minimizes the effects of change and increases stability,
- Speeds understanding,
- Encourages collaborative development,
- Helps clarify issues through graphical representation,
- Lowers the future cost of development by promoting reuse and reducing subsequent development time, and
- Sets the scope and forms the foundation for a technology solution.

Many organizations have still not adopted object-oriented techniques because information technology has been unable to meet the needs of object-oriented applications. The changing speed of business and the Internet are forcing the issue. You must design solutions that continuously change and find a way to make the technology perform.

What is missing, and strongly needed, is an understanding of the usefulness of object-oriented development for business and a consistent approach detailing how to model objects from a "top-down" view. Most organizations have no time to establish a formal approach that is specific, repeatable, and measurable. We share our approach with you in the remainder of this book.

The Basics of Object-Oriented Theory

To realize the benefits of object modeling, you need to apply fundamental object-oriented concepts while building your business solution. We briefly define these concepts.

Class

A class is an abstract entity that defines a name. It has attributes that describe its characteristics and operations that define its behaviors. A class may also have relationships to other classes.

The class is the template that holds the names of attributes and the methods that operate on the actual values stored in an object. The class, though, does not execute the code or change the variables. To accomplish this, you need to create an instance of the class, known as an object. A class may instantiate an object but not vice versa. You may create many objects from the class. Each instance, or object, maintains uniqueness between the many objects created from the class because it contains actual values. Each of those instances executes the same methods (the code that carries out the operation) and has the same attributes. This promotes reuse, a fundamental theme of object-oriented development.

Abstraction

Abstraction means you eliminate details to illustrate the main points of a concept. Abstraction hides data and operation detail through composite levels and inheritance typing to manage complexity. Applying this helps you develop object models in a layered fashion, adding details as discovered. Eventually, the details may become overwhelming. It is at this point that you begin to hide some of them to draw attention to the major concepts represented on the model. This is most relevant when applying inheritance and aggregation; you are able to discuss the superclass or composite without the distraction caused by subclasses and nested aggregates.

Encapsulation

Encapsulation is the packaging of related data and operations, thereby only allowing defined processes to expose the data. Encapsulation distinguishes what an object does (as defined by its interface) from how it does it (its methods or implementation).

Applying an object-oriented style encapsulates processing to minimize the effects of change. Correctly employing encapsulation isolates change, thereby affecting fewer software components than the use of a traditional approach. Minimizing the impact of change, while still effectively responding to it, should be the primary goal of all information technology professionals.

Inheritance

Inheritance uses the terms generalization/specialization to illustrate an "is a" or "kind of" relationship between a superclass and a subclass. Each class in a generalization/specialization relationship must be only one of the types; this represents an "or" relationship. Inheritance shows optionality between classes at the same level in a structure. Inheritance places common methods and attributes at a superclass level for use by all of its subclasses. That is, it allows a subclass to access the attributes and operations described in its superclass. An instance of a subclass is also an instance of all of its ancestor superclasses (those above it in the structure).

Aggregation

Aggregation means one class "has a" or "contains" component classes. Looking at this conversely, a subclass "is part of" a parent superclass. Aggregation represents the classes that make up the whole. The "part" class uses the behavior and data from the "whole" class. An aggregation is considered an "and" relationship to include all of the classes in the structure.

Polymorphism

Polymorphism uses the same operation name for operations that have a similar intent but whose methods differ by specific classes. Let us describe it using the "+" sign example. You can define an operation called "+" that adds together two like-type elements. These elements can be two numbers (1 + 3 = 4) or two character strings ("long" + "hair" = "longhair"). The method within the "+" operation determines the interpretation of the arguments passed. The sender of the arguments does not need to know the "+" method in the receiving class. Polymorphism makes the most sense within inheritance. A subclass may inherit the attributes and method of the operation in its superclass. The subclass then may add to (known as "overloading") or ignore unnecessary detail (known as "overriding") to support its distinctiveness.

To be truly polymorphic, the method has three features: the same name, the same operational intent, and the same signature. It is important to note that the operation name, although the same, may truly represent different ideas. We suggest renaming an operation if it logically differs in another domain. Examples such as "draw a shape" and "draw a gun," or "divide an integer" and "divide a pie" reveal that someone may misinterpret the meaning of these same name operations. We call this operational intent. The method (and its owning operation) must have the same signature. The signature is the name of the method followed by its arguments or parameters. Note that the number of arguments must match, but the argument types may be different.

Object Types

Objects easily categorize into types. We follow the ideas promoted by Ivar Jacobson, Magnus Christerson, Patrik Jonsson, and Gunnar Övergaard in their book *Object-Oriented Software Engineering*[2]. They promoted separating objects into three major types—interface, entity, and control. Many other approaches call these by different names, but we feel these capture the main concept. Understanding the distinction between them is extremely important for capturing the true behavior of the object. Note this sets the foundation for partitioning by style of service.

The interface object coordinates business events outside of the system with those within by making the thin break between the accessible features of the system and its internal workings. Interface objects may interact with other interface objects, entity objects, and control objects. An interface object generally triggers a control object that in turn addresses the contents of entity objects. The interface object may further classify into two types in the external world, user interface and system interface. The user interface object interacts with people using the system. Among its functions are presentation, navigation, and manipulation. The user interface object includes the windows, menus, buttons, and other components needed to communicate with the user. The system interface object communicates with other systems. It provides a gateway for exchanging data between two or more systems.

The entity object deals with persistent data storage (typically through the medium of a database using a database management system) whose values remain even after shutting down the system. Among its behaviors are accessing, updating, and creating objects.

---

2 Ivar Jacobson, Magnus Christerson, Patrik Jonsson, and Gunnar Övergaard. *Object-Oriented Software Engineering: A Use Case Driven Approach*. Wokingham, England: Addison Wesley, 1992.

The control object defines the business rules that regulate business functionality. The control object generally accesses multiple entity objects. The control object governs business transaction sequences, behavior that should not reside within an entity object. Among its functions are decision-making, policy enforcement, and resource coordination.

We reference these terms throughout this book. Our intent is not to provide you with yet another rehash of object theory but rather to give you a quick starting point. For pure object theory or a more detailed explanation of these concepts, please refer to any of the books found in the bibliography.

Introducing the Unified Modeling Language

This section provides you with an understanding of what the UML is and what it is not, the specific diagrams of the UML, and how the UML diagrams support business solutions.

The UML is a notation set for building object models. It is not, and does not assume to be, a methodology of how to use that notation set. It is the standard for communicating the meaning of object modeling diagrams throughout the industry. The various diagrams within the UML support multiple object modeling needs.

We illustrate the specific uses of each of these diagrams to obtain the correct level of detail based on the expertise of the participants and the goals of the tasks. For example, when establishing business requirements, you may only concentrate on high-level Use Case, Class, and Sequence Diagrams. Object modeling architects may use Class Diagrams for generating code and Collaboration Diagrams for prototyping. Furthermore, the level of detail of these models will vary from project to project depending on requirements of system use and risk factors. If an area has been previously unexplored or demands more attention, you may model more detail early on to confirm your understanding. Only then will you have the knowledge to create a truly remarkable solution. Although individually each object model helps to see the business solution from a distinct point of view, collectively the object models interrelate. Object diagrams maintain traceability, the ability to trace objects from analysis to design.[3]

---

3   Ivar Jacobson, Magnus Christerson, Patrik Jonsson, and Gunnar Övergaard. *Object-Oriented Software Engineering: A Use Case Driven Approach*. Wokingham, England: Addison Wesley, 1992, 80.

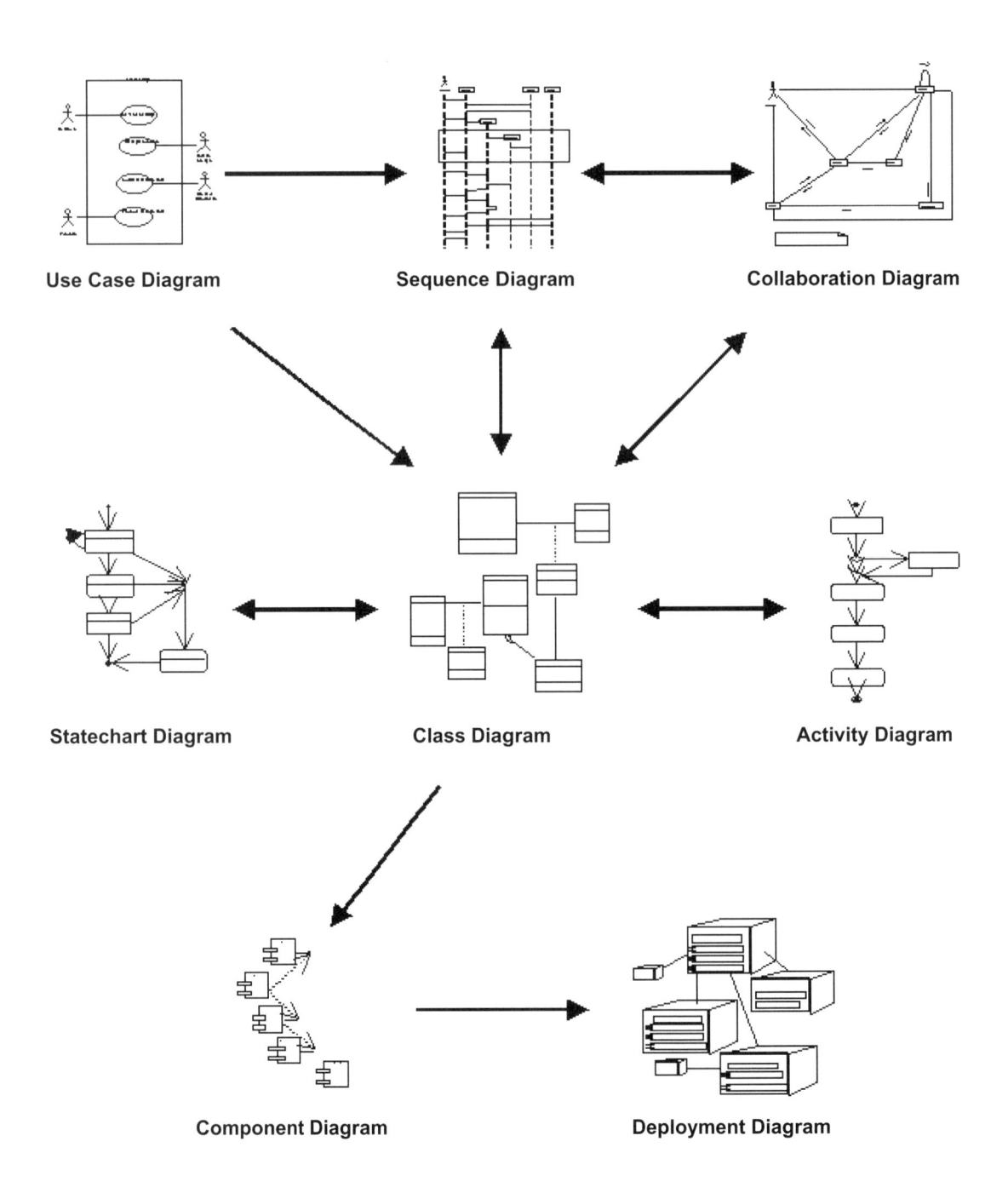

Use Case Diagram   Sequence Diagram   Collaboration Diagram

Statechart Diagram   Class Diagram   Activity Diagram

Component Diagram   Deployment Diagram

Figure 1-1—UML Roadmap

Figure 1-1—UML Roadmap shows how the UML diagrams interact with each other. We describe each of these diagrams and their notations below. We provide high-level summaries of each diagram that highlight the most commonly used features. For more detail, please refer to the complete set of UML specifications.[4]

Stereotypes, Comments, and Constraints

The UML does not pretend to cover every possible modeling situation. The authors of the UML have accommodated extensibility for these situations with stereotypes, comments, and constraints. Stereotypes are a modeling element shorthand to use when categorizing classes into commonly used types. A stereotype is enclosed within guillemets (<< >>). For example, a class designed to communicate with a user may be called a <<User Interface>>. Comments attach textual information to any model element. A comment is enclosed within a rectangle that has its upper right corner folded. Constraints are used to show further conditional meaning that prohibits behavior and is "...attached to a model element, not just to a view of it."[5] A constraint is enclosed within braces ({}). Use stereotypes, comments, and constraints to enhance understanding. We encourage you to be consistent with your defined usage; consistency increases clarity.

Use Case Diagram

The traceability of the UML diagrams begins with the use case. The Use Case Diagram initially sets the boundaries of the business solution. It is the primary mechanism to capture business requirements. The Use Case Diagram is a graphical depiction of use cases and the actors that participate in them. The Use Case Diagram documents external interactions with the system. This includes human, other system, and machine interactions. The Use Case Diagram identifies the expected uses of the system and the behavior needed to support these uses. In our approach, the Use Case Diagram in conjunction with the Class Diagram determines the boundaries for packaging a project into concurrently developed Solution Areas.

---

4 Rational Software Corporation, et al. *UML Summary version 1.1*. N.p. September 1, 1997.
5 Rational Software Corporation, et al. *UML Notation Guide version 1.1*. N.p. September 1, 1997, 16.

*Figure 1-2—
UML Notation
of the Use Case
Diagram*

Use Case Diagram

Actor1
<<actor>>

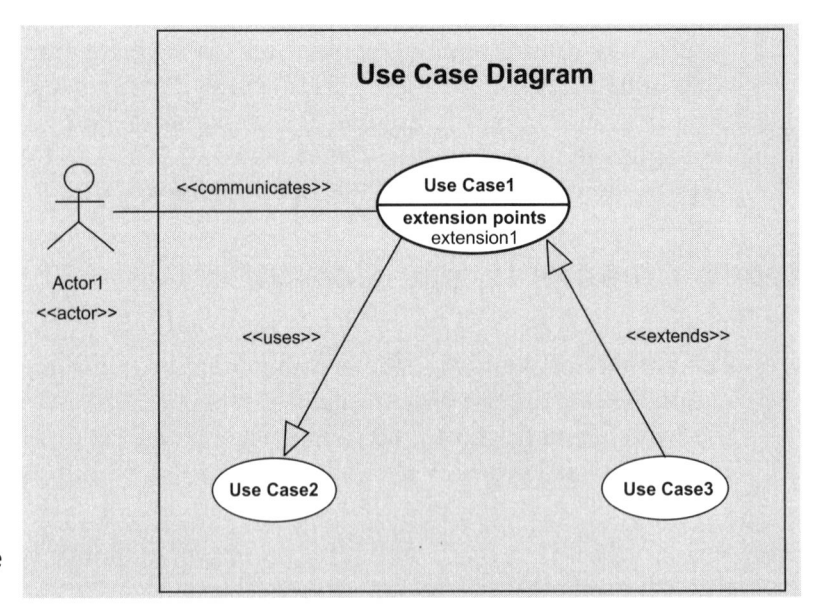

<<communicates>>

Use Case1
extension points
extension1

<<uses>>

<<extends>>

Use Case2

Use Case3

Every Use Case Diagram has at least one use case and one actor (see Figure 1-2—UML Notation of the Use Case Diagram). A use case represents the sequence of actions that the system performs to produce something of value to the actor interacting with the system. The actor may be a person or another external system. An actor may participate in more than one use case and, conversely, more than one actor may participate in the same use case.

A Use Case Diagram may contain three types of associations. A communicates association indicates which actor participates in a use case. The uses association indicates that one use case must include the behavior of another use case and shows mandatory yet commonly shared behavior. The extends association indicates that one use case may optionally include another extends use case under certain circumstances and shows the dependency between them. With extends associations, the use case identifies the trigger or reference to the extends use case within the Use Case Description.

The text behind each use case evolves through refinement from a summary to a detailed description, which then transforms into multiple Use Case Scenarios. A Use Case Diagram does not represent a Use Case Scenario with a model element, that is, a graphical representation. A Use Case Scenario is an instance of a use case (just as an object is an instance of a class). It is comprised of text that details the events and responses to satisfy the use case. Each specific Use Case Scenario provides the vital link to understanding the business solution and the many possible technical solutions that support it.

Class Diagram

Use cases (and their refined Use Case Scenarios) provide the foundation for creating the initial Class Diagram. The Class Diagram is the most important of the UML diagrams. The Class Diagram becomes the pivotal diagram throughout development. The purpose of the Class Diagram is to structure the static nature of classes in terms of their attributes, operations, and associations. Most object modeling tools generate source code only from the Class Diagram.

All of the other UML diagrams provide different points of view from which to identify additional attributes, operations, and relationships that validate the completeness of the Class Diagram. They may help in clarifying a modeling nuance not easily found simply by class diagramming. Most of the other diagrams in the UML exist mainly to feed the growth and change of the Class Diagram, each with a different intent.

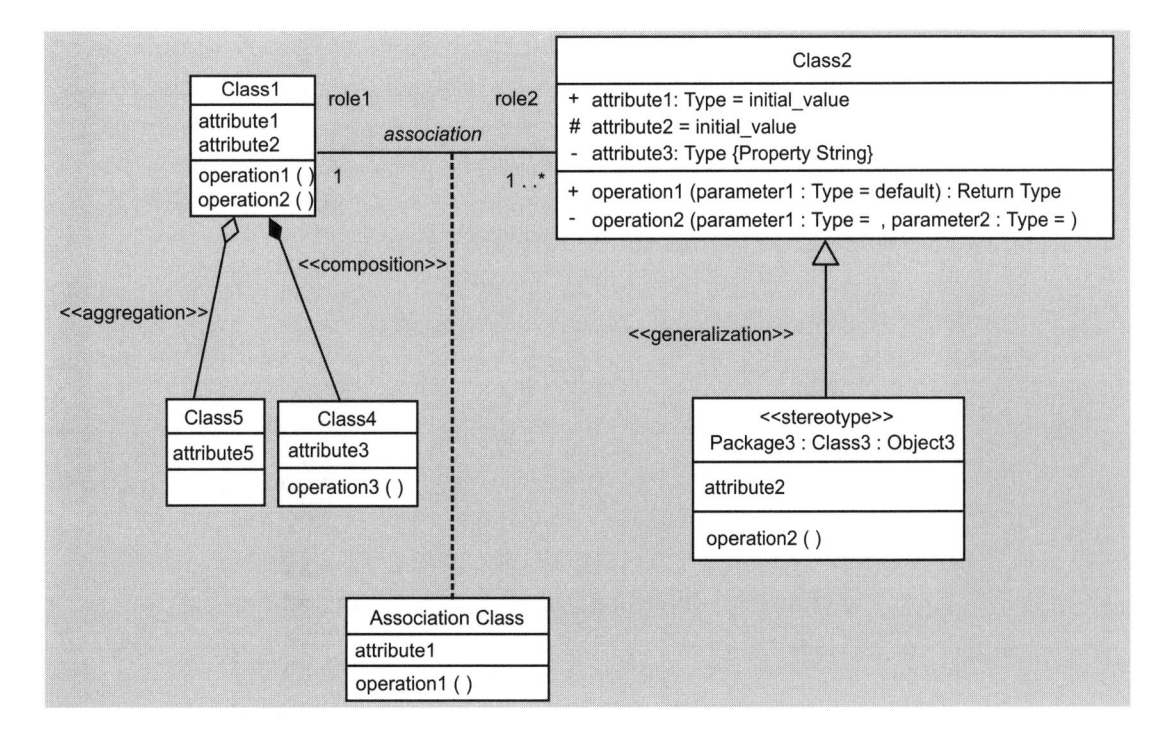

Figure 1-3—UML Notation of the Class Diagram

A Class Diagram consists of classes and the relationships between the classes. As defined previously, a class is a template for objects with similar structure, behavior, and relationships. Each class has a name, attributes, and operations as shown in Figure 1-3—UML Notation of the Class Diagram.

You generally capitalize class names. As work progresses, you add properties beyond the name called attributes and operations. Attribute properties define the characteristics and data of a class, and may include:

1. Visibility (the attribute's availability to other classes; options are public (+), protected (#), or private (-))
2. Type (a language-specific implementation of the attribute type such as character or integer)
3. Initial Value (a default value when instantiating the object)
4. Property String (values that apply to the attribute, such as a range of numbers)

Operation properties define behavior and may include:

1. Visibility (the operation's availability to other classes; options are public (+), protected (#), or private (-))
2. Parameter List (arguments passed to the operation; each argument has its own type and default value)
3. Return Type (a language-specific implementation of the attribute type for the value returned from an operation)
4. Property String (values that apply to the argument in the parameter list)

Associations represent relationships between classes. An association may have a name and two roles. The role specifically describes how each class participates in a relationship with the other class. Each role also contains multiplicity—the zero, one, or more occurrences that participate in the relationship. The asterisk (*) represents the unlimited cardinality.

Some relationships have attributes and operations. When only one attribute applies to the association, it is called a link attribute. For many attributes and operations, you add an association class. The association class cannot exist without the original association.

Recall that an aggregation is a type of association that specifies a grouping of a whole and its part. An open diamond represents a simple aggregation, and the black-filled diamond represents a strong (or composite) aggregation. A composite aggregation has much stronger ties than a simple aggregation between classes in the group; each part must exist for the whole to have meaning.

The triangle represents an inheritance (generalization/specialization) association. It connects subclasses with their specific distinctions to a superclass that defines the similarities.

Sequence Diagram

Use Case Scenarios naturally drive development of the Sequence Diagram. Sequence Diagrams transform the events identified in the Use Case Scenarios into a graphical depiction of the actor's uses of the system. Each event results in a message sent to an object with the expectation that that object will perform an operation. The refinement of the operation and the attributes used in the operation signature (as arguments) on the Sequence Diagram updates the class in the Class Diagram. Identifying and defining operations based on the events provides the traceability back to the use case.

The Sequence Diagram depicts object interaction ordered in time. It identifies the messages exchanged between objects in response to an event, along with the messaging sequence. The intent is to establish the contextual boundaries of a Use Case Scenario. It is a first-pass view of the intercommunication of the classes for a specific Use Case Scenario. The focus is not on immediately capturing operations; the goal is to understand the order of events to complete the scenario. As the order becomes stable, a response to an event becomes a specific operation in the receiving object. Sequence Diagrams are best for complex scenarios and real-time specifications. An advanced Sequence Diagram also shows conditional execution.

As shown in Figure 1-4—UML Notation of the Sequence Diagram, the Sequence Diagram lists objects involved in a Use Case Scenario horizontally across the top from left to right. When you include the class name with the object name, you separate the class from the object with a colon.

You place messages exchanged between objects vertically from top to bottom. Lifelines extend downward from each object. For each step in a Use Case Scenario, one object sends a message from its lifeline to another object's lifeline. The message contains the information needed for the second object to act. In other words, the message triggers action in the receiving object. It is possible for an object to be both the sending and the receiving object (recursion). You may optionally include the actor that participates in the Use Case Scenario as an "object" that sends and receives messages. A step during the Use Case Scenario sometimes creates or destroys an object. Diagram the object's lifeline by aligning the object vertically with the step that instantiates it. Place an "X" at the end of the lifeline at the step that destroys the object.

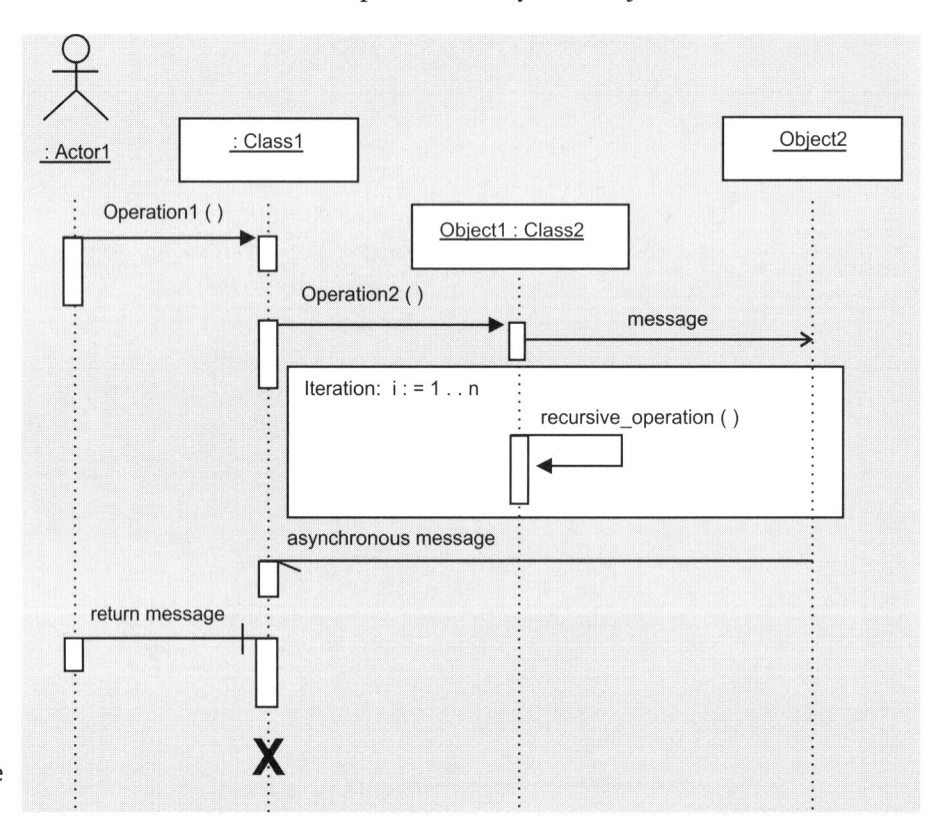

*Figure 1-4—
UML Notation
of the Sequence
Diagram*

A rectangle along the object lifeline shows the duration of the action, called an activation or focus of control, beginning with the incoming message and ending with an outgoing message.

Different arrowheads represent the various message types. A synchronous message, where the sending object waits for the receiving object to return a message, has an open arrowhead. The return message also has an open arrowhead. When the sending object does not pause to wait for a return message, an asynchronous message, you draw an arrowhead with only one open wing. A procedure call (an operation) has a filled-in arrowhead. The return message has no arrowhead and instead has a vertical tick mark placed near the original sending message.

If steps in the Sequence Diagram repeat, enclose the messages with a rectangle to indicate iteration. You then add text to the iteration to note the number of iterations and the exit condition. The format of this text is "[i := 1..n]", meaning "repeat using a variable, i, from 1 to some number representing the limit, n."

Statechart Diagram

The Statechart Diagram models the dynamic state of one specific object. The Statechart Diagram consists of states, actions or activities, and transitions. It identifies the events that cause an object to transition from one state to another. According to the UML, a state is "a condition or situation during the life of an object during which it satisfies some condition, performs some activity, or waits for some event."[6] A Statechart Diagram describes all operations and attributes of a class in response to events. It identifies stimuli that trigger action. Each state on the Statechart Diagram includes the name of the state, any variables that are valid while the object is in the state, and the events that trigger a transition to a new state.

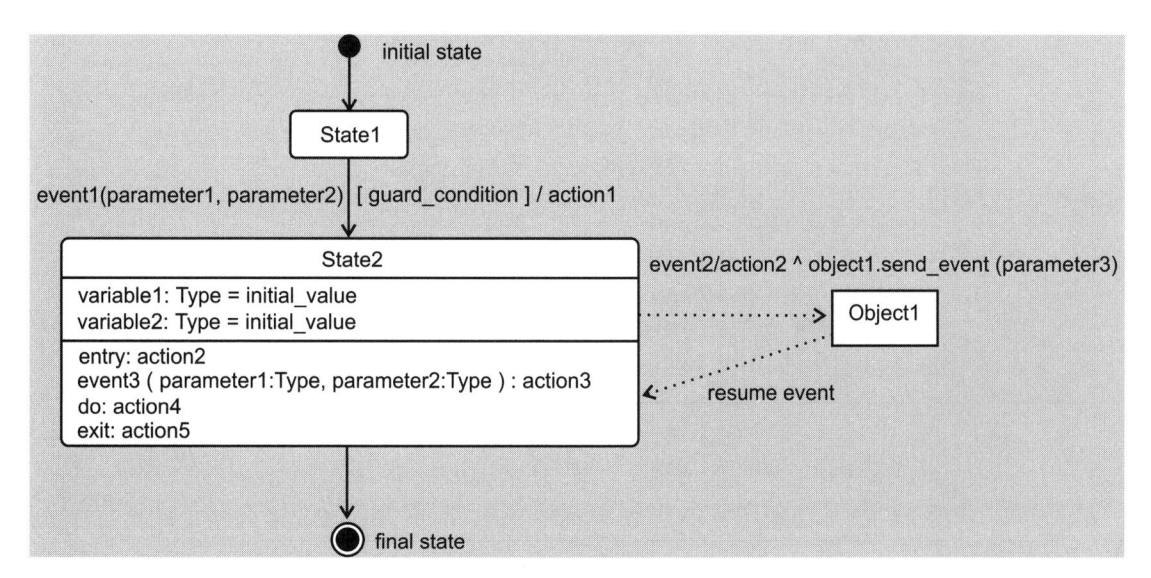

Figure 1-5—UML Notation of the Statechart Diagram

---

[6] Rational Software Corporation, et al. *UML Semantics version 1.1*. N.p. September 1, 1997, 157.

In Figure 1-5—UML Notation of the Statechart Diagram, you see that a rounded corner rectangle represents a distinct state. Every Statechart Diagram includes an initial state represented by a small filled circle and a final state represented by a small circle with a bull's-eye. Initial state occurs when creating an object. Final state occurs when the object ceases to exist.

Except for initial and final states, each state has a name, attributes used within the state, and actions or activities performed. Actions and activities have an event name, arguments, and action expressions. A forward slash (/) separates action expressions from the event name and arguments. Special actions include:

1. Entry—action performed when entering the state
2. Exit—action performed when exiting the state
3. Do—action performed while in the state; external events can interrupt do actions

An object transitions from one state to another when an event occurs and specific conditions are met. A transition is shown with an open arrowhead pointing from the exiting or source state to the entering or target state. A transition has:

1. An event signature that includes a name and arguments separated by commas and enclosed in parentheses
2. An optional guard condition that prohibits state transition until a condition is met
3. An action prefaced with a forward slash (/)

The action executes during the transition. The action may be an operation the object performs, a message sent to another object, or a condition within the object that triggers state change. The action itself may include a signature when the action sends a message to another object. The action expression may include the receiving object and parameters passed to that receiving object. A dashed arrow represents sending a message to another object. This message may be sent from the object while within a state or during the transition itself.

Collaboration Diagram

The Collaboration Diagram depicts a non-sequential view of how objects interact. The Collaboration Diagram supports multiple object modeling needs. One way shows how objects collaborate within a single Use Case Scenario similar to the Sequence Diagram. An interesting interplay occurs between Sequence Diagrams and Collaboration Diagrams resulting in enhanced operations and the discovery of additional attributes. Both diagrams provide differing views of the same information. Both show the implementation of a Use Case Scenario. The Collaboration Diagram filters out the timing or sequential view of the scenario to look at both the static associations and dynamic behavior of objects involved in the interaction. We tend to think sequentially, but sometimes, processes are not as procedural as we assume. Using the Collaboration Diagram may help clarify the context.

You can also use the Collaboration Diagram to show the union of all operations of one particular class. For each operation, it shows the target object of the operation and any other objects that it calls on to implement the operation[7]. The Collaboration Diagram, then, becomes a context for all objects and associations that interact with one object. Because it provides a way to focus only on one particular class, the Collaboration Diagram helps refine the Class Diagram by adding attributes and operations. It also provides a view for what the class does when validating the code behind an operation.

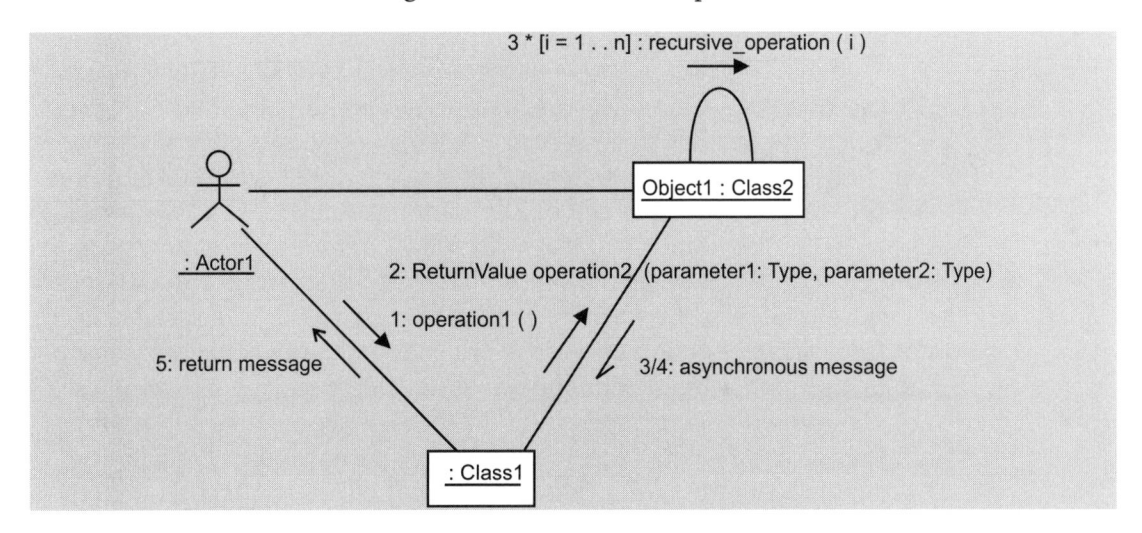

Figure 1-6—UML Notation of the Collaboration Diagram

Figure 1-6—UML Notation of the Collaboration Diagram shows that the notation resembles the Sequence Diagram with objects, messages, and signatures. Each message may include a sequential number

---

7 Rational Software Corporation, et al. *UML Notation Guide version 1.1*. N.p. September 1, 1997, 93.

ordering the steps of the collaboration. Periods separate each number ending with a colon to show iteration. Commas separate sequences and end with a forward slash (/), also known as a virgule. A predecessor in the sequence number indicates that another message must complete before sending this message.

The Collaboration Diagram may show repeated behavior with an asterisk (*), followed by the number of iterations and the exit condition enclosed in brackets, for example, [i := 1..n].

Activity Diagram

Activity Diagrams increase the understanding of complex operations, specifically highly involved operations. Activity Diagrams model this complexity to understand the details within an operation of a class. You then transfer these details into a code to create the method. Sequence and Collaboration Diagrams do not capture this level of detail precisely enough because they only show messaging between objects, not the details behind the scene. Some complex activities may require more refinement in another Activity Diagram that shows its sub-action states and sub-transitions.

The Activity Diagram is a type of Statechart Diagram that specifies an activity of a particular class. The distinction is that Statechart Diagrams represent the whole object, whereas Activity Diagrams typically represent only one operation within an object. Activity Diagram terminology is easily tangled with Statechart Diagram terminology since both use the term "states." State within an Activity Diagram is an action state, which is not the same as the object state. An action state represents the state of affairs of an activity within an operation. It describes the decomposition of action states and transitions within a specific state of the object, rather than from state to state. Decomposing a state does not mean the object changes state. Rather, an action state represents internal processing that occurs during the "parent" action or activity. Internal processing, rather than an external event, triggers the transition from one action state to another. You use the Activity Diagram to show this internal processing. As an example, consider a vending machine. When the consumer inserts money into the machine, the activity of supplying the consumer with a product may traverse through several action states—for example, return change, drop product in tray, advance product line. Yet, none of these action states represents the state of the object vending machine (waiting for selection, delivering product).

The action state can be triggered by:

1. Completion of an operation,
2. Completion of a previous action state, or
3. The availability of an object (a state needed for an action to begin).

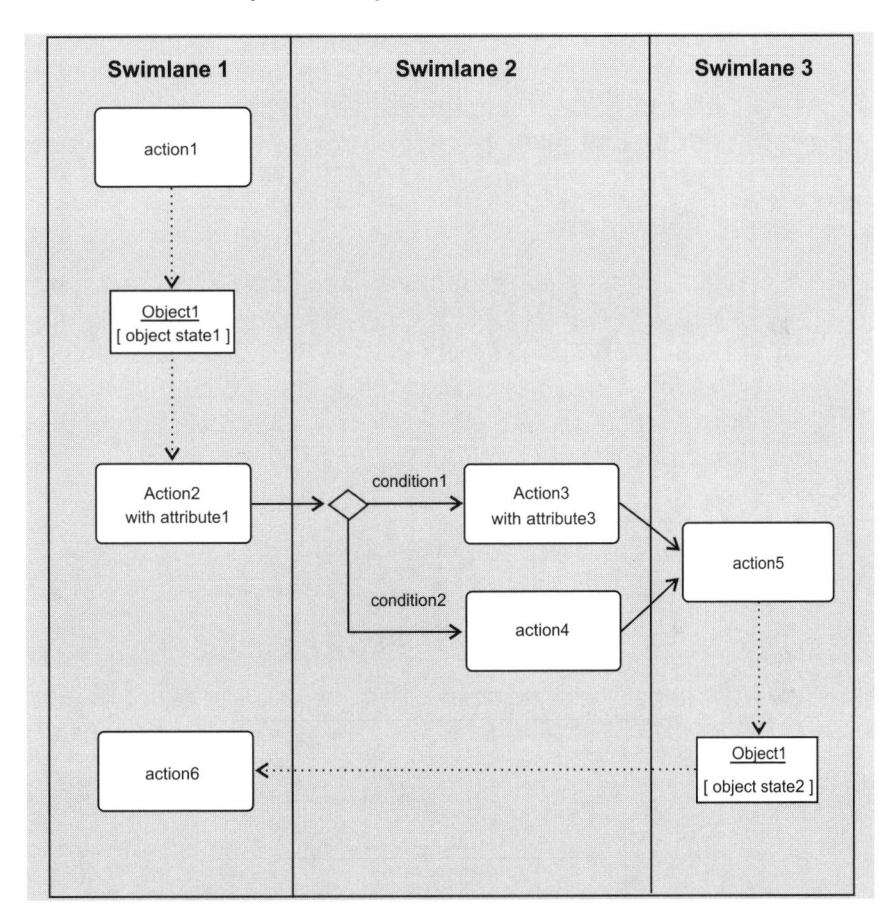

Figure 1-7—UML Notation of the Activity Diagram

The Activity Diagram as seen in Figure 1-7—UML Notation of the Activity Diagram depicts an activity of an object operation with flows between a previous action state and a subsequent one.

The activity consists of procedural steps or operations triggered by internal processing rather than by external events. A specific state of an object or completion of one of its operations triggers an action. An action within an action state is often an operation itself. When an action completes, it may make an object available for a subsequent action. When this happens, the activity has moved on to its next action state.

24 ■ Chapter 1

A rounded rectangle encloses the action; open arrowheads indicate flow of control. It may include the attributes used by an action, but it may only use attributes and links of the owning object (that is, the object for which you are defining the activity).

An Activity Diagram may show concurrency by using the split control branch and the merge control branch. Label these action flows with the condition that triggers the flow. An open diamond provides the notation for a decision point. Remember to label the decision conditions on multiple flows of control for each of the distinct actions.

Component Diagram

The Component Diagram assembles Class Diagram information to create components. Loosely defined, components are groups of objects. The Component Diagram models the software component dependencies for source code, binary code, and executable components.[8] It shows the bundling of objects into software and the packaging, both meaningful at compile time.

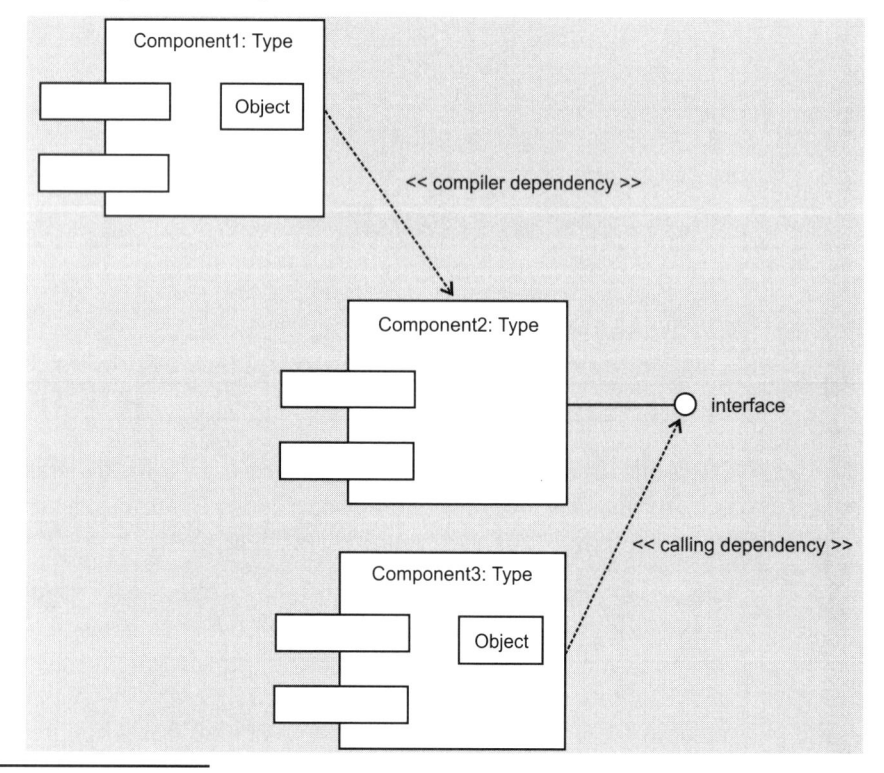

Figure 1-8—UML Notation of the Component Diagram

---

8 Rational Software Corporation, et al. *UML Notation Guide version 1.1*. N.p. September 1, 1997, 132.

Figure 1-8—UML Notation of the Component Diagram demonstrates a component, a rectangle with two small rectangles protruding from its side. A component has a name and optionally a type separated by a colon (:). The component may include the objects it contains.

A dashed open arrowhead from one component to another indicates a dependency from the source to the target. An open lollipop and an interface label may be drawn to the interface of the object to represent a calling dependency relationship. A compiler dependency relationship is represented by a dashed line drawn directly to the component without going through an interface.

Deployment Diagram

Components are "placed" on hardware devices on the Deployment Diagram. The Deployment Diagram models physical processors and devices, security, and the components that reside on the physical processors. The Deployment Diagram represents the partitioning of components and active objects (e.g., a database) to their physical location. It details where to place components within the system's infrastructure. You will most likely create several independent Deployment Diagrams for the various life cycle environments—Development, Training, and Implementation.

The Deployment Diagram uses nodes to represent processors and devices as seen in Figure 1-9—UML Notation of the Deployment Diagram. Each node has a name and optionally a type separated by a colon (:). A solid line from one node to another indicates that the nodes communicate, for example, through a network or channel. A dashed open arrow indicates that a component communicates with an active object. Note that you do not depict a component with a compiler dependency on a Deployment Diagram because the component already belongs to the component executable that compiled it.

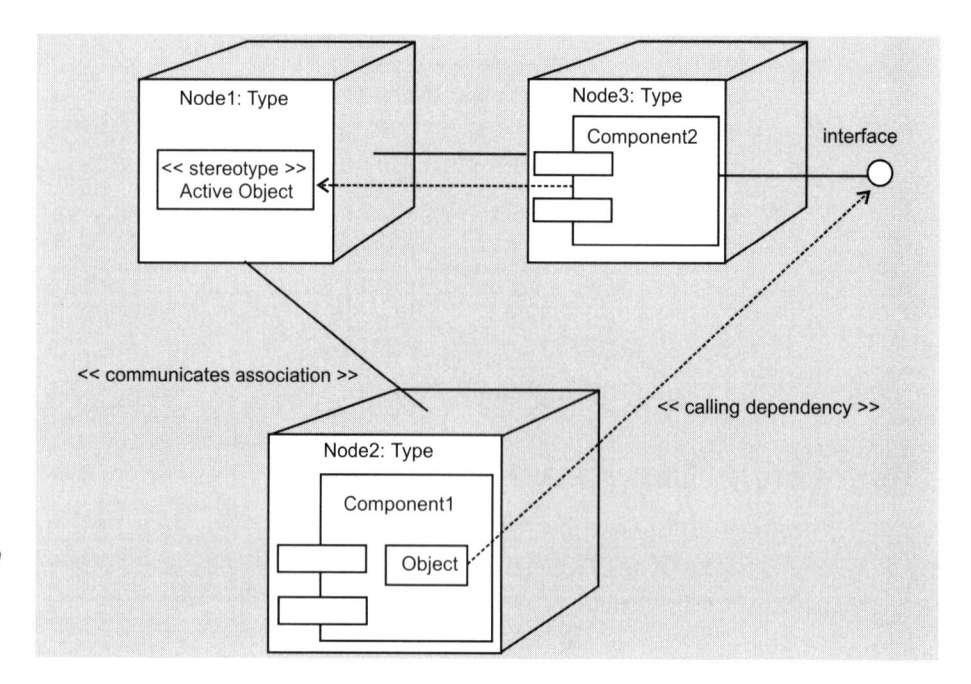

Figure 1-9—UML Notation of the Deployment Diagram

Package Diagram

The UML provides a means for grouping together diagram elements called packaging. You can package other packages, classes, use cases, collaborations, etc. A package shows only the structures it contains. It does not show behavior among its elements. A modeling element belongs to only one package but other packages can reference that element.

A package resembles a folder with a tab containing the name of the package (see Figure 1-10—UML Notation of the Package Diagram). You can elide the contents of the package in which case you place the name of the package in the center of the "folder." If you explicitly show the contents of a package, you place the name of the package on the "tab."

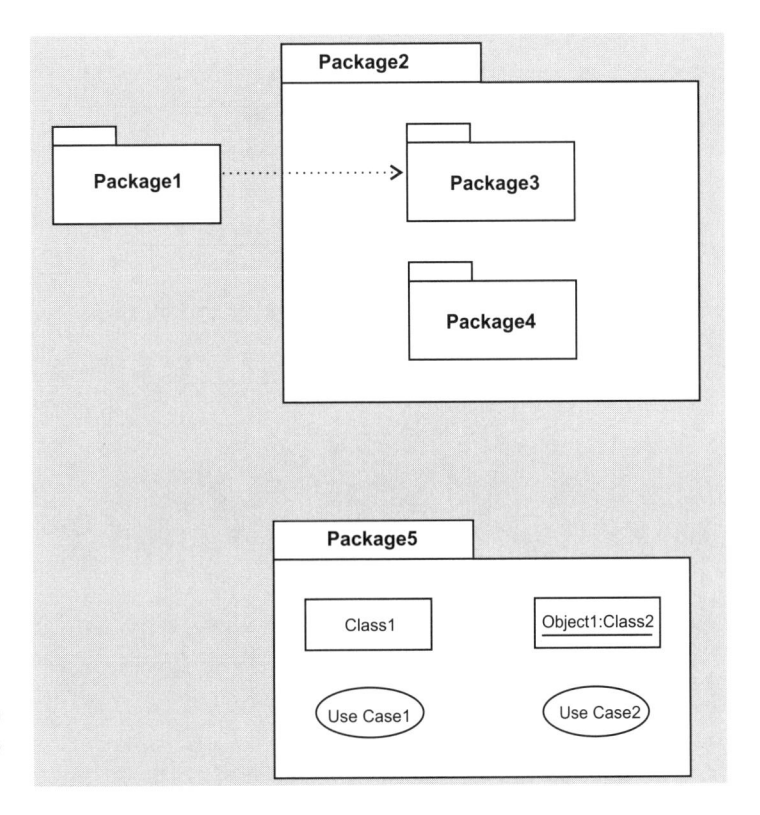

*Figure 1-10—
UML Notation
of the Package
Diagram*

Chapter Summary

We have provided a discussion of the need for object-oriented solutions with Internet considerations, given a brief overview of basic object-oriented concepts, and introduced the UML.

The next chapter presents the differentiators of our approach to object-oriented development leveraging both the UML and the iterative style. We discuss how we incorporate object modeling and how a solid focus on deliverables assists development. We give our viewpoint of the iterative style of development and its benefits. We introduce the importance of including the other vocations involved with the object-oriented development process (such as project management, documentation, testing, training, and infrastructure), and how they must work together to make a complete project. Lastly, we describe the roles used in our approach.

Chapter 2
Introduction to Our Approach

Overview

In this chapter we present an overview of our approach to object-oriented development including:

1. How we incorporate object modeling in our approach,
2. How focusing on deliverables confines development to what is truly necessary,
3. The iterative style of development and its benefits in today's project life cycle,
4. How other vocations involved with the object-oriented development process (such as project management, documentation, testing, training, and infrastructure) interact in a complete project, and
5. The roles needed to implement our approach.

In the early days of object-oriented development, most object-oriented modeling examples centered on how users interact with machines. These examples included vehicles, automated teller machines (ATMs), and recycling machines. Considering how object-oriented technology was born, these examples make sense. O.J. Dahl and Kristen Nygaard[1] introduced object-oriented technology while attempting to model real-world processing of complex physical objects. Most variable information used by a machine exists only while the machine is in use; the machine destroys it when finished. To apply this style to a business solution, information normally saved (such as an account number for auditing) would be lost.

---

[1] David A. Taylor. *Object-Oriented Technology: A Manager's Guide.* Reading, Massachusetts: Addison Wesley, 1992, 16.

We have found one of the best ways to create a clear object-oriented model of the business is to identify and organize the events as described by the Business Area Experts. By identifying business events and defining what the business requires in terms of attributes and operations, we are able to model a solution that naturally follows the structure of the business. We are also able to abstract redundancies, thereby providing a broader applicability and a means to control the absence of structure.

Many businesses now require solutions that consider complex, abstract objects such as classes of merchandise and customer purchasing history. Real-world objects in business usually persist beyond the life of the transaction. This means that within business solutions, entity objects must map to a database and have business rules for maintaining the objects. The mode of managing this complexity must be as flexible as it is firm—flexible in allowing the creative types to develop the proper solution to the business problem and firm in restraining what is impossible to implement or deliver in a "reasonable" amount of time.

Object-oriented thinking has introduced new concepts for building robust, computer solutions. These complex solutions require an ease of understanding; if it is not understandable, then it is not very useful to the business. Many of you readers, and we, can share horror stories of protracted development efforts gone berserk. Though many of these efforts may have been correct in theory, most were impossible to implement due to the lack of understanding by either the Business Area Experts or the developers. For us, removing the arcane and focusing on clarity is foremost in representing the view of what the business needs. It is our hope that this approach effectively responds to this need, given that "defining a standard process was not a goal of the UML"[2] (that is, the approach for applying the UML notation set).

Our approach is a response to the combined influences of object theory, our application of it to business solutions, a focus on deliverables, established techniques, requisite roles, and the iterative style. By following this approach, the project team comprehends the solution and required deliverables earlier in the development process. Subsequent repetition of this approach through increments and iteration builds greater depth of the solution, resulting in higher quality. This means the project team must always be:

---

[2] Rational Software Corporation, et al. *UML Summary version 1.1*. N.p. September 1, 1997, 8.

1. Working with the right amount of detail needed to communicate (abstraction),
2. Designating information and processing to the appropriate object (encapsulation), and
3. Looking for opportunities of reuse (inheritance) and distinction of the reuse (polymorphism).

Our approach adheres to the UML notation and semantics consistently throughout the entire development life cycle. We have chosen to use these diagrams in a way that best supports our development approach.

It is important to understand the business and begin modeling core business events and processes immediately. This may sound like information engineering[3], but the object-oriented twist means you develop both in tandem; not data first, then process (or vice versa). By understanding the complete view of the business in an object sense, you can build consistent, corporate-level subsystems. Why is this important? Well, one of the essential aspects of object-oriented theory is reusability. If you build corporate-level structures first, you can then build applications that have well-defined and solid integration with them. To make this work, you isolate the paths of communications—the messages. The result allows for natural inheritance and makes it easier to select reusable components for future development. If you begin by modeling from applications instead, you risk duplicating effort, creating numerous unnecessary associations between objects, and building an unstructured class library that becomes difficult to use. This leads to unwieldy functional decomposition—exactly the opposite intent of object-oriented theory!

Do not attempt rigorous object-oriented techniques the first time. Neither should you try to capture too much detail right away. Both of these tendencies impede progress. You may want to start with a small team of "forgiving" business experts and shrewd technicians to learn the notation and approach. This team can then disperse and guide future project teams.

If you are new to object-oriented development, you need to learn both an approach for development and a notation to support the approach. We recommend you learn both iteratively. Some teachings begin with notation only and then show you how to apply it. It is difficult to talk about an approach without a standard set of notation through which to

---

3 James Martin. *Information Engineering: A Trilogy*. Englewood Cliffs, NJ: Prentice Hall, 1989.

communicate. The opposite is also true; learning the notation without an understanding of how it all fits together is also difficult. Another way is to learn the notation needed or most used for a specific goal—this is the form taken in this book. For example, if you are trying to scope the project, you may only need to outline Use Case and Class Diagrams. To structure the project, you additionally need class behavior and inheritance. For design, you may need messaging and constraints. We provide the complete approach using UML notation, targeting specific layers of understanding as the goal of each phase.

Most often, IT professionals only address the technology, not business process reengineering (BPR). Experience says you should not try to fix the business process concurrently with any related technology effort. Business first; technology then follows in the form of "projects" using the goals, objectives, and critical success factors as an overarching control mechanism. It requires that a comprehensive Information Strategy Plan (ISP) be in place to ensure adherence to a technological vision. We do not discuss how to conduct a BPR or an ISP. Our approach is concerned with how to conduct a project after a BPR or an overall ISP has completed. We assume the business process works fine and that the technological vision has been communicated. We distill the salient points from BPR relating to a technology solution into our "Problem Assessment."

Some people claim that object modeling is easily understandable for Business Area Experts. This is probably true only for those who comprehend business issues and are aware of the business objectives. The initial steps in object modeling can easily capture the business. However, front-line users still talk mostly in terms of functions—about how they perform their job. You may have also heard that object-oriented programming is not procedural, but we have found that you can readily capture process within the Sequence and Activity Diagrams. This is important! Although object-oriented programming encapsulates information within an object so that an object appears to stand alone, object modeling does not lose the necessary translation of business process. It simply presents it in a different way.

Our approach speaks mainly to a full-scale adoption of an object-oriented style. Realistically, most information technologists already have an existing "system" that requires converting to newer technologies using an object-oriented style. We strongly suggest applying this approach in its entirety to both conversions and "start-from-scratch" projects to reap the many benefits of object-oriented concepts.

Applying shortcuts in the techniques presented here may later result in a mutation that satisfies neither the traditional nor the object-oriented views. This may introduce unnecessary workarounds in the final product. The intrinsic complexities of today's business (and the information systems that support them) drive the need for a clean object-oriented approach.

Our approach promotes reuse of all solution components including business rules, design, code, and test. Code reuse is not the only possibility here; recognize that there is also great potential for model reuse. Object models build upon themselves incrementally and iteratively. Use Case Scenarios drive each testing activity. Object modeling explicitly demonstrates reuse with a "uses" use case. Through the "uses" use case, separate use cases employ a shared sequence of steps. The Class Diagram models the business, generates programming code, and generates database structures. You can reuse code by designing classes to take advantage of abstraction, polymorphism, and encapsulation. Reuse is a goal; you want to develop once and use it everywhere possible. Reuse is especially beneficial with ongoing maintenance of an existing system because you still have the Use Case Test Plan and Test Beds to assist understanding and validation of changes.

Our approach promotes one of the basic object-oriented themes, abstraction, by iteratively refining the levels of detail in a measured time frame. This improves communication during information gathering so that you can postpone details until needed. Abstraction allows you to hide selective details while capturing them. You can then progressively reveal details to guide validation.

Our approach does not include a specific, distinct test phase. Testing should <u>not</u> happen only once at the end of a project just before implementation! Testing occurs continually throughout the development life cycle and is one of the strengths of the iterative style. We advocate holding informal walkthroughs at anytime. We have included multiple confirmation points as part of the approach. Each of the UML diagrams promotes building the others and assists in validation. The inherent traceability across the UML diagrams also supports testing. Use Case Scenarios, in particular, provide the basis for building dynamic models such as Statechart Diagrams and Sequence Diagrams. The use of Statechart Diagrams and Sequence Diagrams refines the Class Diagram. This means that testing implicitly occurs with each refinement and validation of the models. We do promote mandating criteria at the beginning of each phase to test the deliverables. Establishing realistic criteria sets the goals for development, measures progressive refinement, and validates correctness of the deliverables.

Finally, we distinguish between system, application, and project. A system is a packaging of all objects, both hardware and software. An application is the software used to run the system. A project is the measurable process of building systems. One project may initially define a system and many subsequent projects may refine that system.

Focus on Deliverables

Our experience has taught us to concentrate only on the things that are necessary to deliver the final solution. We call these items "deliverables." So, what is the definition of a deliverable? It is a set of information needed to support progress towards the ultimate objective. Common characteristics of a deliverable include information that is repeatable, consistent, and stable. Repeatable means that you can present all information of that type in a similar manner. Consistent means that all deliverables of the same sort are reliably coherent. Stable suggests that you have applied enough detail to make the deliverable resilient to change. All deliverables must pass the needs test—"is this deliverable assisting the goal of producing the final product or supporting us in getting there?" If not, why are you doing it?

Deliverables provide a roadmap of where you are going, a focus for producing results. The completed application is, of course, the ultimate deliverable. To produce the final solution, you deliver units of work and measure progress. These units of work provide value to someone in the business community or information technology services. Focusing on deliverables allows you to assess completeness, plan what is necessary to achieve the next layer of the solution, or confirm that you may begin producing another measurable piece of the solution.

This may require a whole new paradigm for project management. To aid this change in thinking, it may be helpful to illustrate with an example. The old way of thinking tells us to name a task something like "Review Report Design." To help support this task's importance in producing the final product, we need to know more. Which report? Which review (especially since we are iterating through potentially many reviews)? To which deliverable or set of deliverables does it refer? A more appropriate name is one that captures the deliverable, the state it is intended to reach, and the technique to get it there, for example, "Confirm Tested Salary Report Use Case Scenario Using Walkthrough."

This simple structuring gives you enough information to schedule and assign this task accordingly. After putting together a few project plans with hundreds of tasks, you may find that you have duplicated the name of a task. Putting the name of the deliverable and its expected state of completion within the text of the project tasks helps distinguish similar tasks from one another. Fortunately, we have spent a lot of time performing this technique to arrive at our approach. We do suggest that you customize it to fit your own culture and resources. Note that in some cases this naming becomes unwieldy. Use your better judgment to apply to your situation as we have done with the sample project plan included with this book.

Our approach explicitly shows the dependencies and traceability among deliverables. Traceability illustrates the path of deliverables and interdependencies necessary to traverse when change occurs. This is important because change does occur, and you must respond to change effectively. The ability to trace change from the use case to the completed application enables responsiveness. We highlight the traceability of these deliverables as applied to a business solution throughout the approach.

The Iterative Style

Along with object-oriented technology, you may often hear about incremental and iterative development. What is the difference between increment and iteration? Increment is content. Iteration is refinement. Increment means, "to apply one of a series of regular additions or contributions[4]." We use increments to establish smaller scope boundaries within the overall business solution, beginning with the essential and progressing to complete coverage. Iteration repeats specific tasks to attain refinement. We use iteration to control the refinement of increments by the repetition of the specific, measurable, and repeatable tasks in our approach. The goal of the iterative approach, then, is to refine increment content in a consistent manner using controlled iteration.

---

4 *The American Heritage® Dictionary of the English Language, Third Edition.* Houghton Mifflin Company, 1992.

The concepts of iteration and increments arose from the recognition that the sequential building of systems from phase to phase (the waterfall approach) took too long. Each predecessor phase continually delayed the next phase. For example, all analysis had to complete before beginning design, then wait for design to complete before coding, and so forth. The cost of change increased with each later phase. Reflecting newfound change in previous deliverables seldom occurred because of its corresponding cost to rework. The waterfall approach had its biggest failures on large projects. Analysis phases lasting a year or more were common. By the time the project team delivered the system, the system had lost much of its value. The business had changed and left the system behind! We recognize that quality development requires rigorous attention to analysis, design, and code techniques, but we do not promote an explicit separation between them for development as a whole. Rather, analysis, design, and code tasks occur in conjunction with each other as you develop various parts of the system. We have tried explicitly throughout this book to avoid the terminology of "analysis" and "design." There are too many conflicting interpretations of what these are to include. The etymological baggage that goes along with them is much too heavy.

The initial response to the waterfall dilemma was the spiral[5], or iterative, approach. The basic tenets were to break up the development into smaller pieces (increments) and drive out the typical analysis, design, and code in layers of increasing detail (iteration). Advantages of the iterative approach include:

- A means to manage complexity,
- A progressive control mechanism to evolve discovery of content and patterns,
- An ability to identify and accommodate change earlier,
- A higher user involvement in establishing requirements,
- A design that is less likely to deviate from the business, and
- A more robust technical solution.

Object-oriented concepts naturally support incremental and iterative development because well-designed object-oriented code is both stable and reusable. This allows you to build in a layered fashion. As you

---

5 Barry W. Boehm. "A Spiral Model of Software Development and Enhancement." *IEEE Comp. 21 (5)*, May 1988, 61-72.

iteratively refine the detail and incrementally add content, previously written code often requires little or no change. Thus, you can rapidly deploy some components of the solution earlier than others, providing benefit to the business as soon as possible.

Our version of the iterative approach is to take a single topic within the proposed solution and develop everything necessary to implement it by leveraging increments and iteration quickly.

Providing only parts of a solution at a time is not new. However, in procedural designs, the "next" process is highly dependent on the completion of the "previous" process. With object-oriented designs, there is less emphasis on monolithic, chained code. For similar yet different business scenarios, existing code can be reused even if the events in each scenario follow a different ordering. Instead of creating redundant code, developers have an opportunity to leverage existing code by actually reusing the same code without changing it.

Iterative development avoids costly and complex rework because corrections and testing begin early in the development cycle. Another reason to iterate is that it manages risk by exposing it early. The project team assesses and attacks the most pressing risks first, thereby discovering problems earlier. The iterative approach allows the project manager to keep the team focused and to provide direction actively. Iteratively producing smaller increments of a solution means project team members learn skills sooner. Thus, the project team acquires the ability to reuse skills, too.

Traditionally, client/server development meant shortcuts and lower quality solutions. Some developers merely claim to use iteration to build their solutions. They build a prototype, show it to the user, make adjustments, show it to the user, and make adjustments, ad infinitum. You may have heard the developer say, "let's just install it right now and add more functionality later." Iterative development typically meant code some and then review some (and hopefully test some), all without stopping rules and measures of acceptance. This resulted in project overruns and function shortcomings.

Though this approach worked for some, it often got out of control. How long do we let this vicious cycle continue, and when is the project ever complete? With iteration, you must maintain control. You control the iterative approach with a timebox, a fixed duration of time in which to complete a specific set of tasks. Timeboxing is a concept we have applied to ensure delivery of specific deliverables at agreed-upon dates. It constrains the elapsed time to a fixed duration to avoid overruns. Timeboxing allows you to commit to milestones at specific points during development, as you have never done before. In addition, it encourages the entire project team to focus only on the core development process. This reduces the tendency for analysis paralysis, journeying down a path that is either too detailed or extraneous to producing the final product, and causing scope creep. Timeboxing also provides specific breakpoints at which the project manager can assess progress and adjust if necessary.

The first phase of applying the iterative style begins by establishing the strategy for building an increment. All subsequent iterations for that increment begin with an assessment of the current state of the increment against the previous work completed. The purpose of this assessment is to identify and then focus the iteration around the most critical, unresolved risks. Then, by identifying the Use Case Scenarios that encompass the risk areas, the project team can address those risks first.

The greatest paradigm shift when first using an iterative approach requires gearing to the level of detail. Understand that the comprehension of the business solution evolves throughout development. Immediate perfection of the solution the first time through each task is not the goal within the iterative approach. You only explore to enough depth to gain consensus on the solution before continuing. The goal is to build a solution that achieves 80 percent stability with each iteration, with the understanding that discovery of the remaining 20 percent will naturally happen by the last iteration. Once you attain stability, it is time to move on. You want only enough to produce a working solution. This may sound irresponsible, but in fact displays maturity. It acknowledges that you cannot get everything immediately. Your response to any perceived shortfalls is that you are working in a controlled approach and that the final iteration ties up any loose ends.

However, if you do not attain stability, you must consider adding additional iterations to complete; otherwise, you are creating an unstable solution. For example, you might add new operations or relocate several classes from one package to another to strengthen an abstraction. You then proceed to the next iteration only after successfully confirming the change. The stability and the attained level of refinement continue on to the next effort.

Realize that regardless of the subject area complexity, you simply cannot capture everything the first time. You must strive to gain stability in your evolving understanding before moving on to the next iteration.

When do you know you have completed enough to gain stability? There are two basic stopping rules. First, the prescribed number of iterations serves as one type of stopping rule. The second rule uses a simple measure of stability based on changes to deliverables resulting from a walkthrough. Using the Class Diagram as an example, you count the number of classes on the Class Diagram before beginning a walkthrough. You then count the number of classes that were changed or added at the end of the walkthrough. If 20 percent or more have changed, you do not have enough stability to stop and move on. If the rate of change is higher, you may consider adding another iteration to complete. Apply this change measure to all deliverables produced in the timebox. The stability measure stopping rule requires expectation management. The Project Sponsor needs to understand that an additional but essential iteration may delay a planned implementation date. Balance this against the likely delay caused by reworking something that should have been more robust. The Project Sponsor participates in the decision to add any iteration.

We have established a confirmation activity at the end of each phase. At a minimum, you must assess the deliverables at that point to verify stability. When all deliverables have gained enough stability, you are ready to integrate with other concurrent work efforts (the convergence point).

It is important to remember that what you produce during iteration you reuse and refine in subsequent iterations until the final product is complete. For example, you do not "throw away" the prototype. Because of this, it still is important to consider the entire business when object modeling. Major changes such as creating higher levels of abstraction, revising associations between objects, and eliminating objects altogether may make version upgrades difficult to manage. Elegance is not always the best solution.

You measure the acceptable state of the solution at the end of each iteration against predefined criteria established before the iteration begins. These criteria include the depth to achieve. Explore to enough depth to either understand how to provide the functionality or to determine if the functionality belongs in another iteration. You determine depth based on an estimate of the required work to achieve stability within a preset timebox.

So how do you estimate each of the tasks within an iteration? Metrics, metrics, metrics! Based on the Task Analysis, you make your best guess of the amount of work effort for each task. There have been many "formulas" developed over the years like lines of code, function points, and projections from historically similar projects. In the past, you may have estimated three days to develop a GUI application. Should you now estimate only one day per iteration? Was that three days of development only for coding? These estimating techniques do not apply smoothly with an iterative approach because development occurs in smaller portions. In addition, all tasks occur repeatedly and continuously within each iteration. Nevertheless, this is not an excuse to throw this type of estimating out.

To adapt your existing metrics to the iterative approach we suggest you work backwards from iterations to increments. Begin by estimating as you do now, but using the tasks in our approach for each subproject. Allocate extra time for training and the inherent learning curve if you are using new technology. Take the total of the subproject critical path estimates and divide by 120 (three weeks in an iteration) to get the number of iterations needed. Round up unless you are confident and brave! Divide the number of iterations by three to arrive at the number of increments. For any remainder, determine whether it belongs in an existing increment or whether there is enough work to warrant an additional increment for the remaining iterations. This is not an exact conversion, but it does provide you with a starting point from which to refine. Note the three-week iteration is just a guideline. A two-week timebox may not allow enough time to accomplish enough work. Anything much shorter may reduce quality and result in burnout. A four-week or longer timebox may allow extraneous work to creep in and does not allow for expeditious project management.

For timeboxing, a solution of average complexity and resource skill could be completed in three, three-week Build Solution phase iterations. That means, you can state that "in 45 days, this amount of work will be complete." We call this the 360 guideline. Each increment has 360 Build Solution phase hours (three 40-hour weeks equal 120 hours, times three iterations = 360 hours) from the time you enter the first iteration to the end of the third iteration. Recognize that this is not the total estimate for the complete increment, just the Build Solution iterations. For a complete increment, you still must add in time for the Structure Solution phase and the Integrate Solution phase. You must also add in time for the Implement Solution phase. Again, this is elapsed time, not the total number of hours for all resources. When establishing timeboxes, be sure to allow enough time for incidentals. With experience, you may find that your organization responds best with a shorter or longer timebox. We recommend beginners start with a four-week timebox.

If you use very high level percentages to estimate the amount of work in major areas, you could also apply your percentages within each iteration. For example, you could reflect the following in your project plan:

Class Refinement—40 percent

Prototyping—15 percent

Build—35 percent

Review—10 percent

Project Management—additional 20 percent of the total development effort

We would like to give you a standard estimate for every task in this approach. However, the reality is that every project differs depending on resource, skill, availability, and experience. By our use of the term resource, we include both people and technology. People resource refers to not just developers but also Business Area Experts, Users, documenters, Trainers, and support staff. Sometimes you do not have the luxury of estimating based on workload. Your customer (internal or external) may have already decreed the deployment date. In this case, you must work backwards from that end date to some start date and balance the work into manageable pieces. You may need to renegotiate increment content. Any estimating metric will never be exact. Establishing your own metrics is a terrific way to learn how to improve the process. It does take time.

If you are planning to use the iterative approach for the first time, you will likely find a greater learning curve with the first iteration. It generally takes at least one full iteration before the project team understands the strengths and weaknesses of the iterative approach. The strength is that you build as you capture. The weakness is that if the team only knows the waterfall method, they may prefer to wait until one mini-phase completes before beginning the next. For example, programmers often think that before they can begin coding, they must wait until all issues have been resolved, the database created, or the interface coding has completed. We are not advocating writing code before doing good design, but you must strive to complete concurrent tasks through discovery. The team works interactively, constantly fleshing out the details and resolving issues.

The learning curve includes the Business Area Experts and Users. They may need to see the full iteration before they understand how their input helps build the solution. They may think that development is only the responsibility of the Information Systems Department. When they see that the solution requires their input, they often take more ownership of the issues, creating a more thorough test plan, and more closely look at the test results.

Like most projects, the stronger your project team, the shorter the learning curve. Nevertheless, we have found that this approach works best if the team members are flexible and open-minded to different alternatives.

General Techniques

In this section, we present techniques used throughout our approach. Many roles and tasks may use this set of techniques. Some techniques in this group are style-based and are a necessary means to support iterative development. Some cross the multiple vocations of how we as an industry have concentrated staffing.

Most approaches simply discuss the topics germane to their own specialty. If we were to follow this, our book would only include object-oriented topics. However, that would leave you wondering how all of the pieces fit together. For example, the overlap between an Object Architect partitioning the software versus an Infrastructure Architect partitioning the hardware means these two must be in close communication for the solution to be seamless. Otherwise, the Infrastructure Architect becomes frustrated because the partitioning strategy does not work on the deployed technology! This spans the other vocations also; how often has a solution been implemented without proper documentation or training?

Facilitation

We cannot stress the importance of this technique strongly enough. The iterative approach and the use of facilitation are heavily interrelated. It provides the basis for all interactions between the project team and the rest of the business.

Our use of the term facilitation grew out of the notion of Joint Application Design (or JAD) and Joint Requirements Planning (or JRP), formal styles described by James Martin in his monumental work, *Information Engineering*.[6] Variations of this have evolved over the years to include RAD (Rapid Application Development), RIP (Rapid Iterative Prototyping), and JIP (Joint Iterative Prototyping). The latter two purely as acronyms do not instill confidence in the group using it. The last thing you want to happen is someone feeling "RIPped off" or "JIPped!"

The main concept of facilitation is that users and information technology professionals work together in a highly structured setting to capture requirements and design. Shared responsibility for decisions and trust are the cornerstone. The timebox and the goal of delivering a business solution in a limited amount of time bind the team as a whole.

One person, known as the Facilitator, conducts a facilitation session. The Facilitator's sole purpose is to keep the discussion on track to produce the deliverables connected with the current task. When not in session, the Facilitator may help coordinate the work effort and assist the other roles as needed to keep the timebox moving. The Facilitator should get close enough to the deliverable to understand any problem that may occur and must have skill to drive out the details of specific deliverables during session.

There are different ways to decide on the role of Facilitator. One way restricts the Facilitator from having direct responsibility for producing the deliverable in order to remain objective. This means using an additional resource to guide the discussion objectively. Another way assumes the Facilitator and the person responsible for producing the deliverable are the same and objectivity is not an issue. This often occurs in response to the ever-present lack of staff resources. If you have the luxury of an additional resource, try the former. The choice is up to you. The factors to consider are the person's skill level in facilitation, experience with producing the deliverable, and the ability to balance the two tasks while remaining objective.

The Facilitator must always guard against becoming too close to any one solution. The Facilitator can easily lose objectivity and become defensive when Business Area Experts move away from what the Facilitator believes is the "correct" solution. This happens as a natural result of ownership. The direction set by the Business Area Experts is usually the right direction. Remember that the Facilitator is just concerned

---

6 James Martin. *Information Engineering Book I: Introduction*. Englewood Cliffs, NJ: Prentice Hall, 1989.121-123.

with getting it right and a true professional acknowledges the situation and moves on appropriately.

Projects developed using facilitation often stop facilitating when not meeting with Business Area Experts or Users and then resume to review the solution. You likely will find it best to discuss some technical details with less than the full team. This does not mean you need to stop facilitation, though. You can continue to develop jointly, meeting with more of the technically oriented team. When uncertain if the topic is too technical for the Business Area Experts and Users, it is better to err on the side of including them rather than excluding them. Assume that they do have the "ability to understand" and that "they do need to know that information." Continuing to develop with the entire team, even if it concerns a more technical topic, more rapidly produces a high-quality, cohesive solution that everyone understands. The entire team can bring forward their issues, build using the same internal look and feel, and possibly find additional opportunities for reuse.

Project Management

Project Management is one of the most significant techniques in application development. Traditionally, every project has one person managing the project, appropriately called the Project Manager. In our approach, we strive for identifying concurrent units of work called Solution Areas. Solution Areas are essentially independent subprojects. We have additional Project Managers that oversee distinct parts of the solution that are developed concurrently. These Solution Area Project Managers may report to a single Project Manager responsible for managing the entire project.

The project team defines the boundaries of the business need to create a successful business solution on time and within budget. It is important to discover minimum and maximum acceptable coverage of business functionality. This provides alternatives for the eventual scope boundary. Once the boundaries are set, you must stick with them! Changes and additions to scope occur more than deletions. You cannot ignore change, but you must be able to respond to it quickly, efficiently, and objectively.

The biggest challenge early in a project is to keep the focus on the business solution, not the technical solution (past, current, or future). At the beginning of a project, technology experience is irrelevant when defining a business solution. Only when you have a clear definition of the business solution can you begin to bring in potential technology solutions that support it. Rest assured that existing technology knowledge coincidentally assists with the business solution, as technical people have a knack for looking only at the technology. In addition, if technical people are familiar with a particular architecture, you hear a zillion reasons supporting that technology choice. This can hamper the discovery of a better solution. Please note that technology is important to the overall solution, but it must first follow the needs of the business. Technology should never drive the business; business should benefit from supporting technology.

The project team may feel or be limited to a specific deadline. Maximize the time available (see timeboxing). Be up front at the beginning of the project with the expected deliverables the team needs to produce. Be specific on how you measure completeness. Review progress frequently only on that deliverable set and its completion.

Put everything you know related to resources—time, people, money, and task dependencies—into the magic project planning software tool. It gives you an estimated completion date that once revealed to the world will be your expected actual date. Your only hope to meet or change this date is through honest communication of progress through status reports and change requests. This plan becomes an unchangeable fact the longer you leave it alone; so do not let it rest. You must keep it up to date, reflecting the current state of the project. There is no room for optimism or pessimism here, although pessimists seem to be more prepared for contingencies.

Project Managers monitor project plans based on business value, not just on minimizing cost. What is the impact to the business of missing a target date? Document these impacts in the project plan. Tying these dependencies to deliverables helps to understand the impact. The most important point is to get everything to be complete, installed, or delivered at the right time. Easy to say, not so easy to do. Constant communication, if truly possible, only helps but does not guarantee a successful implementation. There is no such thing as too much planning.

When an enterprise embarks on the iterative approach for the first time, it typically wants to test this approach by limiting the first increment to one Solution Area and thus one team. This means the likelihood of developing "with blinders on" increases because the team tends to focus vertically. The team must constantly step back and see how each major decision affects the vision of the entire solution. Sometimes, the team must spend enough time with something outside of the current focus to be able to build the current increment. The Project Manager must balance this by keeping focus on the scope.

Eventually, teams must integrate with multiple Solution Areas. Although our approach has a distinct integration phase, the Project Manager plans frequent integration meetings to share information throughout development. Depending on the size and number of the Solution Areas, this may mean expanding the duration of an iteration to accommodate additional integration meetings. Keeping Solution Area teams informed of issues and designs from other areas minimizes the pain of having one final integration at the end of the increment.

Change Control Management

The only way to ensure the delivery of the right product at the right time is through persistent change control. Notice that we did not use the phrase "on time and within budget." Project Sponsors and Users often criticize information technology professionals for project overruns without acknowledging the numerous changes introduced since the project began. The waterfall method discouraged Business Area Experts from consistent interactions and responsibility for deliverables. Giving responsibility to Business Area Experts and keeping the Project Sponsor in the decision-making role enlightens them all to the causes of project overruns. It is better to deliver what is right than focus the delivery strictly on time and budget. You must ask both of the following questions—"What will it cost our business to deliver the wrong product?" and "What will it cost our business to deliver late with less functionality?"

The original project plan contains only the best view of the effort at the start. A greater understanding of the problem occurs as development ensues. Throughout the development cycle and even after you implement the solution, Users will find ways to improve the solution. The reasons are manifold, including business change, ease of use, and improved technology. Let us just say that we acknowledge that change happens. You still need to manage change to prevent scope creep, to stay on schedule, and to avoid analysis paralysis. The key is to respond to change in a structured fashion by capturing every change and identifying its impact. The project team, Users, and the Project Sponsor must recognize that it takes time to identify the change, regardless of whether or not you ever implement the change.

Perhaps traceability is most valuable during change. You begin with defining what change is needed to strategically reposition the business. Then you determine the use cases and classes affected by this change. Then you apply the iterative approach to absorb and dispose of the change. This may require adding an additional iteration to the already timeboxed increment.

Issue Management

Issues are topics the team members cannot resolve by themselves at the current time and rather than waste the effort debating it, they simply capture the issue and move on. Issues are not the same as change requests; however, an issue may cause a change request to occur. Issues are not tasks, either. They are questions that need answering in order to complete a deliverable.

We have been on countless projects where issues are logged and never resolved. Worse yet, sometimes issues arise that are not even logged! The Project Manager typically manages issues by assembling the right people who can make the decision. To ensure follow-through, you could assign "issues police" or schedule a regular meeting for issue updating. It is important to document the answer to the issue, as issues tend to resurface. It helps to retain the reasons for the original resolution.

Knowing when to push for an answer and when to document an issue and move on is an art. If an issue arises in a meeting and the decision-makers are participating, the issue may be resolved right away. If decision-makers are absent or if there are not enough facts available, it is best to acknowledge the issue and resolve it outside of the meeting.

Training

Traditionally, project teams consider training just before implementing. Throwing a solution at a Trainer right before implementation can inundate the Trainer with information overload. The Trainer then writes the training curriculum from a technical view, not from a business scenario. Why wait until implementation? We recommend including the Trainer throughout solution development. By participating from the start, the Trainer learns the ins and outs and understands how the solution evolved to meet the business needs. The participating Trainer will be better capable of capturing the nuances and more prepared to establish the curriculum.

Someone experienced in training has an eye for bypassing common points of confusion, highlighting subtle shades of meaning that can reach the majority, and setting the pace and content needed for different levels of users. Including a Trainer in the project team not only gives the Trainer more time to absorb the topic, but also allows the Trainer to become comfortable with business terminology and identify areas that may cause confusion. The Trainer also can often offer suggestions to improve the usefulness of the solution during development.

Documentation

It is no revelation that the developer often neglects documentation or a technical writer begins documentation after the solution is complete. The problems here resemble those with Training. The documenter needs to learn about the various business events, hear the words of the Business Area Experts, and recommend considerations for designing user interfaces and information references.

The project team can then test all documentation for readability, applicability, and ease of use at the same time it validates the rest of the solution. How many software products have you used where the documentation did not align with the software functionality?

Infrastructure

Some theorists claim you do not need to know the hardware and software with which you implement. They suggest that you defer infrastructure discussions until "after analysis." It is true that you build your solution from the perspective of the business and its customers, but reality tells us that well-positioned use of technology provides us with opportunities to distinguish the business from its competitors. Sometimes the solution to support the business changes as the project team learns what technology can do to enrich it. Technology may trigger a more creative solution. Again, like documentation and training, it is important to consider infrastructure from the beginning and throughout development. In fact, we encourage all information technology professionals to keep abreast of the latest technologies to have a repository of alternatives for enhancing business solutions.

On the other hand, it is unwise to plan the infrastructure architecture without knowing what the business needs. Projects often begin simply because someone has heard of a great technology that promises to be the silver bullet for the enterprise. It is hard to dissuade the person that the enterprise needs something else. In both cases, understand enough of both technology and the business need before linking them together.

Testing

Project teams often begin testing software <u>after</u> building it. Waiting until this phase of development can delay implementation, produce less than desirable quality, and totally miss the target. Project teams need to focus on providing the right business solution, not a solution with a minimum number of errors. Some project teams have responded to this by identifying acceptable test cases just before implementation. This is not the answer either. Identifying test cases right before testing is not early enough. By this time, the focus is more on the software and less on the business.

So when does testing begin? It begins from the very first Use Case Description and occurs continually throughout development. Therefore, you need to know how much you are testing and what to measure the results against at each step along the way. Each refinement of a use case validates the solution by adding further understanding and detail to support the business. Use Case Scenarios serve as test cases to validate the object models, the classes realized as software, and the entire technology solution. Use Case Scenarios must characterize all events and conditions that occur as they identify necessary preconditions and expected outcomes. Testing continues with each successive refinement exhibited in the models all the way through to the eventual implementation. Testing never really ends; it just briefly suspends until the team makes enough progress to force another round of verification. The final solution therefore holds no surprises of any magnitude.

For each deliverable within a task, two questions often arise: "How can I objectively determine the state of completion for a deliverable?" and "How do I ensure that this deliverable is correct?" With iteration, it is sometimes confusing because performing a subsequent task often adds detail to a deliverable previously considered stable.

To determine completeness and correctness, you must involve Users, Business Area Experts, and Project Sponsors to validate the deliverables. They are the only true judges that a) the business need is correctly defined and b) the proposed solution is adequate to meet the need or at least heading in the right direction. It is better to get constructive criticism early rather than face destructive criticism later. A correctly handled validation acquires the benefits of buy-in and political support strongly needed for budget approval and continuance. If the decision-makers feel the deliverables do not reflect the business, you risk losing them early; winning them back is tough.

We previously stated that we think testing occurs throughout development. How do you accomplish this? Given that the iterative style does not lend itself well to hard cut-off between phases, the response to this is STEM. STEM is an acronym for Solve, Test, Examine, and Measure. This approach promotes interweaving testing techniques throughout development. By interweaving within the approach, the object-oriented theme of reuse continues by reusing test cases and test beds throughout the development life cycle. These same test cases and test beds again provide reuse for regression testing in subsequent version releases. It rarely happens that there are too many STEMs in a project. Apply each of these techniques in an increasing level of formality.

You **Solve** with an informal get-together to discuss an idea of how to model or implement a topic. Although not explicitly stated as a task, we encourage informal discussions at any time during development. You can never have too many brainstorming sessions, as this allows for the free-form exchange of ideas to create solutions.

You validate the solution with **Testing**. Many books have been penned on the topic, but we feel they are still lagging when it comes to iterative development. Most focus on the waterfall approach, where it was easy to tell when to test. We recommend scope testing, which comprises both breadth of coverage and the depth of detail. Correctly discerning the breadth includes more than how much to cover; it also means recognizing the boundary of what you want to test. You test the boundary by identifying the pre- and postconditions for each test case. Depth of detail means identifying the plan for testing all elements within that boundary and specifying the results to measure actual outcome against that plan. Depending on where you are in the development life cycle, the breadth and depth could include classes, clusters of classes, components, subsystems, or the entire system. We have identified specific tasks within our approach for testing the various levels of breadth and depth.

Examine is the next level of formality. When you examine a deliverable, you assess accuracy and completeness against requirements. This requires using confirmation sessions to assess deliverables. You typically conduct a review with the Business Area Experts or Project

Sponsor, expecting them to accept the deliverable. You may also need confirmation from a technical support team. We have had great experience with Business Area Experts, after very little coaching, presenting the solution to the senior management of a major international firm. Since they grew up with the model and were committed to getting it right, it was only natural that they present the solution. When the review ended, we all felt proud. In our approach, we have added a confirmation task specifically for this type of review. Note that holding too many confirmation sessions slows progress by rehashing what you have already accomplished. Perhaps you have many sessions because attendance is a problem. It is better to have full attendance for a confirmation session rather than simply holding more sessions because the discussion is important for all to hear at the same time. All attendees should understand that the intent is to gain consensus that the deliverables meet the expected accuracy and completeness for the particular breadth and depth before proceeding to the next level. Still, those producing the deliverables should attend these sessions with an open mind that change may be necessary.

You apply an objective **Measure** to a deliverable to determine its value to the business. You do not merely validate that it met requirements. You measure both that the deliverable is right for the business and it consistently aligns with sound design principles. In addition, you reassess whether the deliverable meets business value even if it has not changed since the Business Area Experts initially specified the requirements.

Applying an effective measure to verify the level of completion is much more involved. At the beginning of the project, you establish guiding principles for the entire solution such as "the solution must be user-friendly" or "the solution must not require a specific browser." Determine how to measure success for these requirements by looking at the underlying reasons and understanding exactly what it means. The effort to uncover that meaning, though sometimes arduous, holds the answer for the measurement.

Evolving Roles That Champion Business Change

This section examines the roles that make a project succeed and discusses why those roles require evolving skills. We present the roles that people assume during solution development described by their overall purpose.

Information technology is a people business. Sure, information technology includes hardware, but hardware alone does not determine cost and benefits. It also means having the right people. We all try to hire creative, talented, and intelligent people for our organizations and not just in the information technology group. Individuals representing information technology advance their own careers and benefit their organizations when they become Enterprise Agents. An Enterprise Agent understands strategic directions of the organization, stays abreast of technology advancements, and responds by providing technological solutions. The Enterprise Agent builds business solutions that can easily adapt to change, new direction, and evolution inherent in business today. The Enterprise Agent builds solutions that easily apply improvements in technology.

The Enterprise Agent develops a strategic vision and shares that vision with the team throughout the project. He or she trains the project team to recognize the need to respond to rapid change, build adaptable systems, and apply the right technological solution. The Enterprise Agent encourages the team to improve constantly upon the work.

Who is the Enterprise Agent? There may be just one to start with, but over time, all share in developing the vision and making it happen. Everyone on the project team must take on this responsibility, regardless of his or her assigned roles.

Are employees ready for their role? Are they motivated? Do they understand the vision? An enterprise must keep its employees constantly learning, both in formal training and on the job itself. The most successful corporations spend more than one percent of gross revenue on training and education.[7] Jointly developing solutions creates an environment where employees share, improve, and use knowledge.

Role Definitions

What follows is our definition of the roles identified in our approach. We discuss the intention and the overall responsibility of each role.

Our approach includes roles that do not typically match up with a common job title. The difference arises from our distillation of the skills needed to accomplish a development project. Moreover, many of

---

7 James Martin. "Cybercorp: A Business Revolution," In *DCI's Database & Client/Server World Conference Proceedings*, Vol. III, Chicago, IL, December 12, 1996, D35-10.

the titles the information technology industry generated over the last 30 to 40 years are painfully irrelevant compared to their original purpose. Redefining job titles is not within the scope of this approach, but we do encourage you to examine the people you work with and the duties they perform concerning their latest job description and title. You may be surprised at the variance.

Our set of roles came from a detailed analysis of the deliverables in our approach. We looked at each deliverable to find the skills needed to accomplish its completion. We created these roles based on what we felt were logical groupings of those skills. A single person may also fill many of these roles and roles may transcend organizational boundaries.

We do not promote teams segregated by their vocation such as having an infrastructure team separate from a software development team. These vocations represent specialized focuses that influence the complete solution. Although each vocation has its unique characteristics, it is dependent on the others for the team to attain success. No project can afford to wait while one area finishes. That is why we recommend including all vocations on the project team throughout the development cycle. For example, Document Architects begin documenting while the solution is under development. Database Architects test performance as a new Solution Area unfolds. Throughout this approach, we show how these basic vocations weave together and expand concurrently throughout development. We do not wish to convey by our description that these vocations act independently; rather they must interact to develop a complete business solution. The vocations sometimes align with one or more roles. Our intention is not to limit tasks only to these suggested roles but to encourage the entire team to consider the strategic vision as Enterprise Agents throughout development. The following sections describe each role.

Business Area Expert

The Business Area Expert's primary purpose is to provide the team with concise and accurate knowledge of the business. This approach requires multiple Business Area Experts as a resource for discovery and definition to align the business solution to ongoing business needs. Each Business Area Expert actively participates in the entire development process including modeling and validating. Since Business Area Experts contribute to modeling efforts, the models more closely align with the business. When Business Area Experts "grow up with the model" they are perfect candidates to communicate and explain how the model matches the business. They also validate the solution against the original needs and any new needs discovered during the project.

You want to select Business Area Experts that not only thoroughly understand their area of the business, but also see the impact of their business area across the enterprise. They have the most knowledge of the business and have the greatest potential to create a vision. Realize that these people do not remain objective forever; they become part of the project team. This is not necessarily bad, but the developing solution eventually creates a bias. It becomes doubly important to achieve the solution quickly!

> **Tip** Keep your Business Area Experts involved! When preparing for reviews, always provide the materials at least a week ahead of time. Then check in to see if they have reviewed it a few days before the session. If they have not, suggest that they do not attend. It is better to exclude them from the meeting than waste the precious time going over what they could have read earlier. If the majority of them have not reviewed the materials, cancel the meeting outright. Then discuss participation with the Project Sponsor.

Database Architect

The Database Architect provides direction for designing and building databases within enterprise guidelines. The Database Architect also assists with monitoring and enhancing data access. When using a relational database, this person also translates the entity objects from the Class Diagram to a relational data model.

Document Architect

The Document Architect creates all documentation required to support the solution. Skills may include writing, publishing, user interface design, and knowledge transfer analysis.

Infrastructure Architect

The Infrastructure Architect designs, builds, and monitors the development and implementation infrastructures. Skills include network design, operating system installation and tuning, capacity planning, and performance tuning.

Object Architect

The Object Architect is responsible for creating quality object models that are complete and traceable. An understanding of the business helps tremendously. Skills include advanced to expert knowledge of object modeling and development practices.

Object Developer

The Object Developer builds the application from object models. The Object Developer designs, builds, and tests the methods from the Class Diagram using the application tool selected for development.

Project Manager

The Project Manager controls the scope, directs the team, monitors issues, institutes change control, and conducts project status reporting. Depending on the size of a project, one Project Manager may oversee the entire project with additional Solution Area Project Managers overseeing separate Solution Areas. In this case, the Solution Area Project Managers integrate issues, change control, and project plans with the overall Project Manager.

Project Sponsor

The Project Sponsor selects Business Area Experts, sets the strategic direction, makes the final decision for all cost-related issues, and gains consensus support from the rest of the organization. The sponsor may actually be more than one person, perhaps in the form of a steering committee.

Trainer

The Trainer creates training curriculum, enhances training support materials, and trains users. A Trainer focuses on objectives for each type of user group and delivers precisely what is essential to use the system. This person knows when to skim and when to embellish.

Hiring or contracting a training professional provides necessary expertise. Selecting a Trainer from your own company may be a better option than you think, providing the individual has the skills and acquires the tools (and budget) to complete the job. Using someone from your own ranks allows for immediate peer-to-peer communication and credibility. This is a bonus when assimilating a new job function into your culture.

Our slant is towards a Trainer that develops customized, instructor-led curriculum that he or she teaches. This style of training may not be the best for your situation. Explore the many other media and staffing options available, especially for training large numbers of users that are widely separated by geography. For example, training 500+ users across 20 states has different implications than training 50 users located at a single corporate office. The Trainer may coordinate multiple agencies to conduct pre-packaged training at different sites. This skill set is greatly different from those of a Trainer that creates a curriculum. The former is logistics-based (a skill in itself) while the latter creatively develops content. Regardless of the vehicle used for training, the curriculum must quickly allow users to understand how the technology solution supports their business duties.

User

The User depends on the system to carry out his or her job duties. The User may not have had a role in the design or development.

Chapter Summary

We have discussed how we incorporate object modeling in our approach and how focusing on deliverables confines development to what is truly necessary. Next, we presented our case for applying the iterative style of development and its benefits in today's project life cycle. Finally, we described how other vocations involved with the object-oriented development process (such as project management, documentation, testing, training, and infrastructure) interact in a complete project, and defined the roles needed to implement our approach.

Part II

The Approach

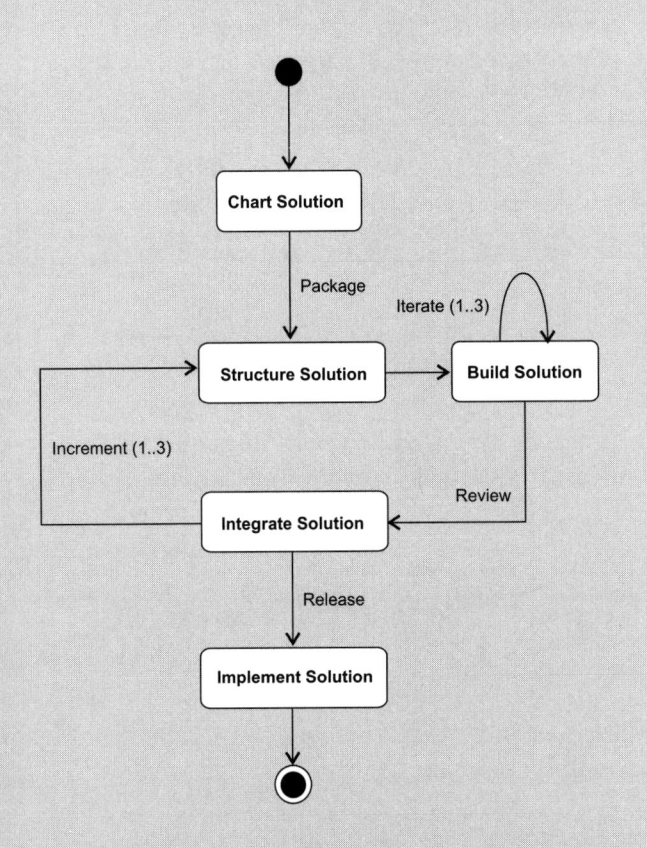

Included in This Part:

Chapter 3: Chart Solution
Chapter 4: Structure Solution
Chapter 5: Build Solution
Chapter 6: Integrate Solution
Chapter 7: Implement Solution

Overview

Part II defines the required tasks that fulfill an entire project life cycle. Each task identifies the deliverable to produce, the roles involved, and the technique to apply. We group tasks by activity themes and group activities by phases. Within each phase, we demonstrate by example the depth of modeling required before moving on to the next. The phases are described in Table II-1—Approach Phase Descriptions.

Table II-1—Approach Phase Descriptions

Phase	Description
Chart Solution	Describes how to set the project scope using object modeling, identify initial requirements, assess the impact of risk, and plan the project.
Structure Solution	Describes how to apply object modeling to translate business needs to understand the work required for building a solution. Suggests ways to package the solution to produce subsystems that can be built in parallel from the core outward.
Build Solution	Describes how to finalize object models for application and database generation, code and test the solution, and validate the solution.
Integrate Solution	Describes how to integrate multiple subsystems developed in parallel with the current released version of the solution.
Implement Solution	Describes how to deploy the solution for version release and obtain confirmation of a completed, useful solution.

Note that this approach represents a template. You adjust the template to create the actual implementation strategy for a project to meet the project and enterprise needs.

Depth of Object Modeling at Various Levels of Development

A development project consists of continual discovery and refinement. The initial work is exceptionally important, as it creates the catalyst that guides all subsequent efforts. As you progress, you refine the various object models to communicate additional detail. You add only enough detail appropriate to the objective of the phase.

In the Chart Solution phase, the Use Case Diagram consists of the actors, the name of each use case, and the summary of the use case. The Class Diagram contains the major classes derived from the Use Case Diagram and possibly some preliminary associations necessary to model the core business. Both the Use Case Diagram and Class Diagram help to identify essentially independent subprojects called Solution Areas. The Solution Areas package together a smaller scope boundary to allow concurrent development.

In the Structure Solution phase, you create the Use Case Description. Note that this description captures only the details of how the actor interacts with the system and not the details of what the system does to carry out events. The work to develop the description adds classes, attributes, and behavior to the Class Diagram.

In the Build Solution phase, you make the transition from the business solution to the technology solution that supports it. You further refine the Use Case Description by creating Use Case Scenarios. Use Case Scenarios distill the events and processing steps into detailed system responses. These scenarios can become complex. To comprehend the nuances of Use Case Scenarios, you model them further with Sequence Diagrams. For objects with many messages in the Sequence Diagrams, you further model that behavior with Statechart Diagrams. In Statechart Diagrams, you define object states, or life cycles, and the activities that transition state. The models capture both short- and long-term information about class state and class behavior (when and how an object changes state). This progression of modeling organizes the structured comprehension of the solution and its complexities.

During the Build phase, you will enhance the Class Diagram to reflect the additional objects, attributes, associations, and operations uncovered through the other UML diagrams. You abstract classes with generalization and specialization. Remember to structure the classes independently of the actual implementation environment; focus on the logical structure of the system. As you enhance one model, you will uncover more detail that affects the other models. You then add interface and control classes, create a prototype using a graphical user interface (GUI) tool, and finally code and test the methods within the classes. You may also use Collaboration and Activity Diagrams to further refine your understanding of the classes. You create the Component Diagram to package the evolving technology solution within the Solution Area. The Build Phase activities and tasks may seem disproportionate compared with the other phases. Although the other phases have fewer tasks, they may require greater duration. We group phases to align with the division of the project team. During the Build Solution phase, for example, you need daily interaction between Architects, Developers, and Business Area Experts.

In the Integrate Solution phase, you integrate the current solution with the previous version and with the components of other Solution Areas. You integrate messaging between classes that communicate across Solution Areas and test the integrated solution. You enhance the Component Diagram to show the integrated Application.

In the Implement Solution phase, you install the solution. You deploy hardware and software, back up databases, and enhance the solution for implementation. You finalize the Component and Deployment Diagrams to reflect the final solution.

Demonstration of the Approach with a Case Study

We provide the case study to help guide you through the approach with examples of the deliverables and discussion of the techniques for producing them.

The case study demonstrates the approach with a clear, single-topic business example, which we find more useful than continually switching examples from deliverable to deliverable. We illustrate the essential deliverables as they evolve through the approach. We do not include all deliverables simply because we cannot produce some deliverables in a book format. We do demonstrate the approach and specifically highlight traceability through the UML diagrams. We explain the major assumptions made to produce the deliverables.

To demonstrate the approach, we have chosen a ticket selling enterprise. The business contracts for and promotes performances, sells tickets, and manages performance locations.

Chapter 3
Chart Solution

Overview

The purpose of the Chart Solution phase is to establish the project scope, package the project into Solution Areas, create or review existing standards, organize the project team, and establish the strategy for developing the solution. The Project Manager must quickly understand the background and distill the main objectives for the system. The entire project team must work to solidify the consensus view of scope as soon as possible. This forges the foundation on which to create the solution.

This phase typically happens just once during a project, although it may repeat for subsequent enhancements or full version upgrades. The deliverables produced here provide the initial framework from which all other deliverables evolve on their way to forming the final solution.

Within our Case Study example, the activities in this phase assess the current and desired state for the ticket selling business.

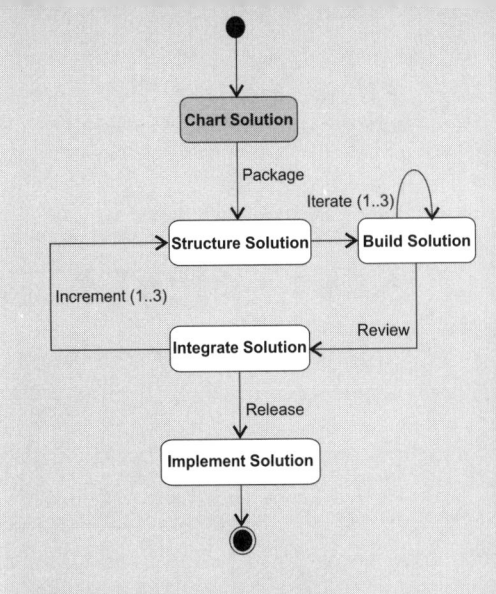

Deliverables:

Change Requests
Class Diagram
Cost/Benefit Analysis
Deployment Diagram
Documentation Approach
Issues List
Problem Assessment
Project Plan
Project Standards
Risk Assessment
Solution Area Scope Statement
Solution Strategy Confirmation
Training Approach
Use Case Diagram

Activities

Establish Project Scope

The purpose of this activity is to conceptualize the business solution and set the boundaries for both the business and technical solutions. Here you see how each of the vocations of documentation, testing, training, infrastructure architecture, and project management must organize their work to achieve the business solution. Organizing the work based on the developing solution helps firm up the scope. At this stage, only talk in terms of the business.

> **Deliverables**
>
> Problem Assessment
> Issues List
> Use Case Diagram
> Class Diagram
> Documentation Approach
> Training Approach
> Deployment Diagram
> Project Standards

The scope must identify not only what is inside the system but also what is external to it. This includes human actors as well as computer systems and machines. You assess a probable solution based on technical, economic, and political considerations.[1] While defining the project, define abstraction at a high level. Identify only the things you can put your hands on.

Tasks:

Define Problem Assessment

Role(s): Project Manager (Facilitator) and Project Sponsor

The Project Manager meets with the Project Sponsor to scope the project from a business perspective. This includes business context, current environment assessment, influences, restrictions, strategy, and business objectives for the solution. The Project Manager summarizes these points using terminology familiar to the business.

Truly understanding the business from front to back can make the difference between a new system that only meets user requirements and a system that absolutely supports the business. It is crucial to define

---

[1] Advanced Concepts Center of Lockheed Martin Corporation. *Object-Oriented Analysis Using UML*, Volume I of I, N.p., n.d., 117-16.

scope in terms of the business's natural boundaries rather than on the artificial boundaries of a system. This may mean that the project scope includes cross-functional areas within the organization. For example, the enterprise may have separate departments for purchasing and stock replenishment. Building system boundaries limited to the purchasing department may prohibit real-time stock replenishment. Imagine reducing the time that you have out-of-stock situations!

There are many ways to elicit the information for the Problem Assessment. If you are of better than average fortune, you may have it provided to you. Otherwise, we suggest assembling whatever background material you can ahead of time and putting together a draft for confirmation in a facilitated session. You cannot accomplish this in isolation, through e-mail, or via routed paper draft copies. You may find it most helpful to observe the actual processes and procedures involved in conjunction with a facilitated session. By experiencing the "problems" yourself, you gain a more complete and accurate understanding of the business needs.

Case Study Turning to our Case Study, we established the following Problem Assessment after discussions with the imaginary case study Project Sponsor:

The current system supports ticket purchasing for concert performances. The system currently implements a two-tier computing environment that limits customer accessibility and simply does not provide the performance needed for online response time. Each location sells tickets at multiple walk-up ticket booths. Ticket agents also take orders over the telephone, and customers are becoming irritated at the amount of time it takes to complete the transaction.

The business establishes contracts for concert services at each performance location. It also establishes contracts with concert performers. Performer reimbursement and seating location both factor into calculating ticket markup. Performers receive a percentage of attendance (that is, a percentage of projected revenue above a guaranteed minimum).

Base ticket price calculations include the cost of the performance plus the standard markup per ticket. A "prime" seating location adds an additional markup to the base price of the ticket. Tickets are generated one week after the performance is scheduled. Ticket price calculations are currently manual. The business wants to automate ticket price calculations.

Five full-time performance promoters arrange all advertising and posters. The business desires to explore other channels for reaching a wider target market.

There are five established locations and plans to acquire at least one new location each year. The setup of a new location is a burden due to the sheer volume of correctly identifying sections, rows, and seats. Determining prime versus non-prime seating is also difficult to establish. Once a location is set up, there are few updates.

The business schedules twenty-four performances per year at each established location and anticipates twelve performances at each new location its first year and twenty-four performances each year following. The smallest location seats 15,000 and the largest location seats 35,000 per performance with 110,000 total seats.

The business accepts payment using cash or credit card. Credit approval confirms purchases paid by credit card.

Customers may reserve tickets at any location regardless of where the performance is scheduled.

Each location supports two full-time ticket agents. Twenty-three additional part-time ticket agents work during peak ticket purchasing. The main office supports four full-time ticket agents, five performance promoters, and a concert coordinator for each location. The main office ticket agents also assist the concert coordinator and performance promoter with common administrative tasks between orders. The walk-up ticket booths are open from 9:30 A.M. to 9:00 P.M. daily.

Ticket reservations occur real-time. Peak ticket purchasing occurs between 6:00 P.M. and 9:00 P.M. local time for 50 percent of the daily volume. Sixty-five percent of reservations for the most popular performances occur within the first two days after the tickets go on sale, also a peak time. The business estimates receiving 3,350 calls the first two days with 1,800 remaining calls before the performance day.

For each performance inquiry, there is a subsequent 80 percent purchase rate. Each purchase averages four tickets. Performances are generally 75 percent sold.

The business currently does not retain individual customer demographics but desires to capture customer baseline demographics for follow-up marketing. When capturing customer demographics, the business intends to standardize addresses for direct mailing.

They anticipate retaining customer demographics for two years from the last purchase and one year for customers that did not follow through with any purchase. Of these figures, the business estimates 50 percent new customers per year and 50 percent repeat customers.

The business averages a 3 percent growth in yearly sales and anticipates this continuing for the next three years. The business anticipates 250,000 customers the first year, followed by 257,500 customers the second year, 265,225 the third year, and so on.

Ticket agents frequently quit so the business needs software that newly hired ticket agents can learn quickly and easily. Typically, these ticket agents lack extensive computer skills.

The business retains all purchase information for seven years. This information is stored at the main ticket office.

The business desires to obtain an Internet presence. The desire to have Internet accessibility is partly due to competition and partly due to its high level of publicity. The latter reason is not a good one. We hope to keep focus on the former reason, that is, have business reasons drive an e-commerce solution. Using the Internet today adds risk due to its immature supporting technology. Riskier yet, the business does not know what it wants on the Internet. The current ideas range from publishing information about ticket locations (for example, open/closed hours, addresses, and telephone numbers) and performance schedules to a full function e-commerce site that supports actual ticket purchasing.

In addition, the business has no idea of the work effort involved in building an e-commerce site. Although our approach has specific tasks for identifying risk at the end of each phase, you should document and act on the risk as soon as you first become aware of it. Therefore, this topic becomes a "threat" in the Risk Assessment (see Confirm Solution Strategy). The nature of this risk pertains to forcing a technology solution as a business solution. In addition, the main objective is to reduce customer wait time, something the Internet may not be able to address.

Knowing of risk may also require issue resolution. In this case, we add the issue "what content belongs on the Internet?" to the Issues List. We identify this issue as the first on our Issues List (we eliminate the columns for open date, opened by, meeting, affected deliverables, owner, assistance, and due date for illustration).

Table 3-1—Issues List

Num	Issue Description	Resolution
1.	What content belongs on the Internet? Options include schedules, performers, concert dates, and locations, with query capability for all of the above.	
2.	Does purchase information need to interface to the accounting system?	Not for the first release. Reconsider in next year's budget.
3.	Will we support payment by check?	No. Checks present too much of a credit risk. Reconsider automated check verification as an enhancement after first release.

We capture other issues identified (yet immediately resolved) in the session as shown in Table 3-1—Issues List. Issue resolution is important to controlling the size and scope of the project. The greater the unknown, the greater the risk and, therefore, the greater the anticipated cost. On the surface, these decisions appear simple but begin to draw a clear boundary around the project. The unknowns encourage the Project Sponsor to postpone a large amount of work until the right time comes for addressing these decisions. The basis for "the right time" in this example includes prioritized business need and budget.

From the Problem Assessment, we can extract the business objectives:

1. Increase customer accessibility to ticket purchasing.
2. Reduce ticket purchasing time for the customer.
3. Increase market share through new marketing channels.
4. Identify customer demographic profiles for use in marketing strategies.
5. Maintain a minimum 3 percent yearly growth in sales.

We want to make sure that the solution aligns with these objectives initially and throughout development.

Create Initial Use Case Diagram

Role(s): Object Architect (Facilitator), Business Area Experts, and Project Sponsor

The Object Architect facilitates a session where the Project Sponsor and Business Area Experts identify the actors and the use cases within the project boundaries. Use cases identify the required uses of the system and the behavior needed to support its uses. Use cases enable the business to complete a necessary function through supporting technology. Actors communicate with the system in terms of the roles that they play in performing the business activity. After the facilitated session, the Object Architect logically groups complex systems into several Use Case Diagrams.

> **Tip:** Including the Document Architect early in use case development allows the opportunity for the Document Architect to gain the business perspective. The Document Architect then can provide beneficial help in managing the meaning of the discussions.

The Use Case Diagram graphically depicts the use cases and the actors involved in the use case. It also documents both internal and external interactions with the system. This includes human, other system, and machine interactions. The Use Case Diagram provides a mechanism for collecting requirements of system use. It helps identify requirements. What you are after is the structure, behavior, and associations within the context of a project scope.

Information documented in the use cases also provides business-level information that is especially useful for managing the testing effort. The business solution begins with use cases, which you use throughout the entire project to develop and measure the progressing technology solution.

At this point, you identify the main business activities as use cases. The Use Case Diagram consists of the actors, the name of each use case, and a descriptive summary of the use case captured in one or two sentences. To get the team started, you may want to list the major business events that occur around a business activity. For example, you might begin a high-level view of business activity with the following events:

1. Customer purchases product
2. Product is promoted
3. Store opens

These types of business events translate easily into high-level use cases.

Another approach for beginning the modeling process identifies the external actors that communicate with the system. Then you ask, "what information does the actor exchange?" This becomes a use case and collectively places each use case on a Use Case Diagram.

The Problem Assessment provides a rich source of background information to prepare for this session. It is possible with experience to define the Problem Assessment and the initial Use Case Diagram concurrently, using one to build the other. You may find it beneficial to begin conversations by drawing a context diagram showing a black box of the system and all external actors that communicate with the system.

What are the factors to use in identifying use cases? The goal for the high-level Use Case Diagram is to keep the number between five and fifteen for any size system. This forces a level of abstraction that is manageable. Realize that you may add more use cases as the project progresses to discover additional uses and extends surrounding the original use cases.

When naming a use case, you may find it helpful to complete the sentence "This use case provides the ability to..." The Use Case Diagrams include a descriptive summary of each use case that clearly states the business's desired result in response to a business event. Summaries corresponding to each use case depicted in the diagram establish an initial Use Case Description for the use case. The summary is a two- to three-sentence explanation of the use case to capture the context discovered in the session. It also provides a quick reference for later in the project when the full Use Case Description becomes larger.

After the first attempt at defining use cases, the Object Architect looks for overlaps or duplication, combining mandatory duplications into a new, separate use case. The relationship between use cases that share duplication is the <<uses>> association. Use cases that show optional behavior are created and diagrammed with the <<extends>> relationship.

There may be a tendency to create use cases with too much granularity. If one use case has similarities with another but answers a "what if" question, you should probably combine them into one use case. If a use case becomes too complex, you can divide it into multiple use cases and diagram it with <<uses>> or <<extends>> relationships.

> **Tip** To remember the direction of the <<uses>> relationship for a use case, the generalization arrow points at the new use case being "used." The direction of the generalization arrow for an <<extends>> relationship points at the base use case being "extended."

There is no direct actor for both <<uses>> and <<extends>> use cases. The actor is either the use case that <<uses>> the use case or the use case that receives the <<extends>>.

Do not create multiple use cases that appear to split the state of a major object. You will likely end up packaging this into one Solution Area anyway. As a means of managing complexity, try to keep everything about the life cycle of an object together in one use case. You then have a better chance at creating single-purpose objects and controlling object refinement. This helps maintain object independence.

Sometimes people want to use a department or title to name an actor. If that is how they work, use that name. Change the name if you find genuine role inheritance occurring between actors.

Case Study One often discussed topic concerns differentiating between an actor that interacts with the business and one that interacts directly with the system. In this case study, this translates to "Is it the customer or a ticket agent that interacts with the system?" The discussion generally leads to other questions such as "Is the customer doing the same things as the ticket agent?" "Are they redundant actors?" "When does the concept of the customer go away to be replaced by a ticket agent?"

The UML provides an actor stereotype called <<case worker>> to distinguish between an actor outside the system and someone who interacts directly with both the external actor and the system. Although you could model both actors, we recommend that you begin with the external actor for three reasons. One, we do not yet know how this will be implemented, nor do we want to impose technology or staffing restrictions now. Consider our Case Study where the customer may want to reserve seating directly without an intervening ticket agent. You can add the internal actor later when modeling begins to consider implementation aspects. Two, the information technologist should focus on the business transaction, not on intermediary (and potentially unnecessary) layers created to accomplish it. This means we must look at it from the eyes of the customer first. Determining how the system or other personnel support the business comes later. Third, the external actor may later become a class. Starting with an actor assists in distilling its behaviors and attributes. We can choose which behavior and attributes to transform into the class representation and which are best left with the actor as we later refine the human/machine boundary.

From the Case Study Problem Assessment, we identified the major areas of the businesses and possible uses of the system. We recognize from the problem assessment that we eventually capture customer demographics. We initially model the customer as an actor knowing that the customer likely becomes a class later. We assume the actor customer interacts with the current <<case worker>> actor, ticket agent. We only show customer for clarity.

Figure 3-1—Initial Use Case Diagram shows the initial Use Case Diagram developed from the Problem Assessment.

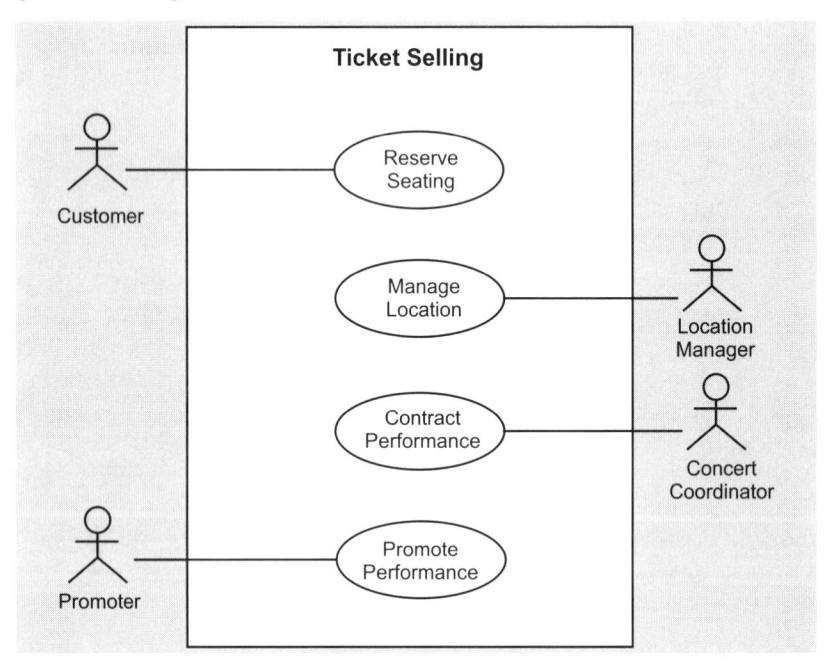

Figure 3-1— Initial Use Case Diagram

Summaries corresponding to each use case depicted in the diagram establish an initial Use Case Description for the use case. The summary is a two- to three-sentence explanation of the use case to capture the context discovered in the session. It also provides a quick reference for later in the project when the full Use Case Description becomes larger. We have used the following template for describing use cases; modeling tools each have their own "fill-ins."

> **Use Case Summaries**
> Name: Reserve Seating
> Summary: Customer reserves seating for a performance. Customer selects seating and performance, pays with cash or credit card, and receives one or more tickets.

Assumptions:
Actors: Customer
Preconditions:
Description:
Exceptions:
Postconditions:

Name: Manage Location
Summary: Location Manager reserves a location for anticipated performances. This includes establishing contracts for maintenance, refreshment, and security services at a particular performance location.
Assumptions:
Actors: Location Manager
Preconditions:
Description:
Exceptions:
Postconditions:

Name: Contract Performance
Summary: Concert Coordinator establishes a contract with a performing artist or group and calculates the ticket price structure based on markup, the performer, and prime seating. The Concert Coordinator oversees the printing of the tickets.
Assumptions:
Actors: Concert Coordinator
Preconditions:
Description:
Exceptions:
Postconditions:

Name: Promote Performance
Summary: Promoter advertises upcoming performance.
Assumptions:
Actors: Promoter
Preconditions:
Description:
Exceptions:
Postconditions:

Note that now the summaries lack detail. This will evolve into the true structure, believe us! You are simply trying to capture the major landmarks at this point. This does provide us with enough information to start drawing the high-level class diagram.

Create Initial Class Diagram

Role(s): Object Architect and Business Area Experts

The Object Architect reviews the Problem Assessment and each use case to extract and define classes. The Class Diagram contains major and possibly some preliminary associations between classes. If available, information on dynamic associations between classes is considered. The Object Architect also models any exchange of information, the dynamic messaging, that occurs between class objects. This includes any expected interfaces to other systems.

The Class Diagram grows in detail throughout the development life cycle. You initially want to focus only on the core business objects to both minimize complexity and maximize understanding. We refer to the core business objects as domain objects. Actors control domain objects. You begin with the obvious real-life objects, avoiding the contrived objects that later support implementation.

To keep it simple, you could look for common nouns used in the Problem Assessment, Use Case Diagram, and use case summaries. These nouns or "things" may become classes or attributes. Not all nouns automatically become classes. With the noun-based approach, most classes are probably of the entity type. There are other means to derive this, but this works for a first-time Object Architect.

You may do this with your Business Area Experts in a facilitated session. As you identify objects, consider how the objects relate to and communicate with each other. You may capture some attributes, operations, and relationships, although this is not your goal at this point. However, if some obvious ones are uncovered, add them to a class. Use attribute types if this helps clarify an attribute, for example, degrees, dollars, etc.

If you have an entity/relationship data modeling background, you may find similarities in these concepts when creating the Class Diagram. You do not want to think only of entities, attributes, and relationships, though. Class attributes can be both static and dynamic (also called operations). Even at this stage, be careful about the classes you identify. Avoid redundancy and classes that are not relevant to the problem domain. Avoid classes that are really roles such as teacher, volunteer, or manager. Instead, create an employee class, thereby allowing that employee to assume several roles. Generalization and aggregation naturally occur as you try to hide detail and encourage broader thinking.

Naming is important—let the Business Area Experts choose the names for most everything. After all, it is their business. There are times, though, that the same name means two very different things and requires them to choose more discrete names. Business Area Experts from different departments may realize they use different names for the same thing. Having them in the same room helps eliminate redundant naming.

Case Study Our first attempt does not try to capture anything but the structure itself, that is, the classes and associations among classes. We do not try to determine multiplicity for the associations, nor do we add any attributes or operations. Though there are many candidate attributes and operations embodied in the references, we concentrate first on the structure. We can efficiently place the attributes and operations after the basic structure stabilizes. Note also that we could have created a class for a Cash Register. We are trying to capture the real-world things in our domain. Each real-world thing has attributes and behavior, whether the "system" needs to incorporate them or not. We postpone the decision to incorporate this until after we gain a better understanding of the business needs and discover more potential solutions.

Figure 3-2—Initial Class Diagram shows the initial classes identified from these use cases.

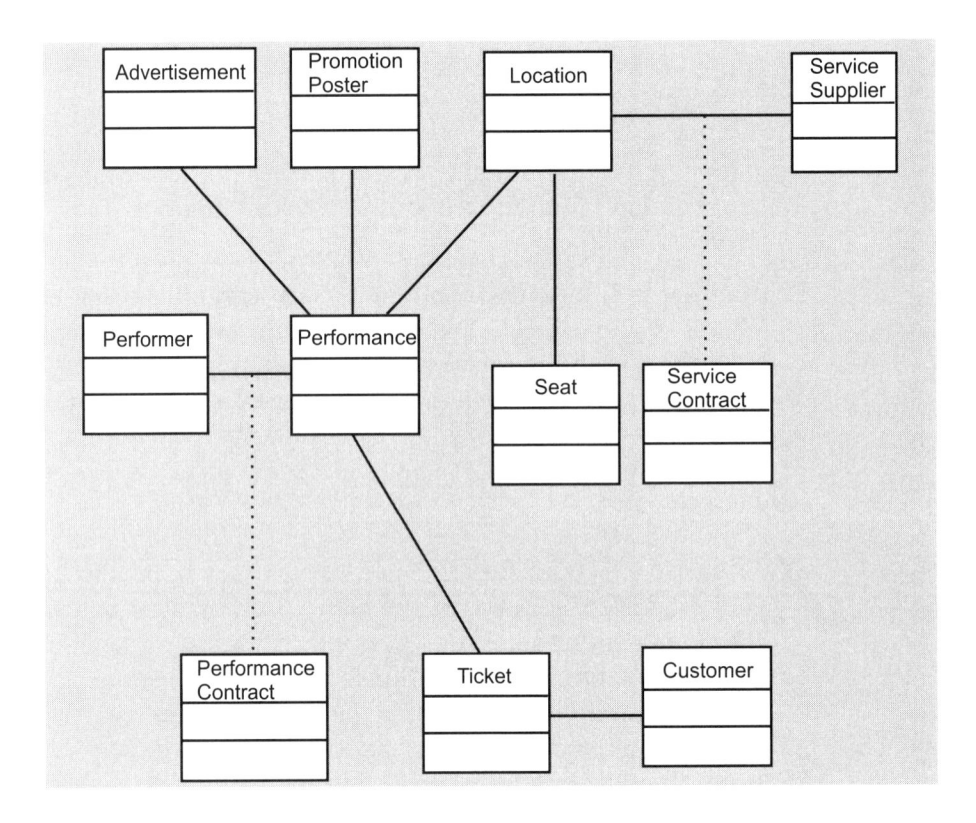

Figure 3-2—
Initial Class
Diagram

Establish Documentation Approach

Role(s): Document Architect, Project Manager, and Project Sponsor

The Document Architect meets with the Project Manager and Project Sponsor to assess which documentation deliverables are required for the solution. Documentation may include a User Instructions Guide and an Information Reference Guide. These individuals identify the purpose of producing the documentation—whether it is for quick reference, establishing user procedures, or building a repository of business information. Initial and periodic measurement of effectiveness can provide justification of the usefulness and clarity of the documentation.

At this time, you plan how to deliver documentation to users both initially and in subsequent upgrades. This includes deciding who has responsibility for distribution, the specific distribution sites, and the document delivery mechanism (electronic or hardcopy). You also determine responsibility for updating future versions of the documentation and how often this occurs.

Case Study Now for the decisions made in our Case Study. Because of the high turnover of ticket agents and their low computer skills, we determine that each ticket agent should have a hardcopy of the User Instructions Guide. The Document Architect continues with the responsibility for document maintenance.

For the Information Reference Guide, the business wants an online terminology description for each user interface. The Document Architect maintains updates to the Information Reference Guide. These updates coincide with other software upgrades. To measure documentation effectiveness, new employees provide responses through a survey.

Establish Training Approach

Role(s): Project Manager, Trainer, and Project Sponsor

The Trainer and Project Manager meet with the Project Sponsor to understand the level of training needed for the solution. This includes identifying the types and number of users, any in-process training efforts, and the potential number of geographic locations. Examining the use case actors reveals the user community and overall responsibilities.

The Project Sponsor specifies measurements for training success. The Trainer eventually incorporates these measures into the Training Curriculum. To measure success, the Trainer issues a survey or test before, during, and after training has completed.

Case Study In the Case Study, the Problem Assessment identified that these ticket agents have minimal computer skills. The discussion uncovers that the current training is unstructured. New hires get a quick overview with the expectation that they learn what they need on the job. There is no consistency across the five locations. We respond with a decision to provide basic computer skills for all ticket agents. Next, we identify common situations that occur with ticket purchasing and describe how the ticket agent should respond to them. Deeper use case analysis obtains the situations and responses through the development of Use Case Scenarios. We then explore how to convey those responses as procedures in a structured training session before on-the-job experience begins. Last, we develop the training in a standardized fashion so that all locations receive the same information.

The Project Sponsor states that users should feel comfortable with the solution one month after training. We decide that the same survey to measure documentation effectiveness will perform double-duty by including measures for training.

Explore Infrastructure Architecture Options

Role(s): Project Manager, Project Sponsor, and Infrastructure Architect

The Infrastructure Architect and Project Manager meet with the Project Sponsor to briefly assess the current architecture, identify geographic access points, and identify any security constraints. They also determine if third-party software participates in any part of the solution.

The Infrastructure Architect then documents the current infrastructure in a Deployment Diagram based on the Problem Assessment, use cases, and the technology strategy defined for the enterprise. At this point, this includes high-level categories such as main operating systems, database management systems, user interfaces, networks, and other infrastructure architecture categories like mainframe, client/server, or Internet.

We recommend stabilizing the devices on the Deployment Diagram as early as possible in the project given the long lead time in approving capital expenses, ordering, and installing. However, remain flexible before committing to any technology platform while you allow the business solution to mature!

Case Study In our Case Study, the business currently has the classic two-tier client/server architecture. They have identified a goal of deploying some portion of the business on the Internet. This greatly affects the infrastructure, as it means minimally adding the web server(s) to the architecture. Regardless of the Internet, the move to a three-tier infrastructure architecture is appropriate due to the performance problems; separating the application services from the database services allows for better performance tuning. The object-oriented style helps us create objects based on their responsibility; ergo the data-intensive entity objects can be "placed" on the database server, while the calculation-intensive control objects can be placed on the application server. We deploy the visual user interface objects on the client machine.

Figure 3-3—Current Infrastructure Deployment Diagram depicts the current infrastructure.

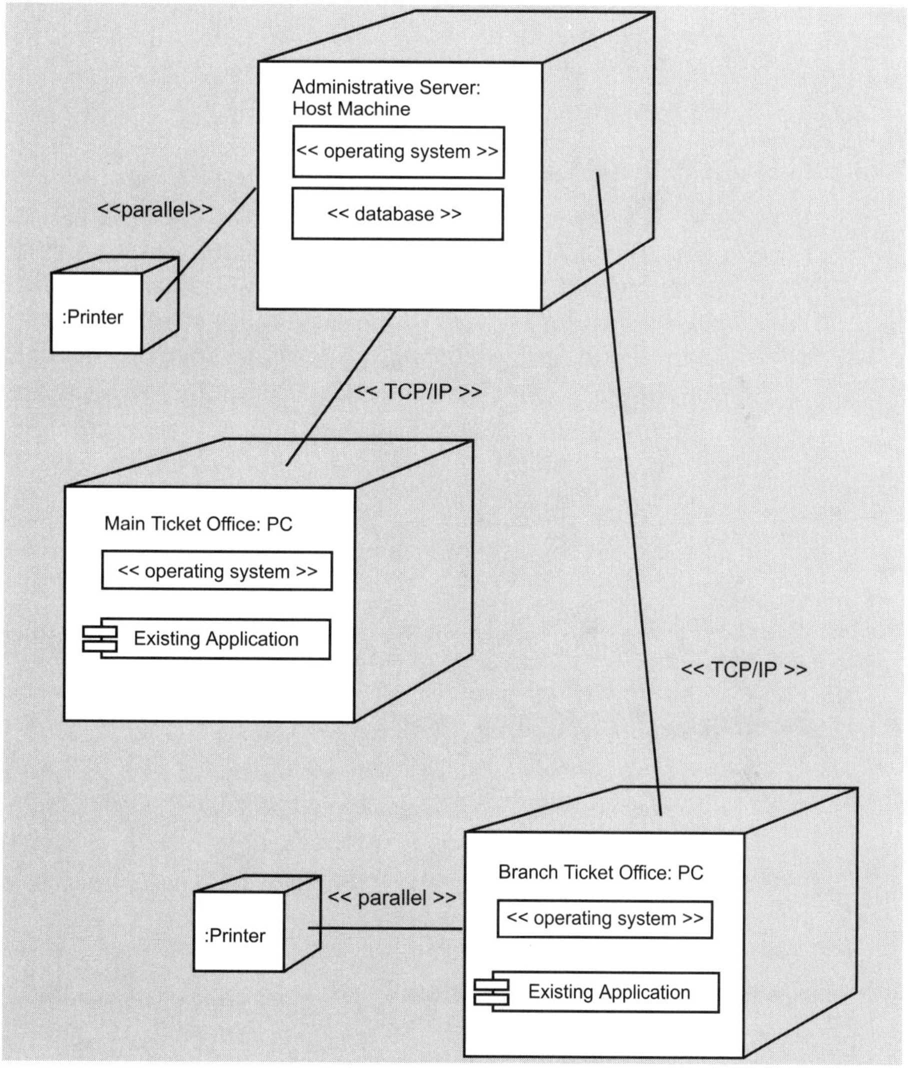

Figure 3-3—Current Infrastructure Deployment Diagram

The business currently manages and supports the computer systems of the branch ticket offices from the main ticket office. The branch ticket offices merely sell the tickets. We discuss if the business should continue this approach for the new three-tier infrastructure architecture. The business does not want to hire full-time staff at each branch ticket office. We decide to continue to support branch ticket offices remotely but consider on-site support during initial implementation.

The impact of adding the Internet simply means the style of the user interface object and its behavior change to conform to a Web browser, thereby minimizing the deployment of heavy-duty interface objects on the client machine.

Establish Project Standards

Role(s): Project Manager, Project Sponsor, Object Architect, and Infrastructure Architect

The project team establishes standards for design, development, and communications for the entire project. This activity may simply confirm standards already in place. Standards that you may address include establishing object model standards, testing standards, error handling, security, and naming. At a minimum, locations and ownership for shared project files containing deliverables (including documents, object models, and source code) need to be set and published back to the team.

Should there be no existing standard (as is often the case), the team must create them.

The Project Sponsor reviews the recommended guidelines.

Plan Solution Packaging and Delivery

The purpose of this activity is to identify natural groupings of use cases and classes. You package these groupings based on both business need evident in the use cases and the classes you distill from the use case summaries. This provides the basis for charting the solution strategy; that is, deciding which use cases provide an immediate benefit to the business if completed first. Packaging supports planning concurrent work options and identifying multiple Solution Areas. The project team further breaks down each Solution Area into a fixed number of increments. Recall that an increment defines content (as the target goal) within the scope of the Solution Area.

Deliverables

Solution Area Scope Statement
Use Case Diagram
Class Diagram
Project Plan
Cost/Benefit Analysis

Tasks:

Develop Solution Area Scope Statement

Role(s): Project Manager (Facilitator) and Object Architect

The Object Architect and the Project Manager divide the use cases and classes into distinct Solution Areas that can be developed in parallel, recognizing that integration occurs before final implementation. The Object Architect then creates distinct Use Case Diagrams and Class Diagrams for each of the Solution Areas. The Object Architect cross-references classes used in use cases and looks for use cases that reference similar classes. The Object Architect groups these into packages. These packages also determine the Solution Area use case and class ownership.

The Project Manager then assesses the packages to divide the project into parallel development and adaptable implementation pieces. Some Solution Areas may be postponed or excluded from the project altogether because they are out of scope.

Remember that objects communicate with one another through messages controlled by the interface of an object. The best object-oriented designs define clear boundaries between systems that communicate through messaging only. Applying this to the business means minimizing the number of messages (coupling) between Solution Areas. The Object Architect's goal is to define a Solution Area that is self-contained and isolates a view of the overall solution; however, it must follow a view matching the business.

Some objects may participate in multiple Solution Areas (especially core business objects like Customer and Product). You must control the evolution of an object by assigning its ownership to a single Solution Area. Identify the "owner" based on which Solution Area first instantiates the object as part of the business solution. Share and integrate the refined definition across all Solution Areas and the enterprise to promote reuse.

Assessing the Use Case Diagram and Class Diagram together avoids a functional decomposition that can arise from referencing use cases only. You apply both of these to look for breaks that can keep similar uses together.

Packaging helps to see which have low coupling (a minimum number of associations) and high cohesion (maximum internal consistency). A

Solution Area tends to have use cases that share objects. Using the visual representation of both the Use Case Diagram and the Class Diagram, you should readily see a small number of links between packages and a high number of links within a package.

You update the Class Diagram and the Use Case Diagram by drawing dotted lines around the classes that have the least number of associations, while keeping in mind the use cases that potentially use those classes. This may take a few passes with the eraser before you get it right. We use packaging to exemplify the Solution Area boundaries on both diagrams.

The traditional scope, time, quality, and cost factors define the number of Solution Areas and their content. You must balance the cost of available skilled resources against the required coverage of the subject matter, date needed, and quality of the solution.

Reality says you cannot do it all at once. Most projects are too big and time constraints too demanding to propose a comprehensive, start-to-end, do-it-all project. Here you have an opportunity to work with smaller units of development. Therefore, you must break up the project to manage complexity, the overall goal being to break the project into concurrently manageable units of work.

You can develop almost anything—concurrently or not—for a cost. There are additional considerations, though, when developing in parallel. To find Solution Area boundaries, press for early understanding of the natural segmentation of the business. Then create the corresponding project to follow the contours of the business too.

The goal thus far was to gain enough background understanding of the business problem to find its natural boundaries. You now divide the project into parallel workloads that minimize conflict during development and future integration.

After identifying Solution Areas, the Project Manager needs to allocate work content across increments. The intent is to ensure full coverage of the Solution Area use cases and classes, balance the workload, and build from the core outward. The first increment provides the foundation for the work performed in successive increments. To quote Johann Wolfgang von Goethe, "Things that matter most must never be at the mercy of things that matter least." The description of the use case and the judgment of the Business Area Experts should sufficiently identify which is the core. You allot extends use cases and use cases dependent on the core to successive increments. Under no circumstance should you split a use case across Solution Areas.

When identifying what belongs in an increment and determining what to develop first, consider the following:

- What gives the business the most value, in the shortest time, with the least cost?
- You cannot wait for other objects to be completed.
- A true object has no dependency on any other object. An object by nature is independent. You cannot assume other objects exist.
- Balance complexity between the number of anticipated resources to build an increment and any time constraints.

Case Study By coincidence only, the Solution Areas line up to one use case per Solution Area. Our identified Solution Areas are:

Solution Area 1: Manage Location

Solution Area 2: Contract Performance

Solution Area 3: Reserve Seating

Solution Area 4: Promote Performance

Figure 3-4—Use Case Diagram and Class Diagram with Solution Area boundaries illustrates the Solution Area boundaries.

For the Manage Location Solution Area, we determine it requires three increments. Although we have only identified one use case, we see an immediate need to set up a location. Part of setting up every location includes defining sections, rows, seats, and "blocked view" seats. This is quite enough work to last one increment. The second increment implements third-party software that supports touch screening for defining location seating. The third increment covers establishing contracts for maintenance, refreshment, and security services. The last two increments can wait if necessary.

The business has determined to enhance the entire system for maintaining performance contracts. Therefore, we decide the first increment for the Contract Performance Solution Area consists of scheduling the date and time of performances and performance cancellations. The second automates ticket price calculations. The third increment retains information about contractual negotiations—payments, penalties, reimbursement, performer concert requirements, etc.

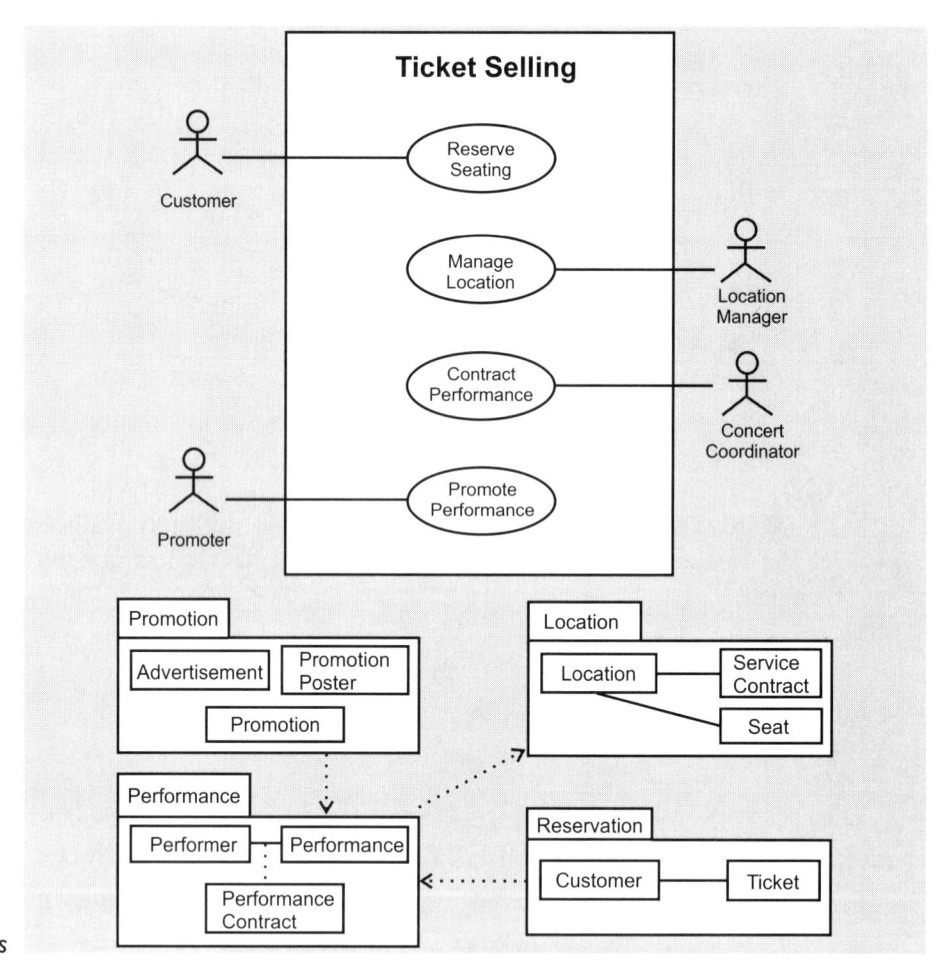

Figure 3-4—Use Case Diagram and Class Diagram with Solution Area boundaries

We plan to develop the Reserve Seating Solution Area in two increments. The first increment contains everything necessary to support ticket purchases. The second increment includes customer demographics and address standardization.

Through further discussion, we resolve the issue of "What content belongs on the Internet?" The Promote Performance Solution Area desires use of the Internet to broaden the target market. The first increment places performance schedules and location information on a static web page. The second increment allows customers to query performance information by performer, location, or date.

We now take the business view in deciding how to coordinate which Solution Area or Solution Areas to address first. Always foremost in our minds is to deliver something of value as early as possible! To make this choice, we look for the area of the business that has the immediate potential of providing value. The business determined that increasing customer satisfaction has the highest priority. The heart of the business is to sell tickets—the main source of customer contact. This time we base our choice on the mechanism with the most opportunity for impact on customer satisfaction and the revenue stream. The Manage Location Solution Area, while important, does not by itself bring revenue into the business. The Contract Performance Solution Area sets the stage, so to speak, for delivering the product (the performance) and establishing ticket prices. The Promote Performance Solution Area depends on the other areas to complete first; you cannot promote a performance that does not exist! The Reserve Seating Solution Area is, therefore, our first choice.

However, looking more closely at what we need to sell tickets, we realize that ticketing information depends on both seating and pricing. We decide to build the core of the Manage Location Solution Area first, then concurrently create both the Reserve Seating Solution Area and the Contract Performance Solution Area, and last develop the Promote Performance Solution Area. Although the Reserve Seating Solution Area needs ticket prices, we believe that we can build most of the Reserve Seating Solution Area and integrate the ticket pricing later because the interface should be minimized to the Ticket object.

Since we decided to build only the first increment of the Manage Location Solution Area, we will need to return with subsequent increments to enhance it later. If resources did not restrict us, we may have chosen to build the Contract Performance Solution Area concurrently with the Manage Location Solution Area because they both build core business objects. The technical view always recommends building the core objects first, but reality says you may have to come up with a creative way to move ahead when the content of the other area is unavailable. Carefully crafting a way to support the business with limited resources is what separates the true Enterprise Agent from the crowd.

Our case study follows the Reserve Seating Solution Area assuming completion of the first increment regarding the seating structure from the Manage Location Solution Area. We later integrate the Reserve Seating Solution Area with the Contract Performance Solution Area for illustration.

Tailor Approach

Role(s): Project Sponsor and Project Manager

The Project Manager puts the tailored tasks into a project-planning tool as a Work Breakdown Structure (WBS). The Project Manager creates the initial work breakdown structure by scheduling the use cases most vital for the Solution Area to the first increment. All subsequent work builds upon this base.

> **Tip** The Critical Path Method highlights the set of tasks which have an impact on the overall project timeline. PERT scheduling is a technique to display multiple dependencies of tasks. The two are used together to view the nuances of scheduling; each can be used to validate the other.

The Project Manager adjusts the tasks in the approach to align it with the project requirements. This may exclude unnecessary deliverables or more likely combine roles and tasks into a grouping that more closely aligns the work to the project "size" or nature. Based on the nature of the application, there may be no need for some tasks or deliverables.

Although we have provided many deliverables, tasks, and roles within our approach, each project may require adjustments based on the business environment. Feel free to eliminate the tasks and adjust the approach.

For example, the project may need Business Area Experts at a greater or lesser level to avoid delays, so a rescheduling of the work could alter the sequence and content of the approach. For another example, the budget dictates that infrastructure architecture changes cannot occur. The amount of time necessary to accommodate changes in the corresponding deliverables forces allocating the tasks and resources differently.

A more common example is that an enterprise already has an established development approach, with a desire to merge our approach with its own to create a comprehensive view of how the two fit together. An organization may also want specific deliverables added. In these last two examples, some negotiation occurs to arrive at a consensus. You may also want to adjust the approach after a "proof of concept."

This task essentially begins the project plan for the project. Now you specify exactly which deliverables are appropriate to accomplish the solution. Your analysis examines the deliverables to see what steps to take to produce them and identifies the skills needed to perform each step. These steps, though, should produce a deliverable. Besides adding tasks, you may also want to combine tasks and condense deliverables. Start by reviewing neighboring tasks to look for synergism or flow, possibly merging multiple tasks into one. Tasks should be on the project plan only if linked to a deliverable that is ultimately connected to the final product. You must identify a deliverable for each task (see Focus on Deliverables). There is no reason for a task unless it is doing something to advance completion of a deliverable and, eventually, the completion of the final product.

When adding or removing tasks, keep in mind available resources. This is not cheating; it is common sense. The Project Manager should not neglect to plan for any support that the system needs before, during, and after implementation. This includes determining responsibility for ongoing support of the day-to-day system use. Some organizations have a help desk or an on-call schedule for support. You may be able to identify the specific persons within the organization who have this responsibility. You may create new positions for support such as a full-time object librarian or an object-oriented database administrator. It is best to identify these positions now to give an organization enough time for training or hiring.

Please refer to the template of our approach in Microsoft® Project 98 format on the CD included with this book. The file contains all of the phases, activities, and tasks in our approach, which you may adapt to your needs.

Estimate Tasks in Project Plan

Role(s): Project Manager

The Project Manager reviews the Solution Area Scope Statement and the calculated critical path for unexpected delays or surprises.

The Project Manager takes the assigned Solution Area packages and estimates the amount of development effort needed for each. The Project Manager then refines the project timeline based on this estimate.

Correctly estimating the amount of work takes up the most time while developing a project plan. To help cross-reference our approach to your estimating, here are some suggestions. Estimating for the Structure Solution phase depends upon the number of use cases and the amount of new infrastructure architecture.

We presented planning and estimating techniques for the Build Solution phase in Chapter 2, The Iterative Style section.

The amount of work required to complete the Integrate Solution phase depends upon several factors such as the number of classes, the number of Solution Areas, and the thoroughness of integration you plan to do during the Build Solution phase. Standard time must include integrating with the previous version and other Solution Areas.

For the Implement Structure phase, consider the amount of training, the number of geographic installation points, and the amount of new infrastructure architecture.

Case Study For the Case Study, we estimated each Solution Area using the 360 guideline. Recall the 360 guideline only covers the three consecutive three-week Build Solution phase iterations, not the time for the additional Structure Solution and Integrate Solution phases that comprise the complete increment. Also, the 360 hours measures an elapsed duration timebox, not 360 total hours for all resources. We apply the guideline as our estimate for each of the two increments for the Reserve Seating Solution Area.

Apply Resources to Project Plan

Role(s): Project Manager and Project Sponsor

The Project Manager and Project Sponsor determine the skills needed and the number of people to fill each role. The Project Manager then assigns people to roles in the Project Plan and levels the resource allocation based on availability and skill.

Once you have the "what" (the deliverables), the "how" (the tasks that need to be done), and the "when" (the estimates), you need to determine the "who." This is just a matter of assigning resources to roles that produce deliverables using specific tasks within the duration estimated. Whew! Simple, right?

Here we have the concept of ability versus availability. Ability means applying the right resource to the right role. Our approach outlines the roles necessary to produce each deliverable. It is therefore imperative that the skills determine which resources to recruit to the project team.

Availability, simply put, means "do not burn out the project team!" Allocate enough people time to get the work done. The (limited) number of resources in the project may force you to reassess the increment strategy. Be sure to accommodate vacations, regular holidays, and some contingency time for emergencies. A tendency is to load the schedule with 40-hour work weeks and schedule tasks in hours. One manager was so enamored with the scheduling software that he went to the quarter-hour level. It only took a few meetings where he himself arrived late to wreck his perfect plan. We recommend scheduling at the day level. Yes, you can do two or more things in a day. However, the care and feeding of a project plan, especially on large, multi-Solution Area projects may bury the Project Manager in too much noise and detail.

Ideally, the Project Manager should assign role experts with experience in specific technologies, soft skills, and business knowledge to a specific deliverable. These resources could be brought in as needed so that they are free to be leveraged in other projects that may require similar skills and experience. This is an example of skill reuse; dare we call this virtual staffing? You may already experience this with roles that require highly specialized skills.

Tip Although we identify the roles that perform tasks, we have found that projects are more successful when a core group of people stay with the full life cycle of the project. Many important nuances and opportunities to build a strong team are lost with turnover.

Often, a Project Manager is unable to recruit the right people when only categorizing by the waterfall roles of analyst, designer, or programmer. With the iterative approach, a team is involved in every life cycle of the project and therefore must have an understanding of how their specific role blends with every other role. The challenge is to fit the available skill sets to the roles. With the number of roles we have identified, you might believe that you need ten or more people to staff a project—not so. In fact, teams may have five or fewer people. We have highlighted the roles necessary for each specific task to assist your skill matching. You may split or combine roles based on resource abilities and the amount of work. It is quite common for one resource to play many roles; on larger projects, however, we do not recommend doing this. It is too easy for the resource to lose focus by being drawn in multiple directions.

In this task, the Project Sponsor determines who within the organization should "own" the high-level business objects. Actors within the Use Case Diagram help to identify these owners. Often, business areas become object owners or already "own" the object. Object owners lead Solution Area development by providing business knowledge, vision, and solution validation. The Project Sponsor obtains resource commitments in terms of actual people, when each person is available, and the amount of time committed. The Project Sponsor reviews the resulting Project Plan and approves or revises it.

You may want to identify metrics for selecting team members and weight the metrics by their importance. Typical metrics for selecting team members include expertise, vision, and availability. You ought to avoid the tendency to section off by department. Find Business Area Experts with cross-functional perspectives (horizontal partitioning). Then balance with select Business Area Experts at various levels throughout the enterprise (vertical partitioning). A team constructed this way brings together vision, cross-functional integration, and operational cohesiveness.

You may need to adjust task duration for learning curves. At this time, you may also want to inventory skills to adjust the plan for training and support.

Case Study For the case study, we select our Business Area Experts from sales, the owner of ticket reservation. We have one person for each role except for the role of Object Developer. This role requires two people to fill it.

Prepare the Cost/Benefit Analysis

Role(s): Project Manager and Project Sponsor

The Project Manager identifies anticipated capital expenditures and expenses. The Project Sponsor specifies benefits, both quantitative and non-quantitative. The Project Manager then calculates the anticipated Return On Investment (ROI). The assessed ROI with the greatest return may cause a change in the increment strategy.

At this point in the project, it may be difficult to determine costs completely. Each Solution Area may uncover major changes to the incremental strategy during the Structure Solution phase. Infrastructure architecture needs may alter based on analysis. Often, though, project teams must propose a high-level cost to a review committee who governs whether or not development may begin.

Certainly, you need to gather hardware, software, personnel, and materials costs. This includes a full projection of support and licensing for a minimum five-year lifetime. You also need to factor in the time value of money in calculating the Return On Investment (ROI). There are at least three major models for assessing the financial merit of an internal investment: payback model, accounting rate-of-return model, and discounted-cash-flow model.[2] Note that the payback model ignores risk and the accounting rate-of-return model ignores the time value of money. The discounted-cash-flow model factors in the time value of money and can include risk if factored into the "minimum" rate of return.

Payback Model

The amount proposed to be invested (the cost) is divided by the amount expected to be gained each year in the future (the benefit), giving the number of years it takes for the capital to be returned.[3]

Accounting Rate-of-Return Model

The Rate of Return = (Cost reduction − Investment)/(Investment)(Years).[4] You compare the rate of return with what the company is paying in capital or other internal investments. If the project rate of return is higher than the preset rate of return, then the project is viable.

Discounted-Cash-Flow Model

This model includes the time value of money. You divide the yearly payback by the discount factor $(1 + i)^n$ to get the present value, where i is the interest rate and n is the number of years.[5] This is the most difficult formula to set up; you may wish to discuss this with your resident spreadsheet wizard.

---

2 Lawrence H. Putnam and Ware Myers. *Measures for Excellence: Reliable Software On Time, Within Budget.* Englewood Cliffs, NJ: Yourdon Press, 1992, 180-181.

3 Ibid.

4 Ibid.

5 Ibid.

These models are just a start in calculating a cost/benefit analysis. Costs are typically easier to identify than benefits when there is an existing record of accomplishment gained through similar project history. The benefit is more difficult to measure than cost when deciding what to include. Benefits may occur by allocating staff to something more profitable to the business. You could also calculate potential revenue gains. Surprisingly, some project approvals are based on the use of new technology just because it happens to be the trendy thing to do. Your financial department may have a different view, so take the time to assemble your justification. Generally, you find the most support and financial backing when the benefits align with the business strategy and objectives.

Case Study To give you an example of a very high-level ROI determination, we consider the cost of investing. Assuming the company's cost of capital (the cost of investing) is 11 percent. This means that you mark up the cost of the investment by 11 percent to cover the "cost of the cost." Although a specific ROI using the payback method in our case study garnered a 9 percent ROI, the intangible benefits of having satisfied customers (decided by the owners) overrides the pure financial view. You can spend large amounts of time coming up with a tangible number. If this helps your case, good for you, but be prepared for the opposite. In our case study, it came down to a gut feel that the benefit is greater than the calculated cost.

Confirm Solution Strategy

The project team reviews deliverables produced thus far and confirms that the project has the appropriate strategy in terms of scope, content, and support. During this assessment, you may find that part or all of the team needs training to proceed with further development. You may need to prepare some initial development hardware, software, and network access for the Business Area Experts, developers, and Trainers. The project team also reviews open issues, risks, and change requests.

Deliverables

Solution Strategy Confirmation

Risk Assessment

Tasks:

Obtain Solution Strategy Confirmation

Role(s): Project Manager (Facilitator) and Project Sponsor

The Project Manager reviews all major deliverables developed within the Chart Solution phase with the Project Sponsor and obtains confirmation to proceed to the next phase. This may result in change to any or all of the deliverables produced so far. It is much better to catch it now rather than halfway through the project.

Assess Risk

Role(s): Project Manager

The best way to assist a project's success is to minimize risks as the project progresses. Of course, understand that you want to address the greatest and imminent risks first. Assessing risk should actually start immediately before the project begins. We note it in all of the confirmation tasks as a reminder.

One very effective technique we have used to organize risk assessment is SWOT analysis. SWOT stands for Strengths, Weaknesses, Opportunities, and Threats. SWOT analysis has its roots in technology impact analysis from information engineering.[6] Projects since the early 1990s have extended and successfully applied this to project management. The Project Manager identifies the project team strengths and weaknesses and the external threats and opportunities. For each of these realized assessments, the Project Manager identifies possible outcomes, both positive and negative. The Project Manager then identifies actions to move weaknesses into strengths and threats into opportunities. The Project Manager also nourishes existing strengths and opportunities.

Although it may take some time to use this technique well, following a systematic approach is the first step to developing this skill:

1. Identify the project strengths, weaknesses, threats, and opportunities. Be specific and identify the people involved.

---

[6] James Martin. *Information Engineering Book II: Planning and Analysis*. Englewood Cliffs, NJ: Prentice Hall, 1990, 119-124.

2. Identify how each of these specific things can help or hurt the project. Prepare for delays, additional benefits, or cancellations. Identify possible outcomes of threats.

3. Identify ways to enhance strengths and correct weaknesses. List specific actions needed to take advantage of opportunities and to respond to realized threats.

Every project has its strengths and weaknesses, depending on resource availability, skill, and motivation. There are also factors external to the project arena that can drastically enhance or damage the solution outcome. These factors include changes in organizational structure, financial backing, technology, legal, and consumer trends. Nurturing strengths, turning weaknesses into strengths, avoiding threats, and taking advantage of opportunities requires innovation, intuition, and planning.

This SWOT may or may not be something you need to share with the project team. One school of thought is that being brutally honest is important and recommends assessing the people involved by name, but keeping the assessment confidential. This is somewhat more compassionate when assessing a person's ability to perform under the current project constraints. Another school of thought publishes the assessment to the entire team so that everyone takes responsibility for the situation and outcomes. The Project Manager assigns individual team members to take each action. Note that the Project Manager is not exempt from assessment regardless of the choice taken.

This is not a one-time task. The Project Manager regularly updates the strengths, weaknesses, opportunities, and threats to keep current with constant changes in the culture and environment. Regular status reporting provides the mechanism for this to occur.

Sometimes there may be so many risk items identified from the above analysis technique that it seems daunting to decide where to start. Here is a set of steps to help you to create your tactical plan for reducing risk:

1. Identify the complete list of risk items.
2. Determine severity, probability, and expected time frame for each risk item.
3. Gain agreement on risk priorities.
4. Attack each risk by its agreed-upon priority.
5. Monitor your list periodically and record progress, additions, and resolutions.

Case Study Table 3-2—Chart Solution Risk Assessment is a sample Risk Assessment created during this phase.

Table 3-2—Chart Solution Risk Assessment

Category	Item	Action
Strength	Team is committed to OO style of development.	Keep team fired up by distributing current articles on OO success, learnings, and guidelines.
	Team members understand the business.	Look to broaden perspectives outside of current way of doing business—send one or two to trade convention and sponsor professional memberships in trade organizations. Prevent developing narrow view.
Weakness	Team is lacking in OO skills	Establish targeted project team training. Consider hiring a "ringer" from outside the company.
	Users lack computer skills	Schedule fundamental computer skills training.
Opportunity	Executive management is highly committed to the project.	Keep in contact with regular status reporting.
	Accounting really likes the idea of better transaction tracking.	Work to firm up reporting and query capabilities as soon as possible.
Threat	Internet as a technology solution driving the business solution.	Specifically identify the purpose of the Internet and determine measurements for success. Align this with the business strategy.
	New technology for the company.	Provide continuous information on what we are doing—outside periodicals, case studies, etc.—to all areas of the business.
	Marketing is disappointed promotions are not first (promote performance).	Go to lunch with Marketing and let them know if they want to chip in from their budget, you could add additional resources.

Chapter Summary

This chapter has explored the activities and tasks vital to setting the scope and tone for the project. We started by defining the boundaries of work from the concerns and business needs expressed in the Problem Assessment. Through concerted efforts branching from all vocations involved, we created the strategic foundation from which the solution grows. We accomplished this by applying a combination of both use case analysis and high-level object modeling. The inherent strength of this approach balances the two styles. Invoking object modeling early in the effort offsets the tendency towards functional decomposition common in use case analysis. Conversely, we leverage use case modeling to keep object modeling focused on the core business processes.

We included the vocations outside of object-oriented development. The project scope now goes beyond a simple listing of desired functions; it now comprises all vocation-centric needs.

We recognize that influences specific to the business require tailoring of the approach and formalizing new or existing standards and procedures.

Most importantly, we have shown how to carve out smaller Solution Areas to manage the size and complexity of the project. Armed with this knowledge, we have sized the project, worked through the cost/benefit analysis, and created the overall project plan with resources.

The next chapter breaks into the Solution Area view of the project. The next level of modeling with Use Case and Class Diagrams forms the beginnings of the technology solution that supports the business. We apply structure to make the Solution Area a self-sufficient team and describe how to plan iteration refinement.

Chapter 4

Structure Solution

Overview

The purpose of this phase is to specify the structure of the business solution as delimited by the scope of the Solution Area. The Solution Area team further describes the uses of the system, which objects support them, and the iteration strategy for building the technology solution that supports the business solution.

Your project may have only one Solution Area, or it may have many of them concurrently creating an encompassing solution. For projects with two or more concurrent Solution Areas making up the larger project, integration is vital. Although our approach has an absolute convergence point in the Integrate Solution phase, do not be misled! Each Solution Area performs the following activities independently, yet they integrate their solutions along the way to ensure a similar vision throughout the entire project, especially during individual builds. One effective technique is to hold a "mini-integration" meeting by role following a facilitated session with Business Area Experts. For example, all of the Object Architects across the

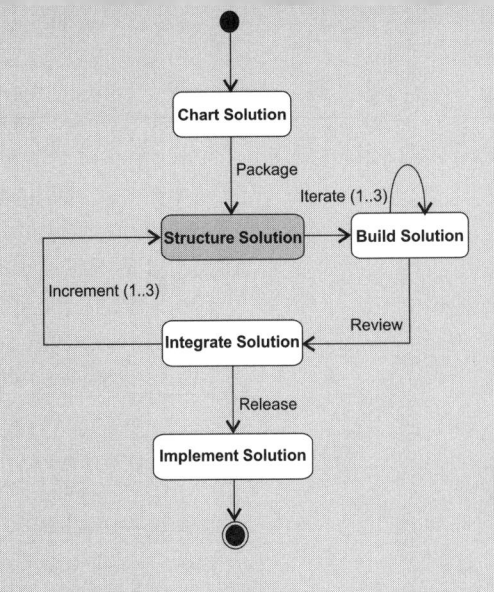

Deliverables:

Change Requests
Class Diagram
Class Library Cross Reference
Deployment Diagram
Development Environment
Information Reference Guide
Infrastructure Acquisition Timeline
Infrastructure Requirements
Issues List
Project Plan
Risk Assessment
Security Restrictions
Software Distribution Procedure
Solution Area Scope Statement
Solution Structure Confirmation
Third-Party Product Evaluation
Training Curriculum
Training Delivery Mechanism
Use Case Diagram
User Instructions Guide

multiple Solution Areas would meet regularly for an hour to compare models, with special emphasis on the shared classes. This cross-functional approach works similarly for all roles. The roles then part ways to produce deliverables and prepare for the next session. Of course, this requires careful planning so that each Solution Area holds similar facilitation sessions on the same day.

You complete this phase once for each <u>increment</u>. This phase sets the content for the increment before plunging into the iterations of the Build Solution phase. After completing the last Build Solution iteration, you return here to establish the content for the next increment. You then follow this phase with the Build Solution phase for the number of its prescribed iterations. Following the last iteration build, you integrate with the current version of the solution and then begin again with the next increment and so on until all increments have completed.

We have chosen to demonstrate this phase using the Reserve Seating Solution Area assuming the completion of the first increment for the Manage Location Solution Area. We specifically show the deliverables and the refinement that results from iteration.

Activities

Structure Use Cases and Classes

The Solution Area team describes each use case packaged within this Solution Area. Note that the Use Case Description merely identifies the events surrounding how an actor interacts with the system, not the detailed system responses to the events.

Deliverables

Use Case Diagram
Class Diagram
Class Library Cross Reference

The initial work concentrates only on the core functionality of the Solution Area and not its exceptions. Naysayers in a facilitated session can delay progress significantly by finding obscure alternative paths and exceptions. Do not humor them or it will turn into a game. The Facilitator acquires a Pavlovian response every time the phrase "but..." is uttered. Only after defining the main steps do you add alternative paths and exceptions as separate Use Case Scenarios.

Tasks:

Refine Use Case Descriptions

Role(s): Object Architect (Facilitator), Business Area Experts, and Document Architect

The Solution Area team creates a detailed description for each use case including preconditions, postconditions, and assumptions. Preconditions and postconditions identify what must be in place before and after the use case carries out its duties. Assumptions are placeholders for the unknown; remove them through resolution before final validation.

Refinement of the Use Case Description uncovers sequences of business events and activities that continue to add detail. This detail eventually becomes a complete Use Case Scenario. There likely will be more than one scenario for each use case. Additional scenarios illustrate exceptions, alternative paths, and error conditions based on the different options available to satisfy the use case. Capture enough information to identify exceptions and alternatives, but do not detail them yet. The core Use Case Scenario details the main path through the complete use case. During the refinement of the description, you may identify exceptions that occur. Embed these in the text itself at the point they are relevant. You may also identify alternatives that you describe in future iterations. Also, record any assumptions you make. Over time, the assumptions disappear as you refine the details. Because use cases are now more fully described, you may notice duplication that allows you to take advantage of inheritance with a <<uses>> type of use case. You can branch out a complex exception case with an <<extends>> use case.

Case Study Considering the Case Study, the next refinement of the use case improves the Reserve Seating Use Case Description. We add qualifying preconditions and postconditions. Note the phrasing of the description, "This use case begins when…" followed by all of the system responses and finishing with "This use case ends when…" This phrasing sets the hard contextual boundaries of the use case and all of the events it includes. It also helps to delimit the human/machine boundary.

Name:	Reserve Seating
Summary:	Customer reserves seating for a performance. Customer selects seating and performance, pays with cash or credit card, and receives one or more tickets.
Assumptions:	
Actors:	Customer
Preconditions:	Performance is booked, location is reserved, and ticket prices are set.
Description:	This use case starts when a customer approaches the ticket booth and requests tickets for a performance. The system responds by confirming information for the requested performance. The system informs customer of remaining seating options and ticket price structures. Customer selects seating area and number of seats. If this is a new customer, the system captures the customer demographics. The customer pays for the tickets. The system collects money, reserves seats, and the customer receives the tickets. This use case ends when the customer leaves with tickets.
Exceptions:	
Postconditions:	Customer demographics and reservation information are stored in the system.

Our beginning statement includes an "and." Why is this important? It shows that one of the components of the statement may be a precondition or may not be useful. If the two are separable, rewrite the phrase to eliminate the compound. In this instance, "Customer approaches ticket booth" is irrelevant, so we remove it.

A question arose at this point: "Is the system keeping demographics without a completed purchase?" Since it is, we decided to make an <<extends>> use case to capture customer demographics. By using the optional form, extending, we can bypass the demographic processing of a repeat customer.

We remove the related "Capture Customer Demographics" text from the Reserve Seating use case and create the new use case. Using the Extension Points notation of the UML, we add the label "new customer," which identifies the location within the Reserve Seating use case where the Capture Customer Demographics use case may occur. Figure 4-1—Updated Use Case Diagram with Capture Customer Demographics Extends shows the new extends use case Capture Customer Demographics focusing on the Reserve Seating use case for emphasis. It extends when a new customer reserves seating.

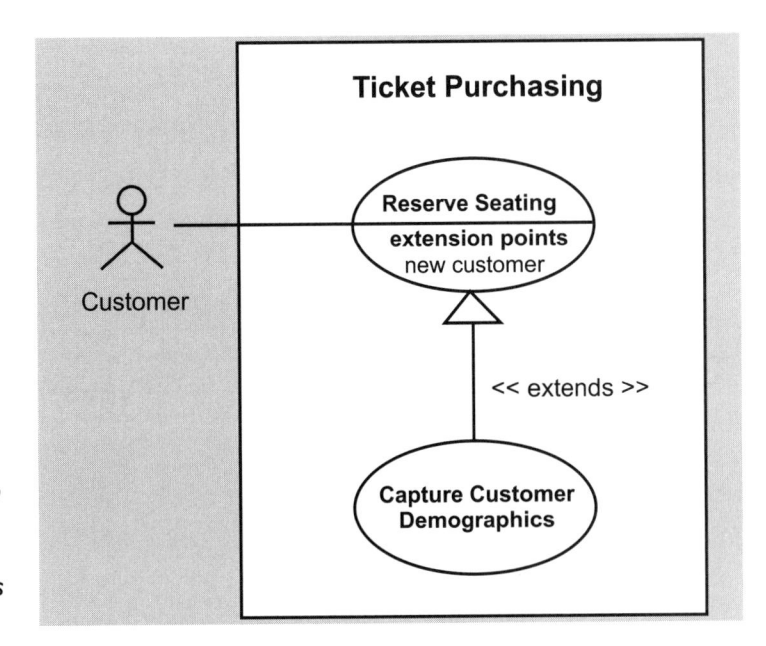

Figure 4-1— Updated Use Case Diagram with Capture Customer Demographics Extends

Ticket Purchasing

Customer — Reserve Seating (extension points: new customer)

<< extends >>

Capture Customer Demographics

In effect, we have just updated the Use Case Diagram to reflect our earlier increment packaging. The customer demographics use case is part of the second increment.

We also look for other business events to identify possible additional scenarios. Through this process, we identify information that helps us determine the number and duration of iterations we need to build each increment. Additional scenarios identified include:

1. Customer cancels the purchase.
2. Different payment types—cash, approved credit, and failed credit.
3. Performance is sold out.
4. Customer requests more tickets for a section than are available.
5. Customer purchases a ticket from one location for a performance at another.
6. Customer purchases different seating price structures.
7. Customer purchases tickets for multiple performances.
8. Customer requests a refund.

After identifying the last scenario, it was determined that the business has a non-refundable purchase policy. We gladly omit this one! The Case Study describes the first four additional Use Case Scenarios in the Build Solution phase. The second iteration covers the Use Case Scenarios 1 and 2; we develop Use Case Scenarios 3 and 4 in the third iteration.

It is important to include at least the scenarios relevant to the core use case in the description. We place these within the description at appropriate places as exceptions so as not to lose them. We review these again before beginning the Build Solution phase as a means to identify iteration strategy.

We update the Reserve Seating use case as follows:

Name:	Reserve Seating
Summary:	Customer reserves seating for a performance. Customer selects seating and performance, pays with cash or credit card, and receives one or more tickets.
Assumptions:	
Actors:	Customer
Preconditions:	Performance is booked, location is reserved, and ticket prices are set.
Description:	This use case begins when customer requests ticket(s) for a performance. The system confirms information for the requested performance. [Exception: Performance sold out]. The customer selects seating area and number of seats. [Exception: The customer cancels purchase (no sale)]. The customer finishes selecting seats. The system sums the prices and applies appropriate taxes. The system communicates the total to customer. The customer provides payment. If payment is by credit card, the system calls for credit authorization. The system collects credit card issuer, number, and expiration date to verify that available credit is more than the total. Charge must be for exact amount only. If credit card authorization passes, the seats are reserved. If authorization fails, the customer has the option to pay with any other payment method. [Exception: Customer declines alternative payment method]. This use case ends when the customer leaves with purchased tickets.
Exceptions:	Performance is sold out: notify the customer
	Customer cancels the purchase: end the use case
	Customer declines alternative payment options: end the use case
Postconditions:	Purchase information is stored in the system.

Structure Class Diagram

Role(s): Object Architect (Facilitator) and Business Area Experts

The Object Architect reviews each use case to refine the Class Diagram further. Each Use Case Description, in conjunction with the Problem Assessment, provides the information for discovering additional classes and associations. The distilled classes at this point still represent the business domain. The goal is to identify and clarify the most common business term for the classes described in the use case and eliminate redundant naming. The Business Area Experts review each of these class candidates to ensure that class names are acceptable and understandable within the business culture. You may optionally perform this work outside of a facilitated session.

> **Tip** For each iteration, the Object Architect specifies the classes to either develop from scratch or incorporate from elsewhere. This is useful as a to-do list, as well as a follow-up exercise after the increment is complete.

At the end of this task, the Object Architects of each Solution Area meet to integrate any classes that might overlap. This ensures a sound, shared structure before building the shared class.

To identify classes:

1. Look for objects that the system needs to remember.
2. Look for domain-specific devices that are required regardless of the software solution such as scanner, cash register, or display terminal.
3. Look for objects that need to provide behavior. Also, identify which objects must remember the results of that behavior.
4. Look for additional objects in classes that currently reflect only one object. You may find specialized classes or parts of classes. [1]

When modeling classes, use the 80 percent rule. That is, model for 80 percent of the behavior instead of creating elaborate models for the 20 percent exceptions. One hint for ensuring fuller coverage of detail is to put oneself "in the shoes of" an object. With associations, think from each object's perspective of the association. Capture that thinking as the role name on the association.

Class Definition You define a class in terms of its attributes and behavior. When defining a class, you may ask yourself, "when does an attribute become its own class?" This answer varies for different domains. You should understand the context of what you mean by a class and its surrounding classes. You should understand how to use the information. One test to distinguish a class from an attribute is to

---

[1] Peter Coad and Edward Yourdon. *Object-Oriented Analysis*. Englewood Cliffs, NJ: Yourdon Press. 1991, 66.

ask if the element answers "how many?" (a class) or "how much?" (an attribute). Another test is to ask if the information always references some other information. If so, it is probably an attribute.

For class behaviors, you assume at this point that every class knows how to create, read, update, and delete objects. At this point, you leave those operations off the diagram to minimize clutter.

Although behavior information is limited at this point, identify class behaviors that uncover potential life cycles of the object. Discovering it now allows you to plan for Statechart Diagram refinement later. Investigate the purpose of each object and look to streamline it while identifying operations. Think of yourself as the object and ask, "what can I do?" ("Ask not what your object can do for you, ask what you can do for your object."—with apologies to John F. Kennedy.)

How do we get attributes and behavior into the correct classes? An object should be limited to doing one thing—carrying out its responsibility—and doing that one thing well. If an object grows too large because it has taken on responsibilities beyond its own, it has lost its ability to maintain stability. That is, it becomes a larger target for change. We want to keep objects small and single-purposed so that when the inevitable change occurs, it has a better chance of remaining intact. Following the Bertrand Meyer shopping list,[2] you ask what the object is responsible for and what might be done with its attributes to determine the object's intent and usefulness. Taking this perspective "bulletproofs" the class against potential change.

> **Tip** When building your models, include text in the class definition that explains questionable things. For example, if there is an exception case that makes an association optional, explain what motivated you to model the optionality. Consistently use stereotypes and constraints as defined in the UML or extend with your own set.

Associations Multiplicity To validate multiplicity of associations, view the Class Diagram with a constant time frame in mind. How long will the relationship persist in this time frame? If the relationship ends

---

[2] Bertrand Meyer. *Object-Oriented Software Construction*. Upper Saddle River, NJ: Prentice Hall PTR, 1997, 770-774.

after a certain time, but you need to retain the history of this relationship, add a history class to store this information.

Scrutinize classes with only one attribute. This "class" may itself be an attribute of another class. If it is a link association, use a qualifier on the relationship to eliminate the multiplicity and give the attribute a home in one of the classes participating in the association.

Inheritance The next pass through the Class Diagram focuses on the object-oriented theme of inheritance. The Object Architect looks for static associations between classes. One type of association is the generalization and specialization of classes. This is known as the "is a" or "kind of" association. This is similar to the concept of subtype/supertype found in Entity/Relationship Diagramming from the data-modeling world.

When considering inheritance, you begin to move to the more abstract. There are two ways of looking at inheritance, top-down (specialization) or bottom-up (generalization). With specialization, you see that certain attributes and operations apply to specific situations, thus indicating a subclass. You put the attributes and operations unique to a class in the lower-level subclass. With generalization, you move redundant attributes and operations to a superclass, or abstract class. Classes that seem to have similar attributes or operations could instead inherit them from a superclass. This abstract superclass may never be instantiated itself. An example of an abstract class is Person. You may want to define name and birth date as attributes for any person. Yet, you would want specific classes of Person such as Employee or Customer to handle specific information unique to these subclasses. For example, Employee may include a hire date attribute and a hire operation that Customer does not need. Inheritance can eliminate redundancy, thereby "cleaning up" the Class Diagram and promoting reuse.

For generalization and specialization, verify that all attributes and operations of a generalized class apply to its specialized classes. Conversely, check if you can promote attributes and operations of specialized classes to the generalized class. Consider how to handle the case of "other." Do you want to have a specialized catchall class or use the generalization class as the catchall? You can choose to create an "all others" subclass or to create any object that is none of the subclasses as an instance of the superclass.

Do not model status as a subtype in an inheritance structure. Although it is true that an object can only be in one state at a time (which sounds like the "or" rule of inheritance), the proper place for modeling life cycles and the impact of state is on a Statechart Diagram. If you implement the classes in separate persistent data areas, you must also create operations to move data from one storage area to another. The Statechart Diagram is specifically constructed to model the dynamic, and it is confusing to model dynamic behavior in separate classes. Rather, you use the Statechart Diagram to understand the behavior of a single object and keep all of that information together. You define the attributes and operations discovered through the Statechart Diagram in the Class template.

To validate inherited classes, ask if an object maps to only one of the subclasses. Is each subclass a kind of the superclass? The inherited classes share commonality with their superclass, but each has attributes, operations, or relationships unique to a subclass. A rule of thumb is to limit the hierarchy level to five plus or minus two. A rule of inheritance is that every attribute must have a value for every instance. If not, create a specialized subclass.

When defining inherited structures, you want to check that you have identified all the subclasses. This is important because you have to decide whether to include methods in the superclass to create an unknown subclass or not.

Aggregation Another association type aggregates classes into a whole and its parts. This is known as the "has a" or "part of" association.

To validate aggregation classes, ask if a class is a part of another class. Are the parts essentially a part of the whole? If the whole does not exist, can the part exist? To validate composite classes, ask if the class is part of another class but can also be a part of a different class or be instantiated on its own.

Case Study The first time around, we quickly identified objects in the problem domain. We recognized possible objects like Customer, Ticket, and Seat from the description. Now we take a more serious look at objects needed to support the Reserve Seating use case. We also look for static associations and corresponding multiplicity as we draw the objects. We name the associations to clarify the meaning.

The discussion in the facilitated session led to fundamental questions in understanding the difference between a Seat and a Ticket and the difference between a Reservation and a Purchase. Out of context, these topics may seem to be a waste of time or irrelevant. The challenge is to make sure that all have the same point of reference. Considering the behavior of these objects across Solution Areas makes this topic very interesting. Do you purchase a ticket or reserve a seat? How do we represent this when a customer could reserve the same seat for multiple performances? The Facilitator decided to capture these as issues and move on as shown in Table 4-1—Issues List from Deriving Classes Out of Use Cases. A later session resolved them and generated corresponding change requests.

Table 4-1—Issues List from Deriving Classes Out of Use Cases

Issue Num	Issue Description	Resolution
1.	What content belongs on the Internet? Options include schedules, performers, concert dates, and locations, with query capability for all of the above.	The Promote Performance Solution Area uses the Internet to broaden the target market.
2.	Does purchase information need to interface to the accounting system?	Not for the first release. Reconsider in next year's budget.
3.	Will we support payment by check?	No. Checks present too much of a credit risk. Reconsider automated check verification as an enhancement after first release.
4.	What is the difference between reservation and purchase?	No difference. We will use the term purchase, since the customer does not reserve a ticket; the customer purchases a ticket.
5.	What is the difference between a seat and a ticket?	The seat is part of a location. The ticket, in the real world, represents a seat. A customer purchases a ticket to attend a performance in that seat.

The resolution of these issues generated change requests illustrated in Table 4-2—Change Request List (we do not show dates, costs, and time for illustration).

Table 4-2—Change Request List

Change Request Number	Change Description	Priority (High, Med., Low)	Benefit	Affected Deliverables	Disposition (Requested, Approved, Denied, Completed)
1.	Issue 4 resolution: Change all references from reservation to purchase.	Med.	Consistency	Use Case Diagram, Class Diagram	Approved
2.	Issue 5 resolution: Clarify seat versus ticket; validate models and correct as needed.	Med.	Consistency	Use Case Diagram, Class Diagram	Approved

Ticket and Reservation appeared to be the same, but Ticket more clearly identified a real-world object. Further, the Ticket is also meaningful only within the context between Performance and Seat. We model this as a link class attached to the association.

We then add the attributes and operations described in the use case. Some attributes require further information, like Customer (do we need first name, last name, and telephone number?). Prototyping in the next phase resolves many of these details. We capture what we can and move on.

Although we initially identified Seat as an object, we know from the Manage Location Solution that it is part of an aggregation of Location. People typically think in terms of layering and abstraction. They visualize the section, then the rows, and finally the seat (to say this a different way, to find the seat at performance time one must know the row and section it is a part of). We leave this as Seat within the case study for simplicity's sake. Later, when we begin modeling for implementation, we may need more specific messaging.

We enhance the Use Case Description again as we learn more about the objects. The Use Case Description sentence "The system confirms information for the requested performance" changes to a more precise meaning "System displays remaining seating options and ticket prices."

The final step in our Use Case Description, "This use case ends when the customer leaves with purchased tickets," is also erroneous. A customer does not have to purchase tickets in order to leave, but we want to be sure the customer receives purchased tickets. We split the sentence into two—"Customer receives purchased tickets" and then "This use case ends when the customer leaves." Refinement means anything can change at anytime! Figure 4-2—Enhanced Class Diagram with Static Structure, Some Operations, and Attributes Added depicts the Class Diagram result for the Structure Solution phase. Note the increased amount of detailed business understanding gained from developing the Use Case Description. Now we have enough to break each increment into time-boxed iterations that provide controlled refinement.

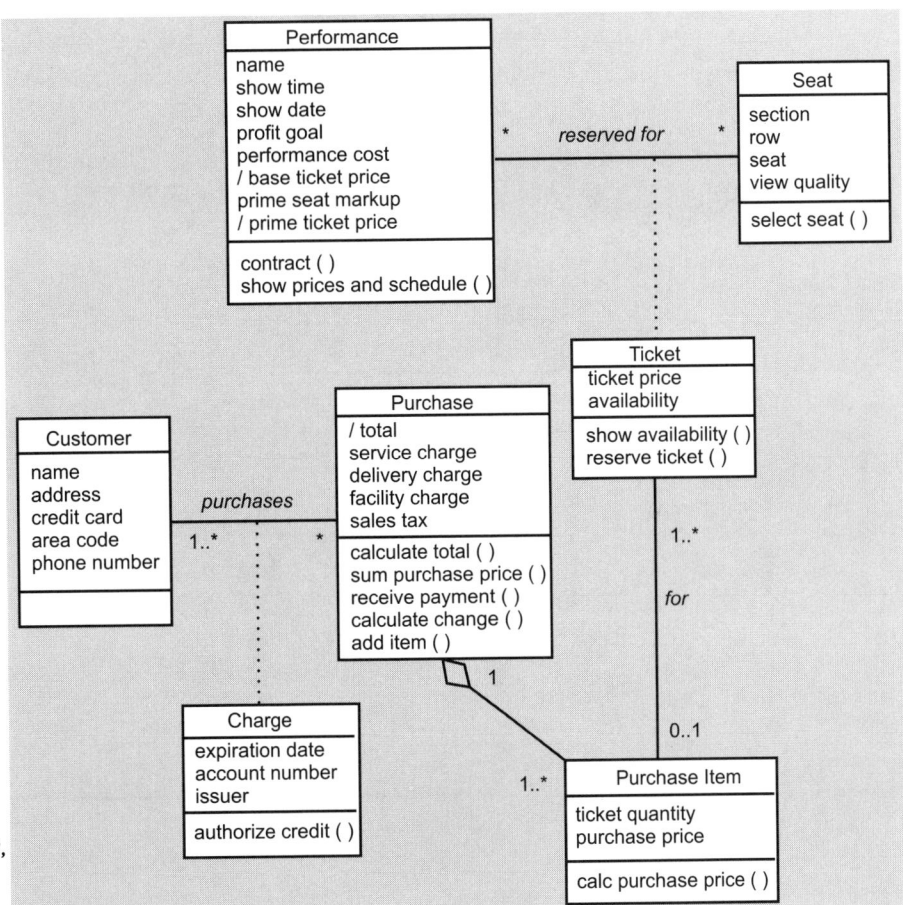

Figure 4-2—Enhanced Class Diagram with Static Structure, Some Operations, and Attributes Added

The Object Architect may also want to refine class packaging to reflect the newly discovered classes. Some classes, like Seat, we recognize are the responsibility of another Solution Area. This is now an obvious target to address in the Integrate Solution phase; staying on top of it from this point forward will save work later. Class packaging also assists the Infrastructure Architect in planning architecture needs. For example, client processors may need larger memory if the user interface has several components with high capacity, concurrency, and complexity needs. Figure 4-3—Class Packaging shows the class packaging, using the same diagram that we used in determining the Solution Areas.

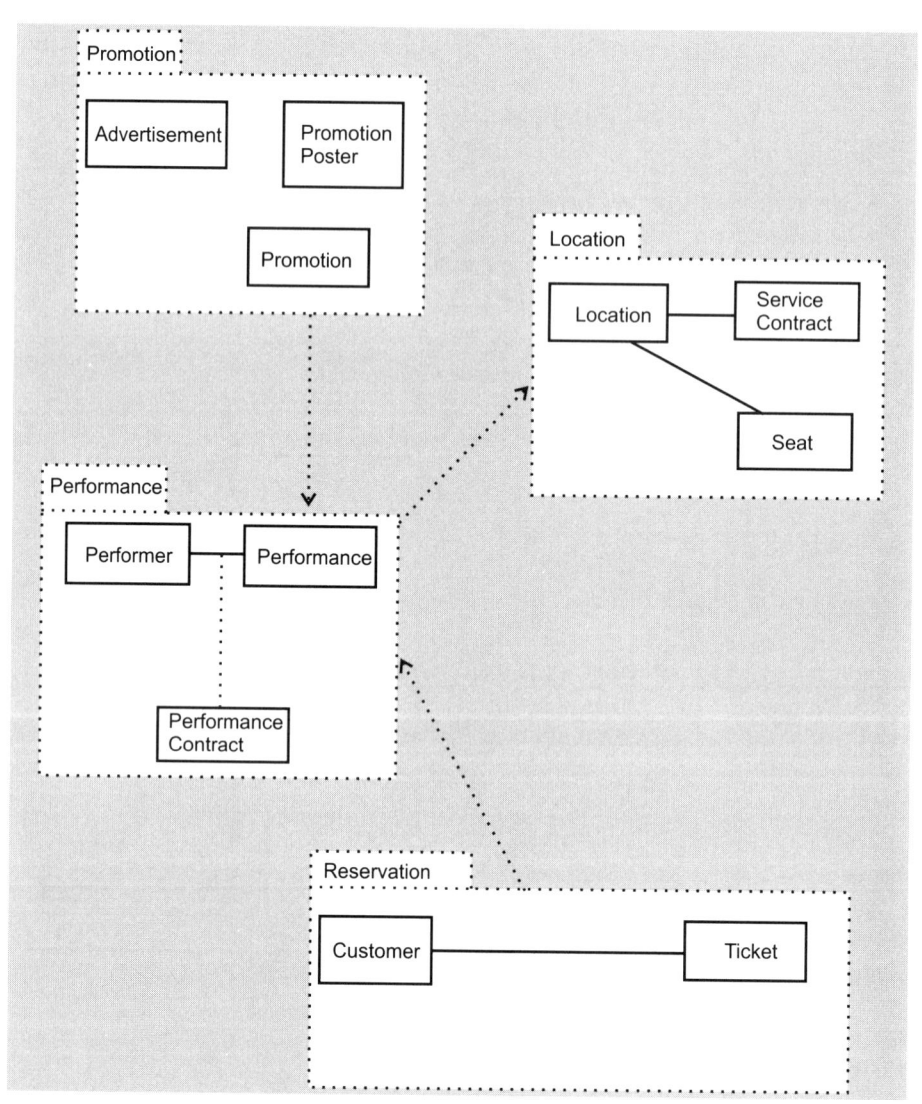

Figure 4-3—
Class Packaging

Select Reusable Classes From Class Library

Role(s): Object Architect

The Object Architect matches the derived classes with the enterprise class library to identify any existing items for reuse. The Object

Architect pays particular attention to patterns of object behavior to synthesize them into a more general class definition. It is important to investigate the class library for reuse. However, without a structured means for this investigation, metamodel management resembles looking for a needle in a haystack. You may find it more cost-effective to build domain-specific views and forego enterprise-wide reusable classes until the resources for proper metamodel responsibility exist.

> **Tip** You may find it worthwhile to research ready-made domains for purchase and customize them to your business solution.

> **Case Study** Since we already built the core Location information, we can reuse classes from the Manage Location Solution Area, specifically the Seat class.

Structure Documentation

The Document Architect structures the framework for each of the identified documentation deliverables. This includes an outline of each deliverable, its distribution mechanism, and maintenance. The Document Architects of each Solution Area meet to ensure a similar look and feel of these deliverables.

Deliverables

User Instructions Guide

Information Reference Guide

Information delivered to users must be planned and architected. The terminology, use flow, and response to user interaction run the risk of being forgotten or delivered in a confusing way without this. Architecting the documentation follows the solution as embodied in the object-oriented deliverables.

Note the documentation deliverables do not have to be in a paper format. They may exist embedded within the application, on CD-ROM, via Intranet, or in other media format.

The foundation for the User Instructions Guide starts with the Use Case Diagram to identify uses and functionality. The Class Diagram provides descriptions for the Information Reference Guide.

Tasks:

Structure User Instructions Guide Framework

Role(s): Document Architect, Project Sponsor, and Project Manager

The Document Architect and the Project Manager meet with the Project Sponsor to define the characteristics of the document that teaches Users how to interact with the system.

Case Study The User Instructions Guide provides a roadmap of procedures that Users follow when responding to business events. That is, each subsystem has a list of use cases; each use case identifies its purpose and lists its procedural steps.

Structure Information Reference Guide Framework

Role(s): Document Architect, Project Sponsor, and Project Manager

The Document Architect and the Project Manager meet with the Project Sponsor to define characteristics of the window architecture to assist Users while using online applications (typically called Help). The intent is to capture the categories of information and the information delivery architecture. They also define how error conditions link to the Information Reference Guide.

Case Study For the architecture of the Information Reference Guide, a Help menu contains the information in a hierarchical Table of Contents.

The categories within the Information Reference Guide include overall window-level information and individual field-level information. Window-level information describes the functional purpose of each particular window and the procedural steps to follow for entering information. Windows that control flow to another window (such as a pick-list window that flows to a detail window) describes the flow to each detail window. Field-level information describes what the field means and how to use the field. In our application, field-level information displays using the right-button down feature of the mouse.

As Users encounter errors while using the system, informational messages should resemble common pop-up windows, but in addition provide a succinct procedure for how to recover from the error. As errors occur, messages display in a pop-up window. One of the button options on the pop-up error message allows the User to link to the associated window- or field-level information reference.

Structure Training

Understanding the audience, the "Users" of the eventual solution, is important to developing the appropriate style of instruction. The Trainers of each Solution Area meet to ensure a similar look and feel of these deliverables.

Deliverables

Training Curriculum

Training Delivery Mechanism

Tasks:

Structure Training Curriculum

Role(s): Trainer, Project Sponsor, and Project Manager

The Trainer and the Project Manager meet with the Project Sponsor to develop the structure of the Training Curriculum based on the training approach and the Problem Assessment. The curriculum addresses the training objectives from which training evolves. The group sets out specific objectives for effectively training the Users to carry out the duties as discovered in the use cases. The Trainer structures and maintains the relationship between use cases and the Training Curriculum for each Solution Area. For each use case, the use case summary provides the main outline of the Training Curriculum.

An experienced Trainer really helps here. The Trainer develops curriculum specific to various user types. People that require training fall into two major categories. The first category consists of those people that perform transactional processing and data querying through the Application. The other category of trainees is comprised of people that ensure operations support and maintain the system. This category includes people who provide user help, maintain the database, and grant security permissions.

The Case Study curriculum has the following topics that begin the outline of the Training Curriculum:

> Computer skills—must be able to operate the basic equipment.
>   Starting the computer
>   Using the keyboard and mouse
>   Printing
>   Shutting down the computer
> Application usage—must be able to perform the duties described in each use case
>   Reserve Seating
>   Customer selects seating and performance
>   Customer pays with cash
>   Customer pays with credit card
>   Customer receives tickets

The User Instruction Guide also functions as a training device because the structure of the curriculum mimics it. The curriculum leads the ticket agent through typical situations and shows where to reference corresponding topics in the User Instructions Guide.

In addition to training needed to use the system, we also discuss creating customer service training for the ticket agents to help them present the "best face" as ambassadors of the company. The group decided this is a good idea but not something this project should address.

Specify Training Delivery Mechanism

Role(s): Trainer, Project Sponsor, and Project Manager

The content (the "what") of the training was set in the previous task. Now, this group brainstorms to come up with the most appropriate vehicle for delivering instruction (the "how") to the User. The Trainer assesses the type and style of information to present, incorporates presentation dynamics, and accommodates both the "levels" of user comfort with computing tools and the potential cultural impact caused by the new work environment. Using this information, the Trainer selects from various means of presenting the instruction (such as video, computer-based training, instructor-led, and lab exercises). The Trainer updates the Training Curriculum to capture the results of the analysis and the decisions made.

The nature of the Application helps select a style effective in maximizing user retention. Recall the Chinese proverb: "Tell me and I will forget. Show me and I may remember. Involve me and I will understand." For example, an application that requires great volumes of reference material or terminology may guide one to a Computer-Based Training (CBT) approach leveraging a hyperlinked glossary. An application with greater "how-to" needs includes classroom exercises. The Trainer selects the delivery medium most appropriate to the content characteristics.

Case Study The Problem Statement highlighted high turnover and minimal computer skills of ticket agents. In response to this, we suggest including the User Instructions Guide in new employee training to provide a quick start on the procedural use of the system.

We recommend teaching introductory computer skills through a purchased Computer-Based Training (CBT) course since it is quicker than creating a course from scratch. The enterprise will determine which Users require this training.

We also recommend role-playing class exercises to immediately test knowledge transfer. We plan to include the User Instructions Guide as a reference in the exercises.

Structure Infrastructure Architecture

The technical infrastructure decisions may be as important as all other project decisions put together. This is especially true with client/server infrastructures where technology offers abundant alternatives for short-term improvement, and yet quickly becomes obsolete. It is important to describe more than just the high-level processors. You must also include the network infrastructure that identifies the communications between the database management system, application middleware, and client. Not all hardware and software fit easily together; any newly deployed

Deliverables

Infrastructure Requirements
Deployment Diagram
Third-Party Product Evaluation
Infrastructure Acquisition Timeline
Security Restrictions
Development Environment
Software Distribution Procedure

application may affect network traffic. An experienced, pliant Infrastructure Architect can significantly enhance the project team. The project needs hardware, software, and networking for which you must plan. There are four main tasks to planning infrastructure architecture:

1. Obtain infrastructure architecture requirements to meet the business solution.
2. Design the conceptual infrastructure architecture.
3. Evaluate and purchase new hardware and software.
4. Plan an implementation and delivery strategy.

Both business requirements and current technical infrastructure determine architecture design. You derive the architecture requirements and technology solution from business requirements. You also assess the current technical infrastructure including hardware, operating system, development tools, network, databases, and management tools. After you have a concept of the proposed infrastructure architecture, you determine gaps between the current and required infrastructures. Additionally, gap analysis includes an inventory of existing skills to identify additional training that the project team may need.

> **Tip** Keep a copy of the original view of the current infrastructure along with major revisions. The history of the decision-making process is otherwise forgotten.

From this analysis, you plan the migration, prioritize requirements, identify the components necessary for multiple projects, and plan the implementation year. You want a standard configuration for all sites including development, training, and testing. It is difficult to test a distributed application adequately when all the tiers are on the same PC.

This activity, more than any other, requires communication among Solution Areas. Infrastructure purchases depend on the needs of the entire project. For example, purchasing a server for each Solution Area may be less desirable than purchasing one server for each Solution Area if capacity allows.

Tasks:

Specify Infrastructure Requirements

Role(s): Infrastructure Architect, Project Manager, and Project Sponsor

The Infrastructure Architect and Project Manager meet with the Project Sponsor to capture hardware and software needs for the solution. Topics to consider include capacity, growth, number of concurrent users, geographic access points, performance throughput, security, backup and disaster recovery, and auditing. The more sophisticated the requirements, the more it costs to build and support a system to meet those requirements.

These factors help determine what is needed for network traffic, processor power, and locations of hardware and software. Ideally, you want to have hardware and software tools each with its own specific purpose. This includes tools for development, version control, and configuration packaging. However, weigh idealism against cost. The complete solution cost also includes the initial purchase, training, and long-term maintenance cost.

The initial attempt to understand the infrastructure architecture begins by determining how the business uses the system. The Problem Assessment provides some business statistics to aid in deciding the infrastructure architecture. The Infrastructure Architect obtains further detail from the Project Sponsor.

The Project Sponsor specifies preconceived performance expectations along with the consequence to the business if deviation from this performance occurs. Performance criteria specify acceptable levels of performance including response, turnaround, and availability. These criteria provide a measurement of the overall solution upon delivery. This includes the number of anticipated users and system availability needs.

Early discussion of performance criteria provides further insight into evolving the solution by telling us what cannot happen. Setting the parameters before further refinement helps us to define a proper measurement for the solution. These parameters serve not to limit scope or functionality, but as a reminder that these items are essential to solving the business need. Use Case Scenarios, developed later, typically illustrate these as exceptions.

Backup and disaster recovery includes determining policies for backing up and recovering data, as well as disaster recovery needs and tolerable recovery periods. The Infrastructure Architect determines what data to back up, the frequency of backup, the retention of history, and the off-site storage of backup data from the business requirements. The Project Sponsor identifies acceptable recovery periods (that is, what is mission critical and what can wait to minimize the impact on business operations).

Case Study We extract the infrastructure-related information from the Problem Assessment and make decisions with input from the Project Sponsor. The criteria stated by the Project Sponsor include:

1. Each location's data must be available from every other location.
2. Data sizing must include projected capacity for the next three years. The Project Sponsor wants to avoid purchasing storage at the last minute.
3. There must be adequate equipment for each full- and part-time staff person.
4. Retention of historical information (customer demographics and purchase information) must allow for online access within 24 hours.

Capacity Using statistics from the Problem Assessment, we derive preliminary capacity needs. Seating capacity currently reaches 110,000 per year, growing at the rate of 20,000 occurrences every two years.

Recall that the business anticipates retaining customer demographics for two years from the last purchase and one year for customers that did not follow through with any purchase. Of these figures, the business estimates 50 percent new customers per year and 50 percent repeat customers. The business averages a 3 percent growth in yearly sales and anticipates this continuing for the next three years. We estimate customer volumes at approximately 250,000 the first year followed by 380,000 the second year, and 390,000 the third year.

Purchase information retained over the next three years means 165,000 purchases the first two years growing to 180,000 in three years.

The capacity considerations show that the infrastructure must adapt to a growing, distributed environment. Sizing the storage and processing power have to match data and transaction volumes including the expected growth.

Concurrency We need to consider concurrent use of the system, because customers may purchase tickets for any performance at any location, and there are multiple ticket agents at each location. Response time is the greatest concern. The spikes for peak ticketing times are also a concern. The Infrastructure Architect must balance between performance and cost. Purchasing equipment to have instantaneous response during peak times means it is underused the rest of the time. The network bandwidth must accommodate peak times without a significant drop in performance. The Project Sponsor sets the expectation of three-second response time during peaks as a target measure.

Concurrency has its greatest impact during peak ticketing when 65 percent of the purchases occur within the first two days after the tickets go on sale. During this peak time, fourteen full-time ticket agents access the system, with an additional 23 part-time ticket agents accessing the system from 6:00 to 9:00 P.M. local time. To handle the average of 3,350 calls in the first two days, each purchase must occur within five minutes.

Determining the performance criteria for the web site must wait for the desired features and content to stabilize before projecting the number of "hits." The Infrastructure Architect adds this to the existing Risk Assessment for follow-up.

Complexity We expect processing to be relatively simple for Ticket Reservations because it processes straightforward transactions, Customer to Purchase to Ticket. Location management could add a bit more complexity to handle the seating tiers. If merely hierarchical, this may not cause too much concern. However, we suspect working with seating information may require several table joins in the database. This always adds complexity to data retrieval and generally requires more database horsepower. In addition, promoting performances may be more complex because it requires many rules to allow for a market-by-market strategy. Contract Performances could also be quite complex. Fortunately, this occurs 252 times a year at most.

Develop Conceptual Deployment Diagrams

Role(s): Infrastructure Architect, Project Manager, and Project Sponsor

The Infrastructure Architect plans the hardware and software needed to support the implementation environment before, during, and after implementation. This includes the hardware and software needed for databases, middleware, the network, backup and disaster recovery, and the user interface hardware and software.

The Infrastructure Architect begins by assessing the current infrastructure architecture documented during the Chart Solution phase. The Infrastructure Architect considers current capacity limits and current traffic flow. This determines not only what is currently available, but also what is missing. The Infrastructure Architect documents the alternative architectures in the initial implementation Deployment Diagram. This view shows descriptions of each hardware and general supporting software such as operating systems and database management systems.

We build the Deployment Diagram in two stages. The first stage represents only the physical hardware and network devices and general support software that make up the three target infrastructure architectures for the project—the Development, Training, and Implementation environments. In this way, we can plan the infrastructure and use the same diagram later to place developed or purchased components on it (when they become available). This minimizes future translation errors and reduces the number of diagrams.

The second stage meshes the software components from the Component Diagram and charts the installation partitioning and security restrictions on the full Deployment Diagram. Essentially, you place the packages from the Component Diagram on the Deployment Diagram to show where to install these items. Typically, user interface classes reside on clients, entity classes on a database server, and control and system interface classes on an application server or middleware. This is not as easy as it sounds, since it forces the team to face issues such as application logic packaging and data packaging.

The Infrastructure Architect and Project Manager meet with the Project Sponsor to select the best architecture. Some of the decisions may direct you to picking the smallest system size based on cost or short-term projected business growth. You want to provide an extensible solution but not force unnecessary purchases. Determining the infrastructure architecture makes assumptions on currently available processing power, popular operating systems, and database management systems. Because economics plays a part in the decision, make sure you include all costs. Besides the obvious costs of hardware and software, remember to include costs for ongoing maintenance, additional resources for system support during development (as well as after implementation), and additional support staff training.

The Infrastructure Architect assists in selecting the development environment for the project. This should align closely with the implementation platform but also include software for documentation, modeling, and programming.

The Infrastructure Architect also works with the Trainer to plan the user training environment. This should also align closely with the implementation platform but includes hardware and software for curriculum delivery. An environment completely separate from the implementation environment is ideal to eliminate performance conflicts between the two.

As you make infrastructure decisions, document all assumptions clearly and as objectively as possible. This process can evoke passionate discussion if left uncontrolled.

Case Study Based on the Infrastructure Requirements and the use cases, we determine that the ticket agents, performance promoter, and concert coordinator need additional or upgraded personal computers (PCs) connected to the application server and a shared database. Given the need to allow customers to purchase tickets from any location regardless of where the performance is scheduled, we recommend one application server located at each location with a central database.

Using the class packaging produced earlier, the Infrastructure Architect considers the processing needs of each application server. Each remote server needs capacity to handle the appropriate volume of ticket purchasing. The address standardization component will also reside on each local application server. The components for Manage Location, Promote Performance, and Contract Performance will only reside at the main ticket office because these functions continue to be performed centrally.

The application server communicates to the central database through a direct line. Although not part of the immediate purchase, the configuration of the web server is included to show the future vision of the infrastructure.

Figure 4-4—Initial Implementation Deployment Diagram identifies the locations for taking reservations. All locations handle ticket purchases. The main ticket office conducts all other business. We have used comments to depict operating system, database, etc.; you could use abstraction to move this to the textual definition of each processor and device to keep the diagram clutter to a minimum.

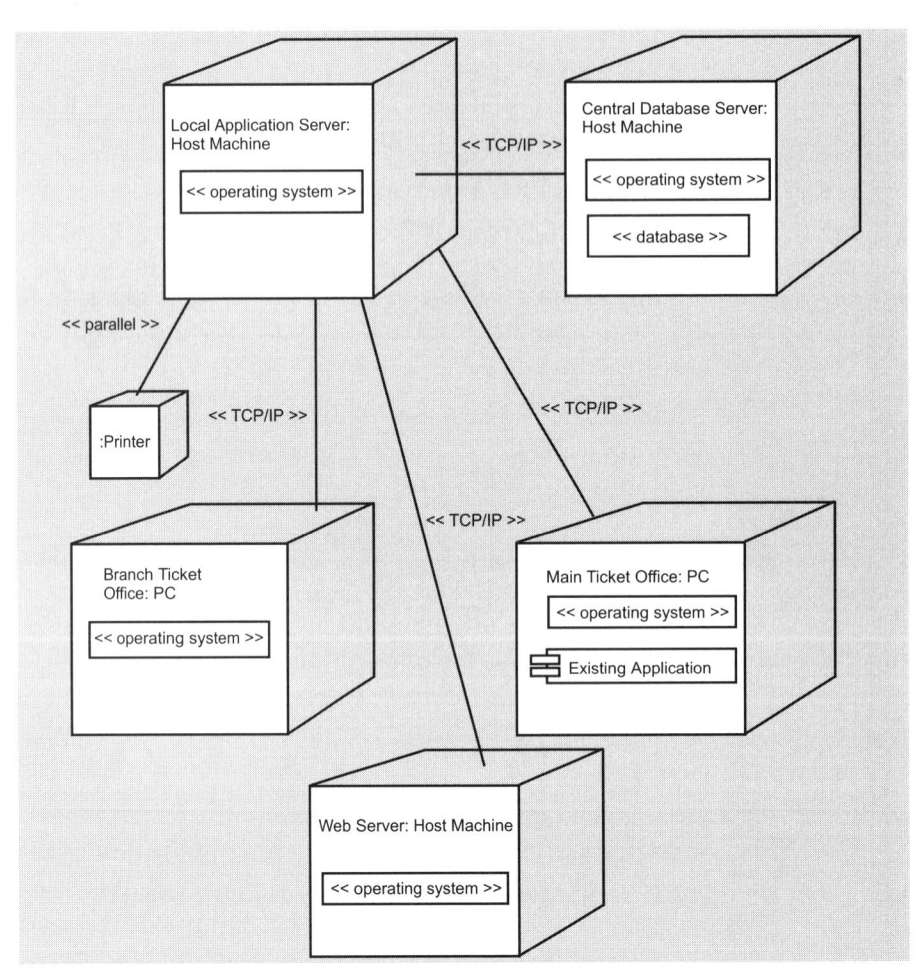

Figure 4-4—Initial Implementation Deployment Diagram

We now determine the development platform. Our development environment mirrors the hardware and software of the implementation environment, as shown in Figure 4-5—Development Deployment Diagram. Additionally, the development PCs will have an object modeling tool and program language software loaded on the appropriate PCs.

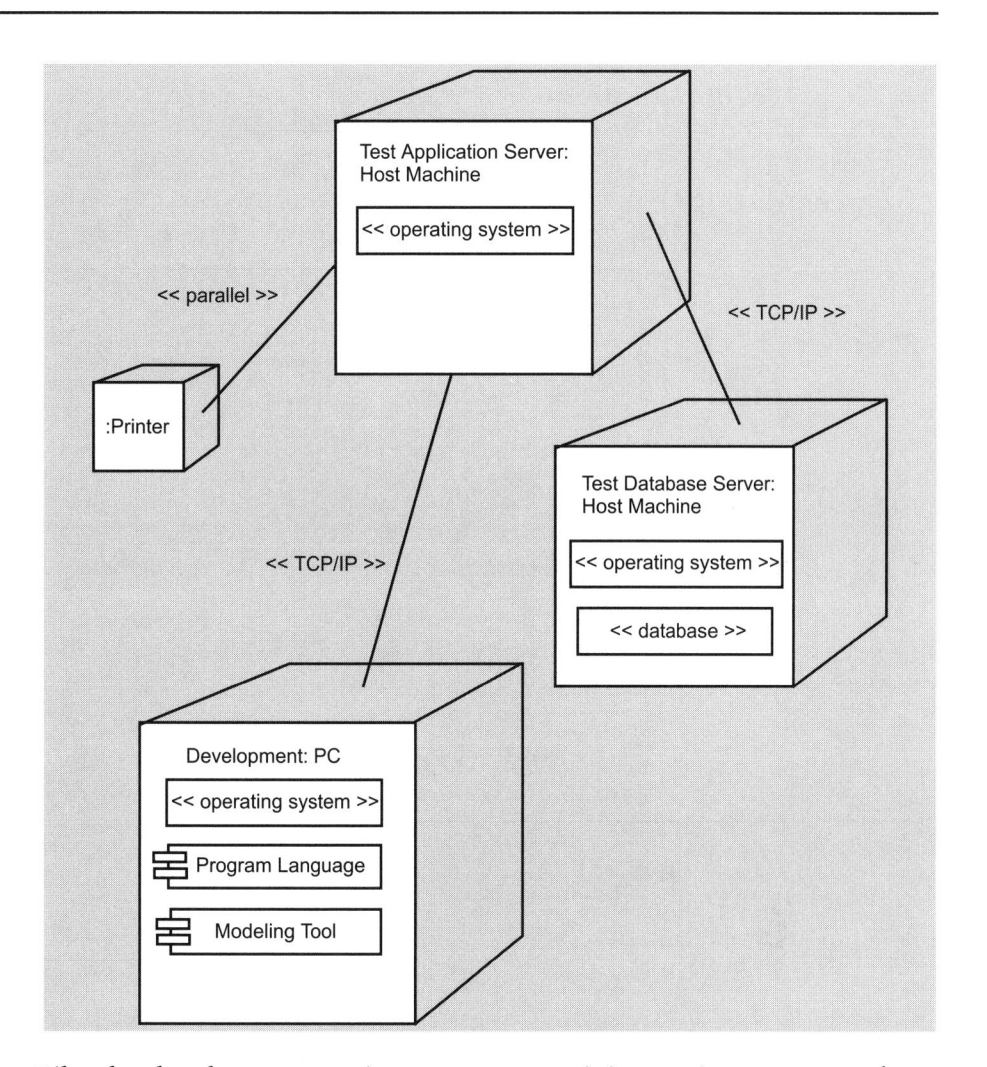

Figure 4-5—Development Deployment Diagram

Like the development environment, our training environment matches the implementation environment, but on a much smaller scale. We decide that the costs of replicating a separate training environment at each location are much lower than the travel costs for numerous ticket agents traveling to a central site for training. The training environment consists of a single, separate personal computer at each location that shares the network infrastructure. We will install the computer skill CBT software on the training PC. The Application will also reside on the training PC at each location. The training database will reside on the central database server in a separate data area from the implementation database. This is illustrated in Figure 4-6—Training Deployment Diagram.

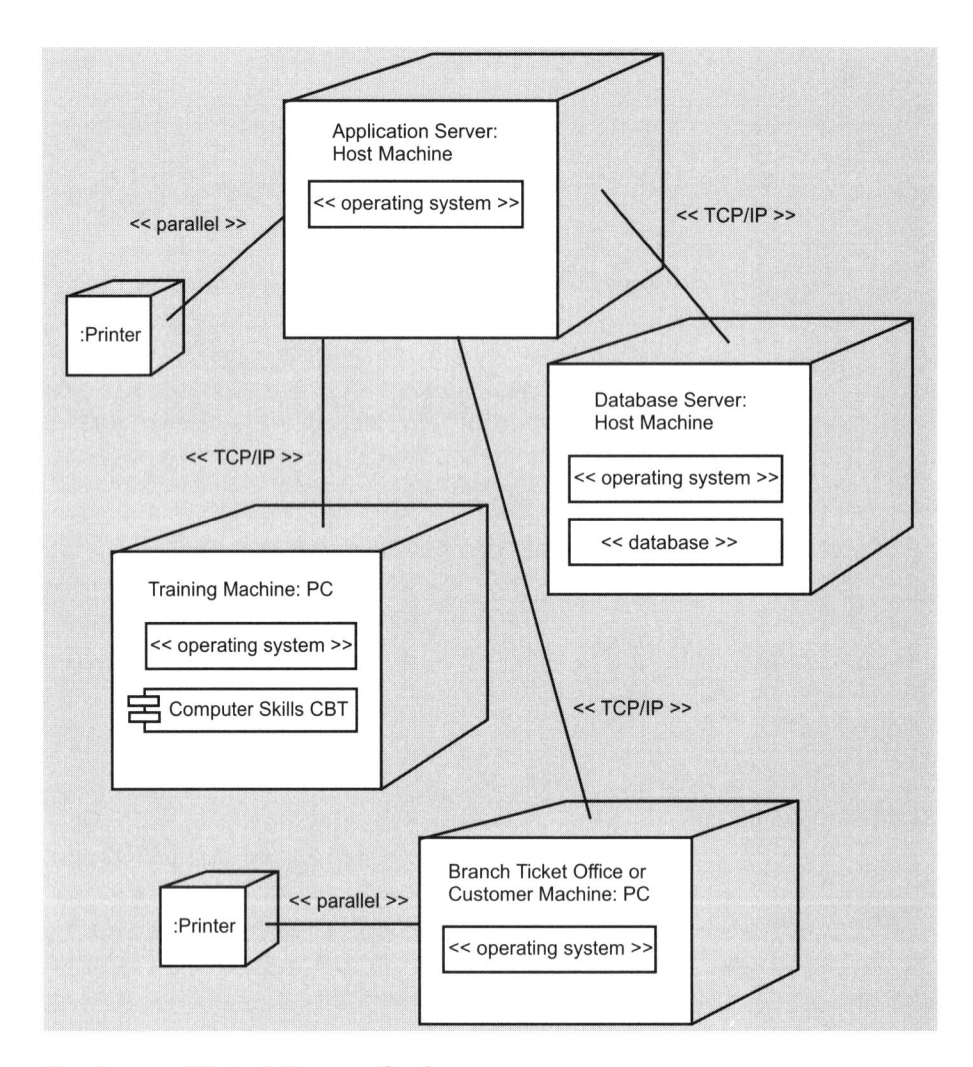

Figure 4-6— Training Deployment Diagram

Evaluate Third-Party Software

Role(s): Infrastructure Architect, Object Architect, Trainer, Project Manager, and Project Sponsor

Consider that you may save significant cost and elapsed time to deployment by buying solutions rather than building them. A purchased solution does not need to have complete coverage of the solution to justify its purchase. Strategic subsets of the solution may meet a partial need that allows you to concentrate resources on the remaining functionality. Be sure to factor in the cost and time to integrate the purchased solution into your Cost/Benefit Analysis. You may be surprised at how a tactical decision to purchase a few components can shorten the time to deployment.

Based on the solution thus far, the Infrastructure Architect establishes the software requirements that third-party software must meet and investigates the software market to find products that meet those specifications. Again, the software may not be a complete solution, just a component that the project leverages. The Infrastructure Architect evaluates each potential product on its own merit and by comparing one product to another. The Infrastructure Architect documents the findings and recommends possible solutions. The Infrastructure Architect includes the necessary copies for the project team in the total purchase and adds in software developer kits if available. The Project Manager presents these findings to the Project Sponsor who approves or denies the purchase.

The Infrastructure Architect enhances the Initial Implementation Deployment Diagram by placing purchased components on processor nodes.

You may need to evaluate and benchmark various products before choosing one or two that work for your system. Determining which products to purchase can seem overwhelming. Prioritize requirements based on business objectives and incremental development strategy. You should be able to trace from your business objectives to your infrastructure requirements. In other words, requirements for selecting hardware and software must have a business reason behind the purchase. This minimizes the temptation of purchasing products that do more than you need.

Adding measurable weights to the requirements provides objectivity when the decision between products is difficult. Unbiased information from third-party review groups can help this process. Investigate products that perform well in your categories of requirements, scale to meet system growth, support open interfaces to other products, and are appropriate to your industry or system purpose. Consider experience, support, training, installation, and product stability. Also, consider vendors that support open standards and are willing to certify compatibility between their products and products from other vendors you have chosen. Some typical criteria include:

1. Level of scalability and seamless interfaces
2. Data capacity limits
3. Limits on the anticipated number of users, concurrent access times, and the ability to access from remote geographic points
4. Ease of versioning and configuration
5. Security

After creating a short list of suitable products, bring in vendors to present their products. Knowing who evaluates the products, ultimately chooses the solution, and negotiates the contract helps people focus on information they need for their role. Establishing a standard list of questions, demo scripts, or scenarios that the products must execute helps standardize vendor presentations. If you only allow a vendor to present the strengths and weaknesses of its product, you may place more weight on what the product does rather than on what you need the product to do. Because you have weighted requirements, you are less likely to sway towards the "bells and whistles" of products. If you have the time, you may want to benchmark how one product compares to another in terms of performance.

The final step is to negotiate price and purchase the product. As part of negotiations, you may want to ask vendors to guarantee performance through a service level agreement. This means the vendor assumes responsibility if the product does not perform as promoted.

For the case study, we have two software packages to research and acquire. Maintaining the customer address list requires an address standardization package. We also need a Computer-Based Training (CBT) package for teaching basic computer skills.

For the address standardization package, the product must provide certified United States Postal Service addresses including rural routes and post boxes updated every six months. It must provide mechanisms for overriding the address that the software derives, processing the exceptions, and recognizing possible duplications. Because the product will reside on the server, it must integrate seamlessly with the custom-built user interface software.

We found two products that meet most of these requirements. We invite the vendors to demonstrate their product specifically showing us:

1. Special addressing such as rural routes and post boxes
2. Exception handling
3. Duplication recognition
4. Change of address update procedures

Before the evaluation, we provide the vendors a list of questions we want them to address. This list includes the company's longevity, financial status, support plan, and any future enhancement. During the evaluation, we rate how well the product meets our requirements using high, medium, and low measures.

We interview vendor references looking for vendor relationships, product strengths, product weaknesses, support, and the impact the product had on the business.

We recommend the one product that best fits the solution based on its overall ranking, customer reference comments, and our intuition. The business negotiates product, maintenance, and support price for all hardware and software before obtaining the financial approval for purchase.

We also need a Computer-Based Training (CBT) package to teach basic computer skills. The Trainer meets with the Infrastructure Architect armed with a pile of catalogs. We received an informal recommendation through word-of-mouth. We ordered an evaluation copy of this package and two others that looked promising. After reviewing the evaluation copies, we selected the package recommended to us.

Establish Infrastructure Acquisition Timeline

Role(s): Infrastructure Architect, Project Manager, and Project Sponsor

The Infrastructure Architect begins with an assessment of what the enterprise already has in terms of hardware, software, and networking. The Infrastructure Architect references the current infrastructure Deployment Diagram and all of the conceptual Deployment Diagrams to identify gaps.

The Infrastructure Architect identifies the pieces to purchase first and those to purchase in the future. This helps distribute initial expenses. The Infrastructure Architect recommends when to purchase the infrastructure components based on development, training, and deployment needs with costs at each scheduled time of purchase for cash flow planning.

After evaluating products, you may feel you know exactly what you want, so why not buy it today? Decision-makers often prefer alternative solutions. Plan different configurations and provide an acquisition timeline for acquiring purchases. Identify the strengths and weaknesses of each configuration. When calculating costs, remember to include costs for supporting each incremental development, the installed system, and legacy systems. Also, identify any costs savings due to legacy systems that become obsolete over time.

It is prudent to consider distributing the cost over time. You must always consider postponing purchases that can wait. Refer back to the Cost/Benefit Analysis and be sure to synchronize that timeline with the Infrastructure Acquisition Timeline. Knowing what to purchase also depends on the current technical environment and possibly on new product release or availability schedules.

The current model may identify a potential need for specialized technology support. New support positions must be hired or contracted for on a retainer basis immediately. Availability of support should coincide with the arrival of the corresponding purchases. For example, you need network support beginning when the network purchases show up. Support for the custom-built software rests with the developers.

Case Study The business immediately purchases hardware, network, and operating system items for employees at the main ticket office so that basic computer skills training can commence. The computer skills CBT course has a quantity discount available, so the business immediately purchases all copies for the main and branch locations. Hardware, network, and operating system purchases for training at the other locations will follow one month later.

The business immediately purchases copies of popular operating system, object modeling, and database products for development. We also recommend purchasing the address standardization product immediately to give us time to learn the interface. The development equipment delivery must occur before modeling and prototyping. In this case study, no existing equipment is available for development use. Therefore, we place the development equipment order right after picking the platform. Equipment needed to imitate the branch ticket office configuration can wait until integration testing.

We plan the purchases for the branch ticket office hardware, network, and operating system (other than for training) to occur just before the solution rolls out to each branch ticket office.

Establish Software Distribution Procedure

Role(s): Project Sponsor, Project Manager, and Infrastructure Architect

The Infrastructure Architect and Project Manager meet with the Project Sponsor to determine the mechanism for distributing software. This speaks to the "hows" of deploying the final product. Here you want to identify how to make software upgrades available and whether to upgrade manually or automatically using "pull" or "push" strategies. For manual distribution, users need instructions and time to install the upgrade as software changes occur. Semi-automatic distribution can use either a "pull" strategy where the user gets the upgrade from some online source and then executes the upgrade without assistance. For a fully automated approach, you could use a "push" strategy. When the user opens the application, it matches the application with the most recent version and upgrades only as needed.

Various automated software development products available in the industry provide a mechanism for maintaining versions of software. A Local Area Network (LAN) supports "push" and "pull" strategies.

At this point in the project, you also discuss the frequency of software distribution. You may want to minimize user interruptions by grouping minor upgrades into a major distribution release.

Case Study In our case study, most Users have limited computer skills. We want to make upgrades transparent to the Users by not requiring them to install their own software. Since the business already has remote locations connected by the network, we will release software upgrades to each application server over the network and automatically download to the client machines when needed.

Specify Security Restrictions for Solution

Role(s): Project Sponsor, Project Manager, and Infrastructure Architect

The Infrastructure Architect and Project Manager meet with the Project Sponsor to determine the security restrictions. Security evolves defined by departments and individual Users. It defines the proper levels and enforcement of access to the system.

Security is an "other" category. Most development projects incorrectly address security at the end. After developing the solution, you have many components. Unfortunately, developers often ignore security while creating reusable components just to make the component more generic.

Our approach started with identifying use cases and actors. The set of identified actors is quite likely to be the same set of roles used in establishing security. The challenge arises from tracing actors on the Use Case Diagram all the way through to the many components created for supporting a single use case.

Access permissions support the inheritance theme of object-oriented development. Some actors can perform the same use case as another actor but not vice versa. When this happens, one actor inherits the same access permissions of the other actor. You typically see this with actors that assume manager roles.

You generally grant access permissions at the component level. We suggest leveraging the robust notation set provided by the UML using a constraint {security level: *level or role name*}. State the required security level explicitly using the notation on the Component and Deployment Diagrams.

Many have tried to establish security to the "field level" within a screen, but it may be easier to accomplish this by creating a separate purpose screen. Another approach is to create security control classes whose sole responsibility is to coordinate access to other classes. The Class Diagram can model these levels in a hierarchy using type inheritance to generalize shared security levels.

How you actually carry this out depends on the operating system and other tools available. The main point we wish to leave you with is to keep the code for security as isolated as possible. Then, as security needs change, you can isolate the change to one easily identified place.

Case Study Anyone can purchase a ticket as a ticket agent. This means having the ability to create Purchases and Customer demographics, but only having read access to Performance and Location information.

Implement Deployment Diagram for Development

Role(s): Infrastructure Architect

The Infrastructure Architect installs the network software, database management system, development software, and middleware software needed for development on appropriate hardware devices. The Infrastructure Architect uniformly configures all software to meet development needs and assigns the security access permissions to the developers.

Train Project Team

Role(s): (Project Team)

Anyone involved in developing the solution receives additional training before development begins. This means everyone, not just those developing models or code. This may occur as formal training from a vendor, training provided internally, or self-paced hands-on training by the individual. Training here consists of specific software tool instruction and any hardware- or network-specific training. The goal is to ensure the project team is comfortable using the technology required for developing the solution.

Case Study The project team attended two different training classes. The Object Architect went to a class targeted to UML modeling and object-oriented concepts. The Business Area Experts, the Object Architect, and the Object Developers attended a class in object-oriented concepts. The Object Developers additionally attended a course in the development language.

Plan Iteration Refinement Strategy

The project team revisits each increment to plan iteration refinement by reviewing the Problem Assessment, use cases, and classes before beginning the Build Solution phase.

Deliverables

Solution Area Scope Statement
Project Plan

Tasks:

Specify Iteration Refinement and Duration

Role(s): Project Manager, Object Architect, and Project Sponsor

The Project Manager and Project Sponsor establish the duration and number of iterations to develop each increment. Iterations function only to increase refinement of the content already packaged within an increment. The Object Architect then balances use case and class refinement equally across the agreed-upon number of iterations to meet the timebox deadlines. Generally, the number of alternative paths within a use case determines the number of iterations. If the number or length of the timeboxes require change, the Project Manager revises the project plan. All of this information updates the Solution Area Scope Statement.

> **Tip** A Solution Area Project Manager can extract a subset of the Project Plan to manage an individual Solution Area. This allows the Solution Area Project Manager to "filter out the noise" of the rest of the project and concentrate on tasks relevant only to his or her own Solution Area.

Recall that you control iterations with hard timeboxes. We used content as our sizing mechanism for determining increments. Iteration sizing uses timeboxes to limit refinement within date boundaries, because otherwise refinement can last forever! It is therefore up to us to determine the level of refinement attainable <u>before</u> entering the timebox. Now that we have a better idea of the content, we can better predict how many iterations it takes to reach stability (80 percent or better).

Case Study For our Case Study, we plan to develop the first increment of the Reserve Seating Solution Area with three, three-week Build Solution iterations. The first iteration (as always) starts with our core scenario. The second adds the alternative paths of a customer canceling the purchase and a customer credit purchase. The third iteration adds exceptions such as the sold-out performance and the instance where a customer selects more tickets from a section than available.

Note that we revisit this phase after the completion of the first increment in order to plan the second increment. The second increment contains customer demographics and address standardization.

Confirm Solution Structure

The project team reviews deliverables produced thus far and confirms that the structure of the solution is sound. The project team also reviews open issues, risks, and change requests.

Deliverables

Solution Structure Confirmation
Project Plan
Issues List
Change Requests
Risk Assessment

Tasks:

Obtain Solution Structure Confirmation

Role(s): Project Manager, Solution Area Project Manager(s), and Project Sponsor

The Project Manager works with the Solution Area Project Manager(s) to assemble the deliverables. The overall Project Manager reviews all deliverables developed within the Structure Solution phase with the Project Sponsor and obtains confirmation to proceed to the next phase. The Project Manager then reviews and updates the project plan to account for the actual time, any uncovered changes, and revisions to the estimates.

Case Study At this point, we obtain the resolution of the issue regarding the move to the Internet as seen in Table 4-3—Issues List at Solution Structure Confirmation.

Table 4-3—Issues List at Solution Structure Confirmation

Issue	Issue Description	Resolution
1.	What content belongs on the Internet? Options include schedules, performers, concert dates, and locations, with query capability for any of the above.	The Promote Performance Solution Area will use the Internet to broaden the target market. The Reserve Seating Solution Area also offers potential where the customer directly purchases tickets through the Internet. Postpone Reserve Seating Internet development until after deployment of the core solution.
2.	Does purchase information need to interface to the accounting system?	Not for the first release. Reconsider in next year's budget.

Issue	Issue Description	Resolution
3.	Will we support payment by check?	No. Checks present too much of a credit risk. Reconsider automated check verification as an enhancement after first release.
4.	What is the difference between reservation and purchase?	No difference. The business does not reserve seats for a performance. We will use the term purchase, since the customer does not reserve a ticket, the customer purchases a ticket.
5.	What is the difference between a seat and a ticket?	The seat is part of a location. The ticket, in the real world, represents a seat. A customer purchases a ticket to attend a performance in that seat.

The impact of this decision on the current Solution Area simply postpones the development of the Internet as an alternative path within the Reserve Seating use case.

Assess Risk

Role(s): Project Manager

The Project Manager considers risks specific to the Solution Area. Some risks may occur on both the overall Project Manager's SWOT and the SWOT created by the Solution Area Project Manager. How each manages the risk may differ, though. Although all Project Managers continually update the Risk Assessment based on progress reporting, this task provides a checkpoint for review based on the results of this phase.

Some of these items change quickly while others may remain the same for quite a while. The key is to focus on moving the weaknesses to strengths and the threats to opportunities as soon as you can. Be sure to keep in mind the strengths and opportunities, considering that they may disappear without proper attention.

Case Study For the Case Study, the SWOT focuses only on the Reserve Seating Solution Area as illustrated in Table 4-4—Structure Solution Risk Assessment.

Table 4-4—Structure Solution Risk Assessment

Category	Item	Action
Strength	Team is committed to OO style of development.	Continue to provide opportunity and education that applies to individuals' immediate responsibilities.
	Team members understand the business.	Look to broaden perspectives outside of current way of doing business—send one or two to trade convention and sponsor professional memberships in trade organizations. Prevent developing narrow view.
Weakness	Team is lacking in OO skills.	Establish targeted project team training. Consider hiring a "ringer" from outside the company.
	Users lack computer skills.	Schedule fundamental computer skills training.
		Note: Staff had two-day training. Now they want their equipment sooner!
Opportunity	Accounting really likes the idea of better transaction tracking.	Work to firm up reporting and query capabilities as soon as possible.
Threat	Internet as a technology solution driving the business solution.	Resolved. No Internet development for the near future. Revisit after first implementation.
	Technology is new for the company.	Provide continuous information on what we are doing—outside periodicals, case studies, etc.—to those concerned with reservations.

Chapter Summary

This chapter has taken you through the next layer of use case and class diagramming to firm up the Solution Area boundary and content. We detailed the Use Case Descriptions to pull in more of the business and identified the core, alternative, and exception scenarios. We have enhanced the Class Diagram by capturing the attributes, operations, and associations from the use case. We have thus stabilized the view of the business solution.

We started the growth of the infrastructure architecture vision and illustrated the thought processes to begin the documentation and training vision. All vocations supporting the business solution now have the basic understanding of the Solution Area to create their specific deliverables.

Finally, we have demonstrated how to lay out iteration refinement before beginning the Build Solution phase.

The next chapter shows you how to build the technology solution iteratively using prototyping and the full set of UML diagrams. We show how these deliverables support each other while progressing towards the complete definition of the business solution with supporting technology.

Chapter 5
Build Solution

Overview

This phase coordinates object model development with the actual building of the solution through durable prototyping. By durable, we mean software that lives beyond initial viewing. You define events and interactions that occur between objects for each Use Case Scenario. You define object behavior, life cycles, and the activities that transition objects from state to state. Interface classes and control classes begin to unfold. You repeat this phase multiple times through iteration. If you follow our suggestion of delivery using the "360 guideline," this phase repeats three times for every increment (with each iteration lasting three weeks). After completing the last iteration, you move on to the Integrate Solution phase.

It is within this phase perhaps more than any other phase where the tasks influence multiple object models. As you enhance one model, you uncover more that affects the other models. You leverage Use Case Scenarios to validate and check other deliverables. You do not need to wait for full coverage of all

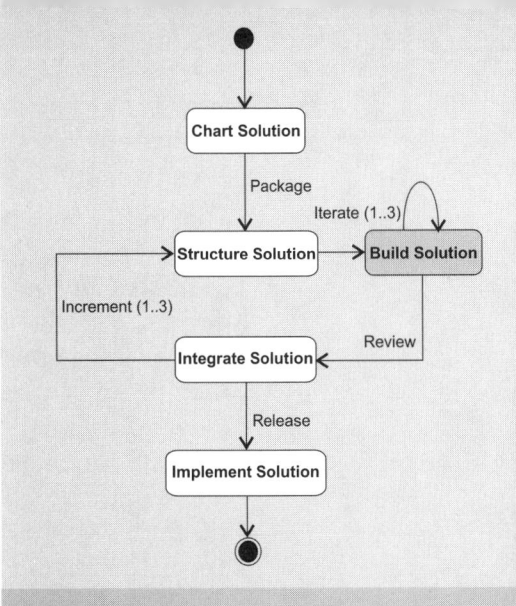

Deliverables:

Activity Diagram
Application
Change Requests
Class Diagram
Class Library Cross Reference
Collaboration Diagram
Collaboration Test Beds
Collaboration Test Plan
Component Diagram
Information Reference Guide
Issues List
Logical Data Model
Project Plan
Risk Assessment
Sequence Diagram
Solution Area Database
Solution Area Database Structure
Solution Build Confirmation
Statechart Diagram
Training Curriculum
Training Support Materials
Use Case Scenarios
Use Case Test Beds
Use Case Test Plan
User Instructions Guide

scenarios before beginning this validation. For example, start with the core scenario to gain overall context, then jump immediately to Class Diagrams, Sequence Diagrams, or Statechart Diagrams to flesh out the details. With the iterative approach, the sequencing of activities and tasks is less important in this phase. Please note that we are presenting them in an approximate order. There is no prescribed series in which to complete the deliverables, especially within dynamic modeling. To gain the benefits of iteration, you should "go with the flow" and capture whatever, whenever! To place bounds on the free flow of ideas stifles the creativity necessary to generate truly magnificent solutions. To those nervous with the threat of project anomie, remember that the timebox and deliverables bind the structure. We do, however, suggest you try the following order at least the first time through. Recognize that over time, understanding how to select the most appropriate diagram varies with the type of information you need.

Our case study example takes you through the first iteration. We describe the impact of iteration resulting from the second and third iterations and include the results from the second increment at the end of this chapter.

Activities

Model the Solution

This activity mainly focuses on refining the Class Diagram with dynamic modeling. Dynamic modeling includes Sequence, State, Collaboration, and Activity Diagrams. You accomplish Class Diagram refinement using the various capabilities of the other UML diagrams through prototyping and facilitation. The tasks in this activity specify object behaviors and reveal additional attributes to support that behavior.

Deliverables

Use Case Scenarios
Use Case Test Plan
Class Diagram
Sequence Diagram
Statechart Diagram
Collaboration Diagram
Activity Diagram
Component Diagram
Class Library Cross Reference
Application

Build Use Case Scenarios

Role(s): Object Architect (Facilitator) and Business Area Experts

The Object Architect works with the Business Area Experts to understand the dynamic behavior of the objects by refining use cases. The Object Architect uses the scenarios as a basis for creating and validating all other deliverables, so this step is the vital link between the static and the dynamic definition of the solution.

You create the Use Case Scenarios from the sequential list of the events in the use case and then add the objects influenced by these events. You apply each of these Use Case Scenarios as input for creating Sequence Diagrams in the next task.

You obtain your list of events from the Use Case Description. Unlike the business events originally identified in the Chart Solution phase, these events occur as a response to the higher-level business event. You easily identify and refine additional events as part of examining each business event. This is the desired result, but it can get very frustrating to iterate back and add more events in an area you thought you already understood. This is good! It shows that you are gaining greater understanding of the detail. Break each event down one by one and treat each one in its own right. The final set of steps eventually stabilizes.

Discussion naturally surrounds the procedures that an actor performs to use the system. You order the steps sequentially into paths that take you through the use case. Each complete path becomes a Use Case Scenario. Each Use Case Scenario describes a complete interaction with the system. There are potentially many scenarios, depending on the specific events that change the way the system responds to the events. Common paths are covered such as initialization (an employee is hired), termination (an employee quits), and continuance (an employee's annual review). You always develop at least one scenario to represent the core scenario. Create additional scenarios for each complex path; the simplistic paths do not require scenarios, but they do aid in understanding the complete business situation. Also explore "what if" conditions, but limit this to the 80 percent rule to avoid analysis paralysis. The big challenge in this activity is to get the correct level of detail.

Exceptions and alternative paths become their own short lists of scenario steps. You may decide to develop additional scenarios for alternative paths and exceptions. The difference between an alternative scenario and an exception is that with an alternative scenario, an actor chooses to use the system in a different way. With an exception, the system forces the actor into a different path. Examples of additional scenarios include customer cancels purchase (an alternative) and customer requests tickets for a sold-out performance (an exception). Judging which scenarios require further detail improves with experience. Again, ignore exceptions and alternate paths the first time through.

Our goal is to derive the essence of the Use Case Scenario. Start by taking the Use Case Description and breaking it apart, one sentence at a time. For the sentences with "System responds by…" you potentially create many scenario steps, replacing "System" with the object or objects participating in the message exchange based on their responsibility. Do not get too hung up on the precise nature of what each object does in response; that comes next. At this point, you are simply interested in identifying the overall messages in the interaction.

Within scenarios, you may include the triggering events, occurrence, frequency, and location. Identify the time if the scenario occurs because of a time-driven event. Identify each object involved in a scenario, describe how those objects are coordinated, and define how they communicate with one another.

Now we must detail the system responses by extending the sequential steps to the classes that participate in the behavior. Each of these events involves two objects, the source and the target. If not, the event requires rewriting to obtain more detail. In some cases, the target object is the same as the source object. This may not flow easily the first time through because there is a lot of detail to uncover. Discovering new objects forces you to rewrite your list of scenario steps repeatedly. Do not spend too much time on format and be sure to focus on content. As you gain understanding, the true steps appear. Phrase the steps in loose sentences of "object source = event = object target." The event may naturally resemble an action the target object should take in response to the event. To communicate the action, the object sends a message to another object requesting the object to do something. Generally, if an object sends a message, the receiving object performs an operation.

You want to sequence these operations to show when they occur over time; you are organizing the main order of operation. You add any operation you uncover to the Class Diagram including all behavior and information naturally connected with the class.

It is common early on to misunderstand the difference between message, operation, and method. A message is a communication between objects triggered by some event. An operation is a service that an object can request. A method is the instantiation of an operation, that is, the program code for performing the behavior of an operation.

Case Study   This section explores the first iteration of the Reserve Seating Solution Area. The Case Study takes you through each of the iterations. Remember our first goal is to discover as much as we can about the core scenario. The second iteration focuses on alternative paths. The third and final iteration concentrates on the exceptions discovered in the first two.

We repeat the Use Case Description here for easy reference.

Name:	Reserve Seating
Summary:	Customer reserves seating for a performance. Customer selects seating and performance, pays with cash or credit card, and receives one or more tickets.
Assumptions:	
Actors:	Customer
Preconditions:	Performance is booked, location is reserved, and ticket prices are set.
Description:	This use case begins when customer requests ticket(s) for a performance. The system displays remaining seating options and ticket prices. [Exception: Performance sold out]. The customer selects seating area and number of seats. [Exception: The customer cancels purchase (no sale)]. The customer makes next selection. The customer finishes selecting seats. The system sums the prices and applies appropriate taxes. The system communicates the total to customer. The customer provides payment. If payment is by credit card, the system calls for credit authorization. The system collects credit card issuer, number, and expiration date to verify that available credit is more than the total. Charge must be for exact amount only. If credit card authorization passes, the seats are reserved. If authorization fails, the customer has the option to pay with any other payment method. [Exception: Customer declines alternative payment method]. Customer receives purchased tickets. This use case ends when the customer leaves.
Exceptions:	Performance is sold out: notify the customer
	Customer cancels the purchase: end the use case
	Customer declines alternative payment options: end the use case
Postconditions:	Purchase information is stored in the system.

We have the following core path for a cash purchase scenario:

> This use case begins when customer requests ticket(s) for a performance.

This triggering event starts the Use Case Scenario. For the steps in this scenario, all customer (actor) steps go through the system interface.

> The system displays remaining seating options and ticket prices.

We break down the definition of "system" into the messages between objects that participate to carry out the response. Our phrasing of the scenario steps becomes:

1. The Interface asks Performance to show event information.
2. The Customer selects a Performance from the Interface.
3. The Interface requests all available Tickets for that Performance.

We follow with the next sentence from the use case.

> The customer selects seating area and number of seats.

This implicitly means that the Customer initiates a Purchase of Tickets. The steps to carry it out are:

4. Customer initiates Purchase.
5. Customer selects Tickets.
6. Purchase creates a Purchase Item.
7. Purchase Item requests selected Tickets to change availability.

Returning to pick up the next sentence from the use case, we have:

> The customer makes next selection.

This last step signifies an iteration for purchasing multiple tickets. It is called a continuation condition. We do not mind that the customer selects more and more tickets! But, alas:

> The customer finishes selecting seats.

The Customer has just implicitly completed the Purchase. The next step stops the continuation of the iteration.

8. Interface requests total from Purchase.
9. The system sums the prices and applies appropriate taxes.
10. Purchase sums the Purchase Items including standard charges and taxes.
11. The system communicates the total to Customer.

12. Purchase returns the total to the Customer through the Interface.

The last step requests payment from the customer, followed by:

> The customer provides payment.

In the core scenario, this translates to:

13. Customer provides payment (cash) amount.

Finally:

> Customer receives purchased tickets. This use case ends when the customer leaves.

"Customer receives purchased tickets" is not necessarily something the system does, but it gives us pause to consider if it is worth exploring. Technology could assist the delivery of tickets. Further discussion makes this issue number six on our Issues List combined with other implications collected during scenario building, as shown in Table 5-1—Issues List. We also add this to our Change Requests but agree to postpone delivery of this function for now.

Table 5-1—Issues List

Num	Issue Description	Resolution
1.	What content belongs on the Internet? Options include schedules, performers, concert dates, and locations, with query capability for any of the above.	The Promote Performance Solution Area will use the Internet to broaden the target market. The Reserve Seating Solution Area also offers potential where the customer directly purchases tickets through the Internet. Postpone Reserve Seating Internet development until after deployment of the core solution.
2.	Does purchase information need to interface to the accounting system?	Not for the first release. Reconsider in next year's budget.
3.	Will we support payment by check?	No. Checks present too much of a credit risk. Reconsider automated check verification as an enhancement after first release.
4.	What is the difference between reservation and purchase?	No difference. We will use the term purchase, since the customer does not reserve a ticket; the customer purchases a ticket.
5.	What is the difference between a seat and a ticket?	The seat is part of a location. The ticket, in the real world, represents a seat. A customer purchases a ticket to attend a performance in that seat.

Num	Issue Description	Resolution
6.	Can we have tickets printed at the time of purchase? Are purchases allowed for tickets at other locations? (Currently, tickets are preprinted, so the ticket has to be mailed to the customer or shipped to the purchase location.)	

Developing the scenario uncovers much information that, of course, finds its way into the Class Diagram and the Use Case Description. Our core scenario now provides the basis for beginning dynamic modeling.

Build Sequence Diagrams from Use Case Scenarios

Role(s): Object Architect (Facilitator) and Business Area Experts

The Solution Area team begins dynamic modeling by selecting only the core and the more complex scenarios and validating their completeness and accuracy with Sequence Diagrams. The purpose is to diagram the object interactions connected by events explicitly. You already know which objects and events to include from your work developing the scenarios. Now you list the scenario steps ordered by time from top to bottom on the Sequence Diagram. List the objects involved on top from left to right. The order of the objects is not important.

Not all Use Case Scenarios require a Sequence Diagram. Select those that are worthwhile. If one scenario differs only slightly from another, adding another diagram adds little value to understanding.

> **Tip** A good way to build Sequence Diagrams and still keep your Business Area Experts involved is to use CRC Cards. This not only tests your Sequence Diagram (and helps build it), but allows you to quickly identify needed attributes and operations.

Sequence Diagrams place the bulleted lists of object-message-object interactions from the Use Case Scenario into a stepwise progression of operations and messages. Now you explore how objects interact with each other. It is here that we add the dimension of time to the definition of objects. You document the sequences and communications using the Sequence Diagram. It shows where an event originates and to which object to send a message.

The first object that starts the interaction is the controlling object, also known as the controller. Control moves from source object to target object. The target becomes the source, and control passes to the next target object in event sequence until the end of the Use Case Scenario. A scenario must have a complete chain. However, you may jump to another object for an obvious gap. This mostly occurs when ignoring return messages.

For each step in the scenario, one object sends a message to another object. To illustrate this, you draw an arrow from the sending object to the receiving object. Above this arrow, you place the name of the message. This message often becomes an operation representing the action that the receiving object takes in response to the event. You can optionally include any attributes and return values in the operation's signature. If no operation occurs, surround the message in quotes.

> **Tip** Sometimes it helps to first place only the messages on the Sequence Diagram, then replace the messages with operations. You may want to use this with teams new to object modeling or still uncomfortable with the concept of class responsibility.

As you place objects and messages on the Sequence Diagram, you may uncover additional objects to add to your Class Diagram. An operation may identify new attributes that you also place on the Class Diagram. At this point, postpone identifying attributes that are implementation-specific such as identification keys and derived values. You do want to capture attributes that change in response to events. This includes association values and link attributes.

Next you specify "what if" sequences, action sequences, conditions, branches, and looping. You can identify when objects are instantiated (created) and destroyed (deleted). At this time, postpone adding the obvious operations like create, read, update, and delete unless they are pivotal to the understanding of the Sequence Diagram. They sometimes get in the way of understanding main functionality.

You may wish to eliminate the return marks, as they are not required. The returns pose a potential danger by forcing a "called procedure" view; fortunately, an object is not required to wait for return from a message. We suggest indicating returns with a messaging arrow. The receiving object can then respond to this new message as it receives it rather than forcing a procedural wait.

Case Study We place the scenario steps on the Sequence Diagram as a first draft preparation for the facilitated session. During the session, we refine the Sequence Diagram and identify the operations that respond to each step. The first challenge entails the differentiation between the customer events and the user interface boundary. The first iteration simply creates a controlling class named Interface to act as a placeholder. The Interface class eventually decomposes into several interface classes; the Prototype User Interface Applications task details the user interface objects. Figure 5-1—Sequence Diagram with Operations shows the resultant Sequence Diagram with operations added.

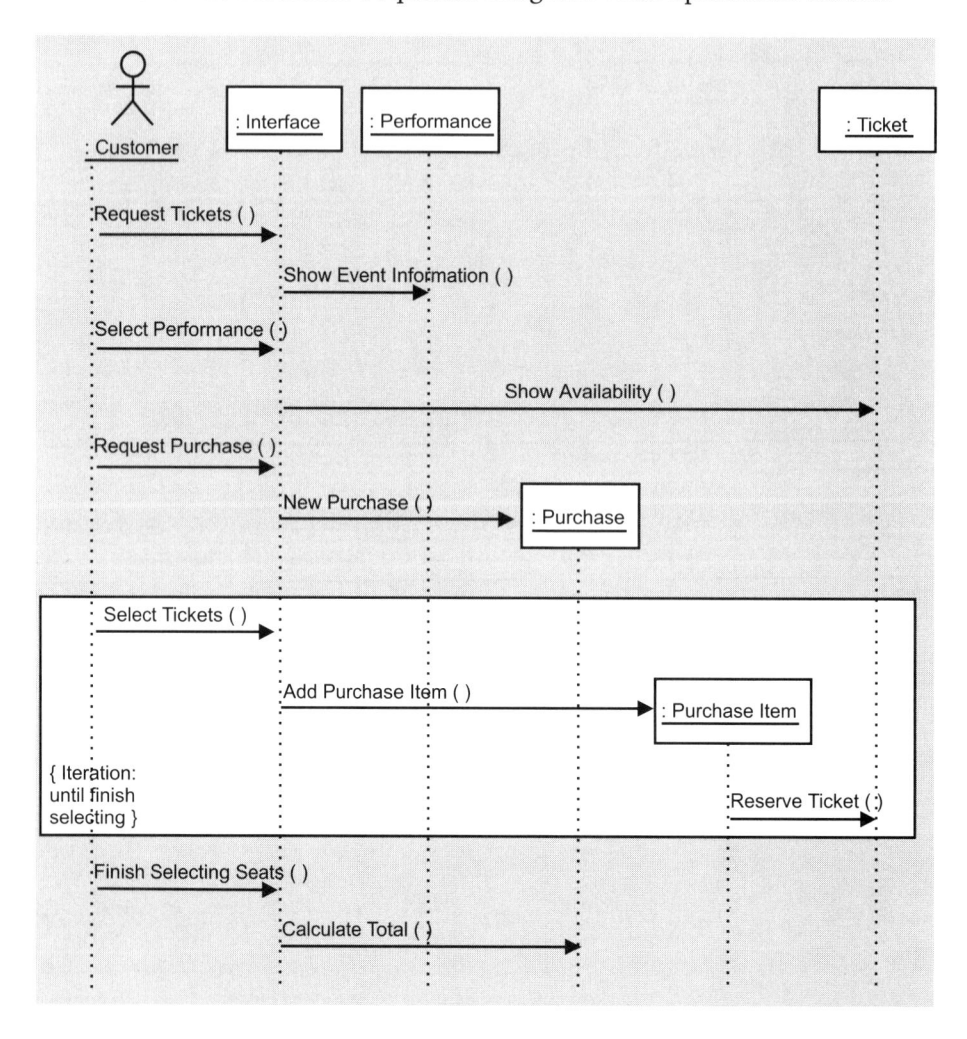

Figure 5-1—Sequence Diagram with Operations

Notice the added operations in Figure 5-2—Class Diagram with Operations. The Class Diagram now includes these operations and other discovered relationships and attributes.

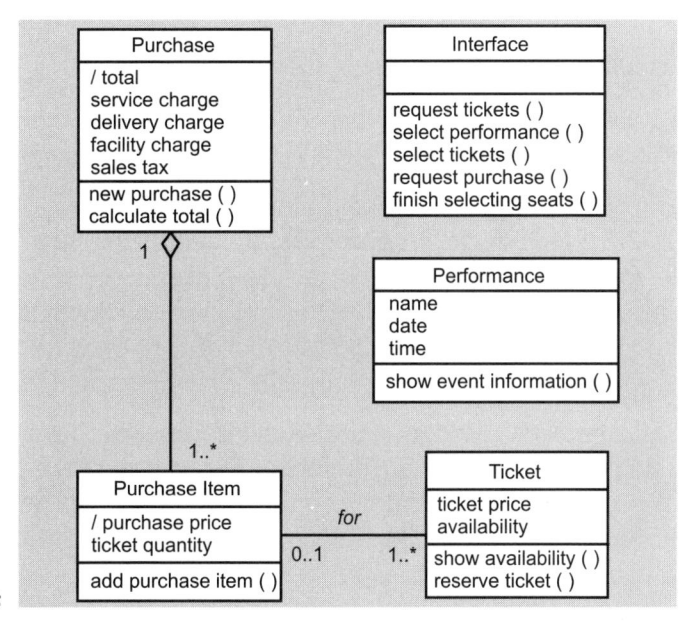

Figure 5-2—Class Diagram with Operations

Purchase
/ total
service charge
delivery charge
facility charge
sales tax
new purchase ( )
calculate total ( )

Interface

request tickets ( )
select performance ( )
select tickets ( )
request purchase ( )
finish selecting seats ( )

Performance
name
date
time
show event information ( )

Purchase Item
/ purchase price
ticket quantity
add purchase item ( )

Ticket
ticket price
availability
show availability ( )
reserve ticket ( )

Leverage Reusable Classes from the Class Library

Role(s): Object Architect

The Object Architect matches additional classes from the class library to the updated view of the Class Diagram for this iteration. During this phase of iteration, these classes generally are implementation-specific classes such as window components.

Case Study Since we are using Visual C++ 6.0, we know that we can use its generic form and control objects. We could additionally build project-specific or enterprise-specific versions of forms or control objects. For example, we may decide to place an existing control with a standard size on a form in a repeatable location. These project standard classes set the same user interface "look and feel" throughout the project.

More interestingly, since we assumed that the first increment of the Manage Location Solution Area is complete, we can now select the implementation classes built during that increment. This includes utility classes such as error management and standard user interface classes.

> **Tip** Instead of using the classes as we build the Reserve Seating Solution Area, we could wait until the Integrate Solution phase and integrate the two Solution Areas then.

Prototype User Interface Applications

Role(s): Object Architect (Facilitator), Object Developer, Business Area Experts, and Document Architect

The Solution Area team begins building the user interface classes following the User Interface Layout established in the Structure Solution phase. You typically do this in a facilitated session with a graphical user interface (GUI) tool. Business Area Experts specify the information needed to accomplish a specific task, format and display that information graphically, and define the flow between GUIs.

The Solution Area team then adds further detail to object interaction and associations through facilitated, rapid prototyping. Prototyping provides an excellent technique for determining how these windows should interact, which attributes to add for entering information, and which control buttons to add for signaling events.

Controversy sometimes arises over whether or not to prototype. Advocates of prototyping claim:

- The user and developers see the solution more clearly.
- The user sees the results and wants something different.
- The user sees the programming work behind the solution.

Opponents of prototyping claim:

- The users think the solution is ready to implement.
- The prototype is "throwaway" work.

We do not advocate the use of throwaway prototyping unless the tools used for prototyping are not the same tools used for the final solution. As long as tools and staff resources remain at a premium, we feel you ought to build upon work efforts and not dispose of them.

> **Tip** Instead of a GUI development tool, you can also prototype using a white board. This allows you to demonstrate behavior quickly that is otherwise difficult to represent.

Prototyping is much more than just placing buttons and fields on windows. The purpose of prototyping is to provide a communication vehicle to comprehend the business solution using technology to assist that comprehension. During the session, you attempt to capture the behaviors of buttons that both control flows to other windows and alter the state of an object.

We cannot emphasize enough the importance of quickly using a tool to display how a screen or report looks. We do not recommend attempting full-scale coding at this point because you have not yet fully defined the business objects. These business objects are vital to your entire application and building them based on the user interface rather than the other way around can result in a sloppy business object with a loose interface. Interface objects should merely provide the editing and formatting of attributes for core business objects. Nevertheless, prototyping at this point often helps Users clarify what they need. This visualization provides a vital communication vehicle for discovering and validating the details. Although building the actual code to support behavior occurs out of session, a tool often provides an excellent vehicle for documenting the behavior behind each control button.

> **Tip** To manage expectations, discourage developers from writing code during prototyping sessions. Emphasize that at this point the prototype is just a picture that assists with communication.

We place this task here simply because this is the earliest point at which you have enough information to begin effective prototyping. You have already created the bulk of the business domain (control) classes from the Use Case Scenarios and Sequence Diagrams; all that remains is the interface and entity classes. Earlier in the process prototyping was premature; you needed a solid understanding of the business domain before attempting to make the visual interface work. To do otherwise may have forced you into rework. Certainly, you may use prototyping later to clarify understanding and refinement once you have formed this basis. Also, consider prototyping in conjunction with Statechart Diagram refinement.

As you prototype, you uncover interface classes. You add interface classes and their attributes, operations, and messages to the Class Diagram to incorporate inheritance hierarchies and aggregations. Given the potential for reuse of these types of classes and the current complexity of the Class Diagram, it may be necessary to keep them on a separate set of diagrams to minimize diagram clutter.

Prototyping should include not only the interface classes, but the control and entity classes as well. In fact, the knowledge of how all objects interact (including the "less visible" objects from the control and entity classes) builds a more robust solution. Letting the interface objects drive the design decisions results in overlooked reusability, less encapsulation, and poorer performance. During prototyping, you may discover many alternatives for how objects could interact. You decide whether the interface class does the work or if it communicates with a control class that owns the behavior. Which alternative you choose depends on how you decide to balance performance and reusability.

You now determine how to handle "lists" of multiple objects instantiated from the same class. Since we are using Visual C++ 6.0 with Access, we will use simple DAO recordsets at the data layer to group them. This is older technology, so we will use vectors everywhere else, e.g., at the business layer.

Still, you must determine if you really need to collect objects. Currently, Section provides the count of available seats, which is sufficient for purchasing tickets. If you determine that you later need to retrieve multiple Sections from the database, you may create a means to collect the instantiated objects at that time. That is the key to object-oriented development—know the general direction you are heading and minimally build what you need today. What you think you need tomorrow may change when tomorrow finally arrives. Do not put it in until necessary.

Sequence Diagrams provide an excellent place for beginning prototyping. They help identify which objects you need and the messaging between them. You could also use a Collaboration Diagram to isolate the view if the messaging between objects becomes too complex. For example, selecting available seats requires several objects to interact. Typically, the user interface controls the user event processing.

> **Tip** You may find prototyping helps drive the Sequence Diagram rather than the other way around.

Case Study In the Sequence Diagram, you see many messages sent to and from the Customer. The system really ought to edit and format these messages. We provide a GUI application to control the Reserve Seating use case that replaces our stubbed-in Interface class. The Application consists of three classes, known as forms in Visual C++ 6.0, for altering attributes, displaying lists of ticket information, and displaying final purchase totals. You can call one form from inside another form. Each form itself is a class.

To reserve tickets, we realize we need to communicate performance information and the number of available seats to the Customer. We also need a means to record the purchases. We decide to use three forms to reserve tickets. The first form, Ticket Taker, starts the Application and contains the other two forms. The Performances form shows performance information we want to reuse from the Contract Performances Solution Area. For our purposes during prototyping, we merely identify the information we need. We need to integrate this information with the Contract Performances Solution Area later. We do not need to wait until Integrate Solution, though. We can work with the other Solution Area project team to get basic class definition and interface information.

On the Performances form, we list the locations of performances and the dates and times of the performances. After the user selects available tickets, the Performances form displays the available seats by section. It is here that we discover a major object, Section. We find it more efficient and user friendly to identify the number of available seats by section rather than list the specific seat itself. We follow the definition of Section from the Manage Location Solution Area and suggest that the Contract Performances Solution Area may want to determine pricing by Section rather than by Ticket.

Finally, we include a command button, Add, to add the ordered quantities to the order.

On the Order form, we capture customer demographic information and the individual purchase items, and display the order total. We make a decision that the form itself has this behavior rather than the Purchase object because we derive these totals. We include command buttons for creating a new order, accepting the order, canceling the order, and removing an item from the order. With the Remove function, we realize we need another method for unreserving a Ticket.

As part of the prototyping session, we reserved screen "real estate" for known future items such as charge card information. Although this is not part of our core scenario, it does not hurt to capture the obvious to avoid rework later. We add a new form, Order, for managing ticket purchases. Figure 5-3—Initial User Interface After Prototyping depicts the visual development of the GUI. Note that at this point there is no code behind these items.

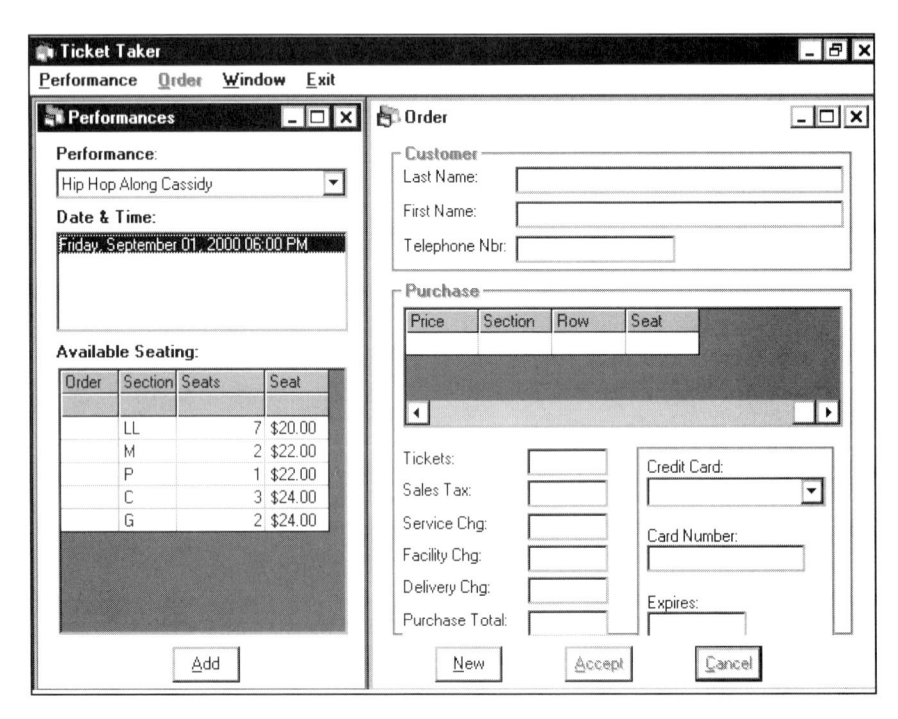

Figure 5-3—Initial User Interface After Prototyping

Figure 5-4—Interface Class Diagram After Prototyping shows the enhanced interface classes.

Figure 5-5—Control Class Diagram After Prototyping shows the enhanced control classes.

Build Solution ■ 151

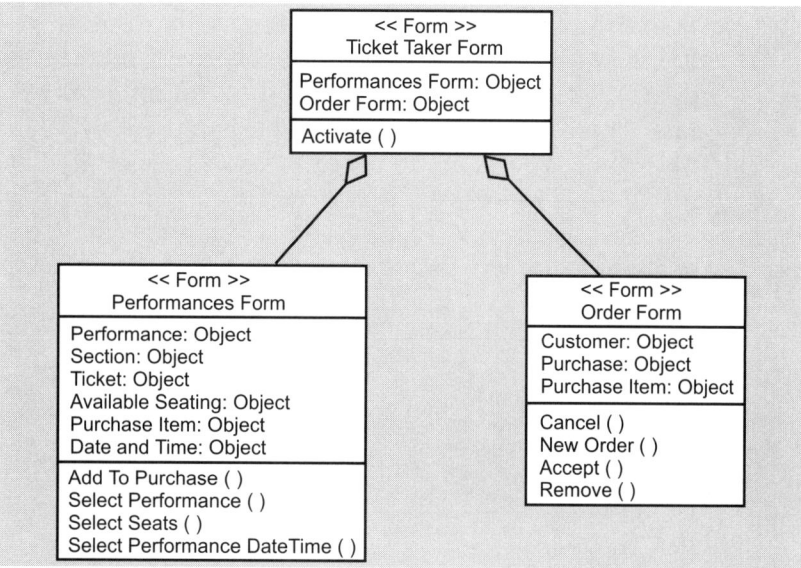

```
              << Form >>
             Ticket Taker Form
        ─────────────────────────
        Performances Form: Object
        Order Form: Object
        ─────────────────────────
        Activate ( )
```

```
        << Form >>                              << Form >>
     Performances Form                         Order Form
──────────────────────────              ──────────────────────────
Performance: Object                     Customer: Object
Section: Object                         Purchase: Object
Ticket: Object                          Purchase Item: Object
Available Seating: Object               ──────────────────────────
Purchase Item: Object                   Cancel ( )
Date and Time: Object                   New Order ( )
──────────────────────────              Accept ( )
Add To Purchase ( )                     Remove ( )
Select Performance ( )
Select Seats ( )
Select Performance DateTime ( )
```

Figure 5-4—Interface Class Diagram After Prototyping

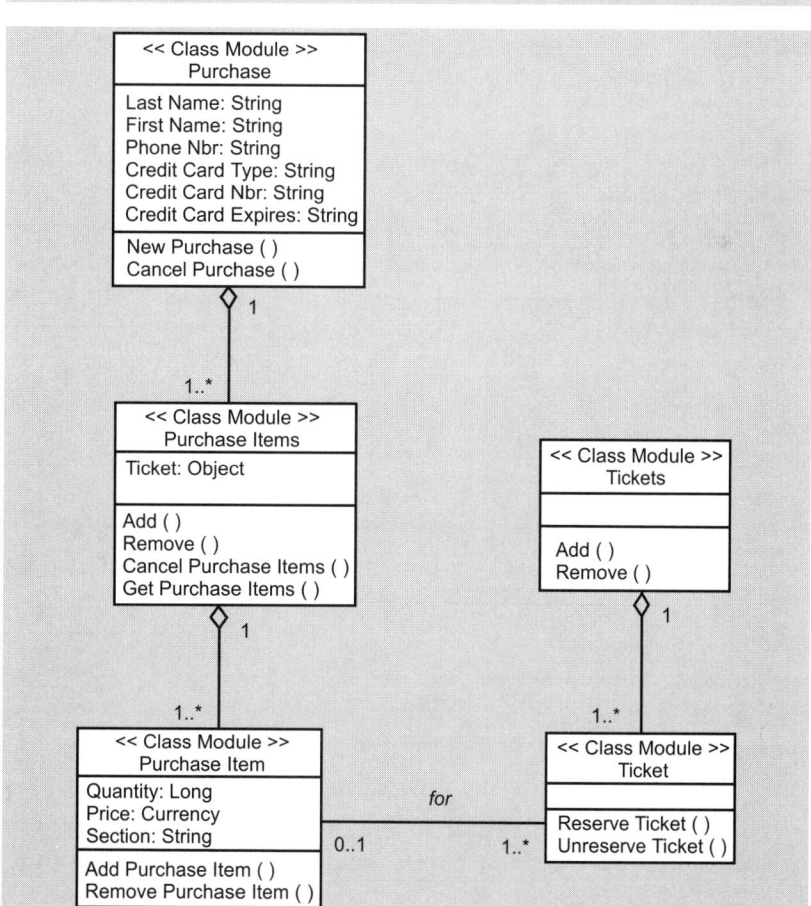

```
          << Class Module >>
                Purchase
        ─────────────────────────
        Last Name: String
        First Name: String
        Phone Nbr: String
        Credit Card Type: String
        Credit Card Nbr: String
        Credit Card Expires: String
        ─────────────────────────
        New Purchase ( )
        Cancel Purchase ( )
```

```
       << Class Module >>
         Purchase Items                              << Class Module >>
     ──────────────────────                               Tickets
     Ticket: Object                                 ──────────────────
     ──────────────────────                         
     Add ( )                                        ──────────────────
     Remove ( )                                     Add ( )
     Cancel Purchase Items ( )                      Remove ( )
     Get Purchase Items ( )
```

```
       << Class Module >>                            << Class Module >>
          Purchase Item                                    Ticket
     ──────────────────────         for           ──────────────────
     Quantity: Long                                ──────────────────
     Price: Currency                               Reserve Ticket ( )
     Section: String                               Unreserve Ticket ( )
     ──────────────────────
     Add Purchase Item ( )
     Remove Purchase Item ( )
```

Figure 5-5—Control Class Diagram After Prototyping

From Figure 5-6—Entity Class Diagram After Prototyping, you can see that the entity classes closely resemble the control classes. The dbPurchaseItems class manages the collection for the Performance class. The behavior within these objects differs significantly from the like-named objects in the control classes. The entity objects communicate directly with the database but perform no coordination of object behaviors other than manipulation of information to and from the database.

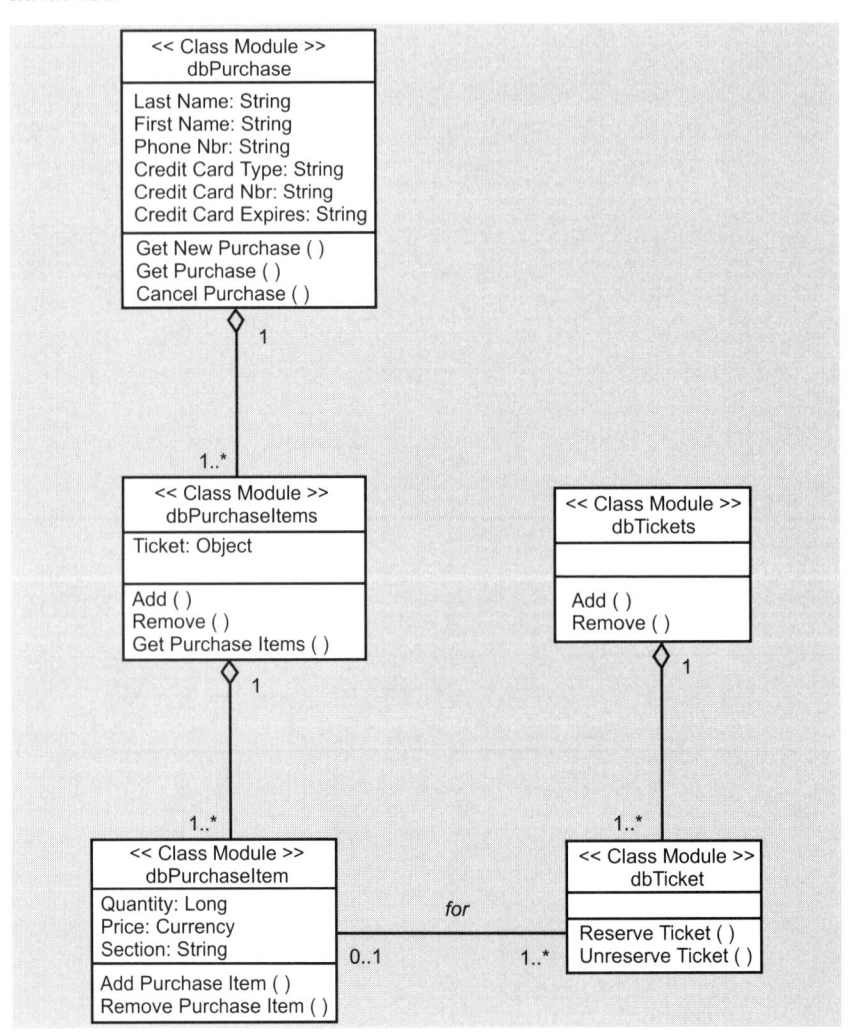

Figure 5-6—Entity Class Diagram After Prototyping

```
<< Class Module >>
dbPurchase
-----------------------------
Last Name: String
First Name: String
Phone Nbr: String
Credit Card Type: String
Credit Card Nbr: String
Credit Card Expires: String
-----------------------------
Get New Purchase ( )
Get Purchase ( )
Cancel Purchase ( )
```

```
<< Class Module >>
dbPurchaseItems
-----------------------------
Ticket: Object
-----------------------------
Add ( )
Remove ( )
Get Purchase Items ( )
```

```
<< Class Module >>
dbTickets
-----------------------------
Add ( )
Remove ( )
```

```
<< Class Module >>
dbPurchaseItem
-----------------------------
Quantity: Long
Price: Currency
Section: String
-----------------------------
Add Purchase Item ( )
Remove Purchase Item ( )
```

```
<< Class Module >>
dbTicket
-----------------------------
Reserve Ticket ( )
Unreserve Ticket ( )
```

Although subtle, the Purchase entity class has determined a need to differentiate between a new purchase order and one previously created. The Purchase control class does not need this differentiation. It merely needs to get a Purchase object.

We make decisions about whether we should immediately update the database, or collect the information and update at the end of a logical unit of work. Updating immediately reduces complexity and functionally makes more sense. Delaying the reservation of a ticket could result in another user reserving that same ticket first.

You could send a message from PurchaseItem directly to the Ticket object to improve performance, but this does not follow sound object-oriented thinking and may eventually lead to cumbersome workarounds.

Notice we have drawn no static associations between classes in each of the interface, control, and entity object types. Static associations should occur only within an object type, not between object types. This allows for portability from one processor to another. Statically associating classes between groupings means that one type of processor must know about a different kind of processor. This results in a dependency that restricts flexibility in deployment and portability.

Build Statechart Diagrams from Sequence Diagrams

Role(s): Object Architect (Facilitator) and Business Area Experts

The Solution Area team reviews the most common or "master" objects to identify potential content changes that occur either over time or due to business events.

You use Statechart Diagrams to gain understanding of the dynamic behavior of a specific object. The development of the Statechart Diagram in a facilitated session provides an effective communication tool for identifying states, events, and activities. A Statechart Diagram generally uncovers additional attributes and operations.

> **Tip** Modeling a Statechart Diagram in a facilitated session with Business Area Experts is an excellent mechanism for clarifying the sometimes sticky nuances of an object life cycle. Complete the finer diagramming details outside of the facilitated session.

The UML bases much of the Statechart Diagram on Harel diagrams.[1] Though typically applied to real-time solutions where the change in state is often more important than the object itself, a concentrated effort of reviewing a busy object may reap great rewards in understanding precisely the nature of its behavior.

From the whole set of completed Sequence Diagrams, you look for objects that are busy with messages. Busy objects are excellent candidates for further diagnosis using Statechart Diagrams. Examples of states include "bought," as in a product purchase; "ordered," as in quarterly reordering of a water purifier; and "totaling," as in a register summing a sale.

> **Tip** Whenever you hear the team refer to "status codes" as an attribute of an object, you likely need a State/Transition Diagram for the class of that object.

You discuss the events that transition an object from state to state to determine any significant impact on the object. "A state is a condition during the life of an object or an interaction during which it satisfies some condition, performs some action, or waits for some event."[2] Ways of identifying state are to look at the results of change activated by time or an event. The receipt of a message from another object is one type of event. You ensure complete coverage of all the possible life cycle states for an object by deriving them from all Sequence Diagrams that reference it. Each time an object receives a message, you create a new state for the object. That is, the receipt of a message is a transition event that causes a change in state. Note that some events do not cause a change in state (known as self-transition events). Generally, for each change in state, or transition, the object performs an operation. Operations translate to actions and activities that occur after receiving the message. You add these operations to the Class Diagram along with any attributes affected by these operations.

You repeat this process for all of the incoming events for the object across all Sequence Diagrams. Then, generalize similar states and events to provide the full view of the object life cycle. Conceptually, you create a single Statechart Diagram that shows all of the object's

---

1 David Harel. "Statecharts: A Visual Formalism for Complex Systems." *Science of Computer Programming* Vol. 8, 1987.
2 Rational Software Corporation, et al. *UML Summary version 1.1*. N.p. September 1, 1997, 104.

merged states and events. You massage some of the events to combine and clarify them into a more generic structure; this is valuable as long as it does not get out of hand. We find that you can spend a lot of time on Statechart Diagrams; keep your life cycle analyses only for the classes that are truly busy.

Keep in mind that a state change may potentially occur from more than one event, and transitions from state to state can be continuous and looping. The transitions through a Statechart Diagram do not need to be single-threaded or sequential.

Sometimes, the change in state sends a message to another object. You may wish to show the messages to other objects on the Statechart Diagram to illustrate these linked interactions. Using the UML, you can define a message using a dotted line to another object on the diagram. From the viewpoint of the sending object, we are not concerned about the state of the receiving object. Any activity resulting from sending the message is the sole responsibility of the receiving object. This helps us to avoid creating public operations (operations that depend on knowledge of other classes).

Assess cohesion while building the Statechart Diagram. Often, an object may have significant operational activity with very little change in its attributes. Conversely, a data stream can be continually affecting the object (as in a transaction processing system) with very simplistic operational characteristics. Any class that has an apparent imbalance between its attributes and operations (low cohesion) is worth further investigation to make sure it is well founded and modeled correctly. If there are many states that use only distinct sets of attributes and those attributes are minimally affected by the other states, recognize that the state may need to be "in a class all by itself" (every pun intended). The goal is to have an object do one thing—carry out its responsibility—and do this one thing well.

Case Study We look across all of the Sequence Diagrams created for scenarios and note that the Purchase object receives many messages. This is a candidate for exploration using a Statechart Diagram.

Figure 5-7—Statechart Diagram for Purchase depicts the Statechart Diagram for Purchase. This view includes only the dynamics from the Reserve Seating Use Case. Note that canceling a purchase stops the life cycle of Purchase, but we added the Canceled state to the object in order to "back out" the purchase transaction using a void operation.

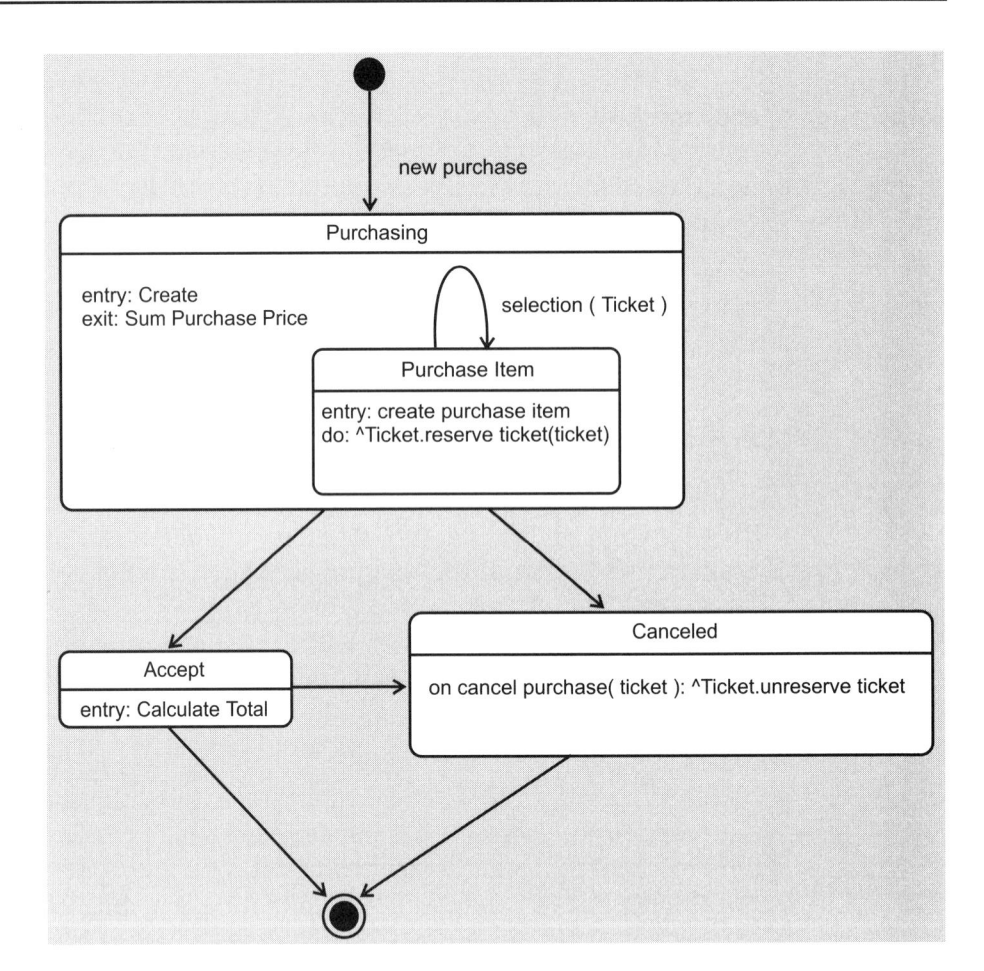

Figure 5-7—Statechart Diagram for Purchase

Build Collaboration Diagrams

Role(s): Object Architect

The Object Architect documents the interactions organized around the objects in a Collaboration Diagram. Additional "what if" scenarios may manifest themselves, necessitating updates to previous models.

The Collaboration Diagram provides an additional aid in designing the operations behind the events from the Sequence Diagrams. It allows you to refine the operations and include the operation signatures, while looking at the "big picture." The strength of this view allows you to view all of the interactions for the objects within this collaboration. The Collaboration Diagram filters out the sequential nature of the events to help visualize how an object participates in a specific collaboration.

The Collaboration Diagram, Statechart Diagram, and Sequence Diagram all depict behavioral aspects of the system. The Statechart Diagram focuses on one object at a time. The Sequence Diagram includes all objects involved in a sequentially described interaction. The Collaboration Diagram graphically shows information relevant within a specific context, typically a Use Case Scenario. Both the Sequence Diagram and the Collaboration Diagram show objects and messages, but the Collaboration Diagram additionally shows attributes involved, including the static relationships of objects. Relevant objects may not directly participate in message exchange, but may indirectly be affected or accessed. Like the Sequence Diagram, you may want to include the actor that invokes the action. The Sequence Diagram lists steps from top to bottom thereby inferring sequence. The Collaboration Diagram explicitly labels messages with sequence numbers. They both support the same types of messages.

> **Tip** We have found the Collaboration Diagram especially useful for planning and documenting test cases. The Use Case Scenarios and Sequence Diagrams work sufficiently for user acceptance testing, but Collaboration Diagrams allow us to more thoroughly test smaller collaborations of behavior for collaboration testing.

Case Study Figure 5-8—Collaboration Diagram shows the view derived from our Sequence Diagram.

Adding attributes provides another validation opportunity. In the step that returns the ticket prices, we had to ask ourselves, "When did the ticket prices get in the database?" Our precondition for the use case listed this, and we realized that this responsibility came under the Contract Performance Solution Area.

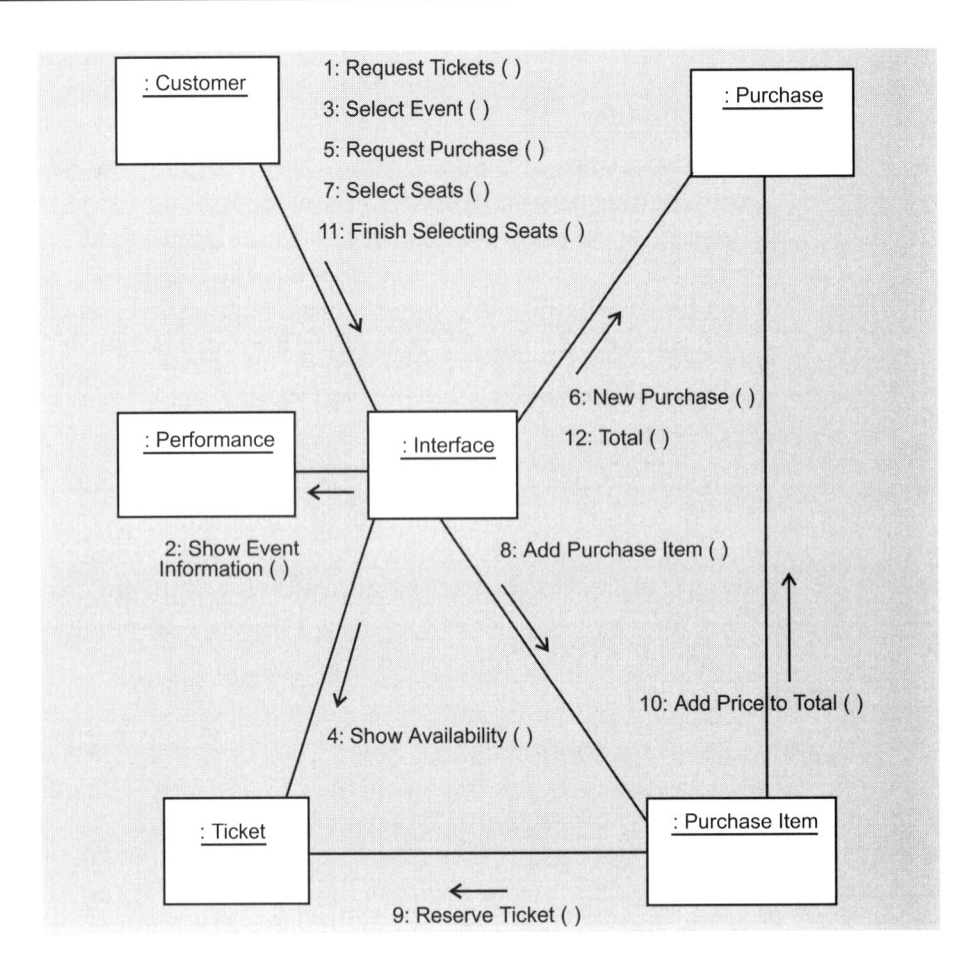

Figure 5-8—
Collaboration
Diagram

Build Activity Diagrams

Role(s): Object Architect

The Object Architect creates Activity Diagrams to clarify detailed business logic and the algorithms behind it. The main benefits of an Activity Diagram are that Activity Diagrams show possibilities for concurrency (parallel) steps and decision points to show optional control branching.

The most complex operations require Activity Diagrams to detail the steps for creating the methods. We recommend using Activity Diagrams only for complex algorithms where the actions are not immediately obvious. Only the most difficult operations qualify for this work.

Consider each step within the algorithm a substate of the algorithm itself. The step is either an action state (typically a single process step within a single operation) or a wait state (a delay caused by the expectation of an event outside the control of the object).

Case Study When you have an operation like Calculate Total that has a lot of internal processing, you may want to model this operation using an Activity Diagram. In our example, we show no wait states (more typically found in real-time systems). Remember not to confuse action states within an Activity Diagram with the state of an object. Technically, the activity state of an operation (that is, which step is executing at a point in time) may have an effect on its owning object's state, but there is no object state transition.

Our Reserve Seating example produces the following Activity Diagram from the Calculate Total operation within Purchase.

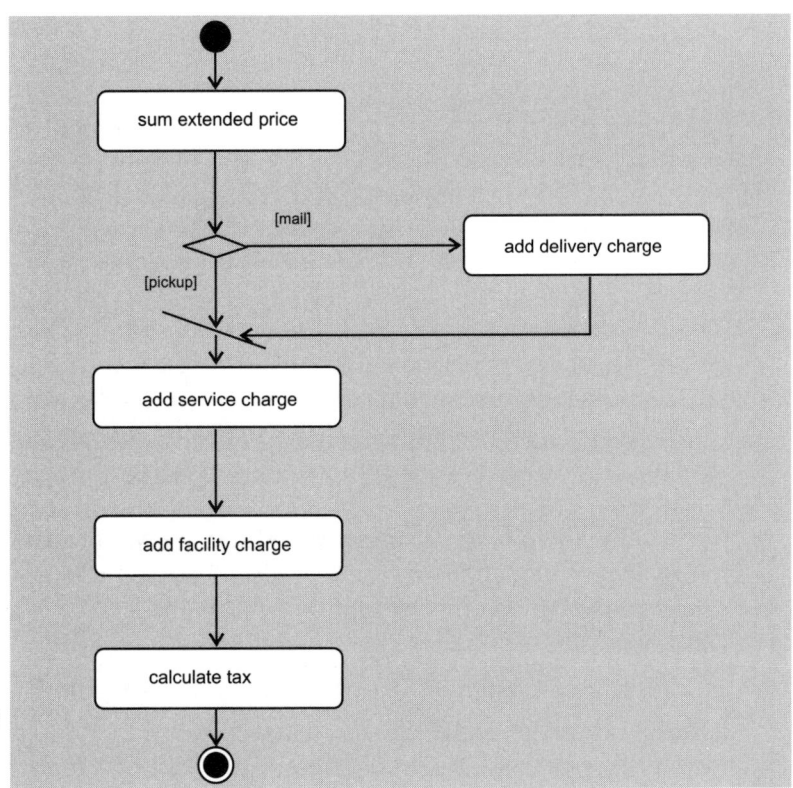

Figure 5-9—Activity Diagram for Purchase::Calculate Total shows the Activity Diagram for Purchase::Calculate Total.

Figure 5-9—Activity Diagram for Purchase:: Calculate Total

We originally modeled this operation with the Purchase class. At implementation time, we moved the method to the interface class Performances form as a trade-off between performance and a pure object view. Note this restricts reuse because it moves business logic to the interface class; if another use case needs to perform the same logic, it has to be written twice or pulled back to the control class. This turned into a theoretical discussion between the Object Architect and the Object Developer. We agree to leave the Calculate Total as coded but add a change request to reconsider in the future. We discuss more implementation decisions in the next task.

Assess Class Diagram

Role(s): Object Architect

During the final stages of design, the Object Architect may:

- Specify the navigation direction on associations
- Decide on public, package, or private visibility of operations and attributes
- "Invent" implementation-dependent classes

Implementation-dependent classes communicate with the database, are specific to the GUI or reporting software, or improve response. This is where you apply the class stereotypes of <<interface>>, <<entity>>, and <<control>> by types of objects. Some of this has already occurred while creating the user interface during prototyping.

> **Tip** Aligning individuals with the responsibility to develop one of the object types (interface, control, and entity) may increase reusability because individuals do not need to know the specifics of another object type. They can then focus on a smaller set of objects with similar kinds of behavior.

In Visual C++ 6.0, the user services layer, business services layer, and data services layer contain the interface, control, and entity classes respectively. We use this terminology to communicate with the Object Developers.

The Object Architect may also add implementation-specific attributes and operations to entity classes. This is the time to add the operations for create, read, update, and delete. Also, identify any remaining derived attributes. Decide either to update them on demand when accessed or when triggered by an event.

To identify additional control classes, look for processing that requires multiple entity objects to make a decision, calculate, or act. Control classes capture the rules and procedures of an enterprise. For example, an enterprise may give a 10-percent discount for payment of a bill within one month. You want to localize this kind of information to one place for maintaining consistent organizational policy. Identifying control classes can seem hazy at first. Any attribute and operation that definitely belongs neither to an interface nor to an entity class should become a control class. A control class typically handles transaction-related behavior and communicates with multiple objects. The reason for this is that control classes are the most likely candidates for initiating change. As you go through this process, ask yourself if a class is doing too much or has too many roles or too much responsibility. If so, you may need to create another class. An object-oriented theme is that each class should do one thing—carry out its responsibility—so that it does that one thing well. A busy class may have taken on too much responsibility. There are a number of things to look for in a busy class, all related to cohesion:

- Is the class doing too much? It may be a candidate to split into multiple classes.
- Is there hidden multiplicity, such as occurs with a master/detail relationship? This anomaly can force the class into aberrant behavior, such as elaborate code to maintain attributes of the detail. The attributes and operations may be better off in a new class or part of an aggregation.
- Are there many attributes that are never set with a value or only set in one state? Those carried along for the ride are likely to need a separate object, with the new object possibly containing previously undiscovered attributes and operations of its own.
- Sometimes real-world objects are just naturally busy. You want your model to reflect the real world.

You do not want to break a class into multiple classes arbitrarily just because it appears to be doing too much. Rather, the guideline of "an object should do one thing—carry out its responsibility—and do that one thing well" applies within two further constraints.

First, reassess if the class is representing a real-world object. Can that object be broken down into smaller components in the real world? If not, keep it intact. On the other hand, if the real-world object consists of smaller components (for example, an aggregate "part of" structure), then disassemble the object following the real world. Use this new structure and delegate the responsibilities to the corresponding objects, again matching to the real world.

The second constraint refers to the responsibilities of the object. Are all of the responsibilities truly the duty of this object? Assume your object is lazy and, thinking like a lazy object, look for other objects to which to delegate the responsibility. This may give you clues to arrive at a more appropriate positioning of behaviors. If all else fails and the busy class truly represents the real world, leave the class as is. The only other option is to change the world!

Besides creating implementation classes, the Object Architect looks for ways to improve performance, minimize coupling between objects, and minimize messaging parameters. Some ways to improve performance include:

- Minimize the number of messages sent from object to object.
- Flatten a class hierarchy to minimize the "made-up" methods written only to gain access to a subclass.
- Pre-allocate an object at program startup rather than during transaction interaction.

Assessing classes means measuring coupling and cohesion. *Coupling* refers to the number of associations and messages between objects. The goal of coupling is always to minimize this number. One method to manage this is to find the average number of associations in the model, and target those areas that have higher than average coupling. During a walkthrough, be sure to review any areas with coupling higher than the average.

Cohesion measures how tightly bound the attributes and operations are within the object. The goal of cohesion is always to have high cohesion. This concept has similarities to normalization from the relational model. Though not speaking directly to cohesion, Bertrand Meyer's shopping list advice for discerning class features, which include both attributes and operations, is applicable (brackets added for emphasis):

S1   The feature must be relevant to the data abstraction represented by the class [roughly first normal form].

S2   It must be compatible with the other features of the class [roughly second normal form].

S3   It must not address exactly the same goal as another feature of the class [roughly third normal form].

S4   It must maintain the invariant of the class.[3]

An object with high cohesion means the operations fully use the attributes and no single operation references only a distinct "set" of attributes. An object with low cohesion is a candidate to split into multiple objects. Remember that an object should do one thing—carry out its responsibility—and do that one thing well. Low cohesion means the object is doing too many things.

So how do you measure coupling and cohesion? There are many simple formulas to assess:

Internal Cohesion Measure—Count the use of attributes by different methods within the class. Low use indicates accidental or inappropriate abstraction.[4]

External Coupling Measure—Count the non-inherited associations between classes. It indicates the degree of modularity and test complexity.[5]

Method Invocation and Cascading—Count the number of methods directly available to a class. It indicates the degree of complexity in relation to other classes.[6]

Inheritance Depth Measure—Count the number of ancestor classes a subclass has. Use it to measure the shape and size of a class structure.[7]

Inheritance Breadth Measure—Count the number of descendants a superclass has. It indicates design influence of the superclass.[8]

Weighted Methods Per Class—Count the number of steps in an operation. Add one for each of the following steps: a simple value assignment, an IF statement (count an ELSE as an additional step), an iteration loop, and a function call. Do this across the entire enterprise model. Then divide this number by the total number of operations in

---

3   Bertrand Meyer. *Object-Oriented Software Construction*. Upper Saddle River, NJ: Prentice Hall PTR, 1997, 772.
4   Chidamber and Kemerer, as cited in Keyes, J. "New Metrics Needed For Software Generation." *Software Magazine*, May 1992.
5   Ibid.
6   Ibid.
7   Ibid.
8   Ibid.

the enterprise model. The result is a target value to minimize; the goal is to lower the average.[9]

Lack of Method Cohesion—Count the number of operations that use distinct sets of attributes within the signature. Then subtract the number of operations that use common attributes. The lower the resulting number, the better. Find the average number of common attributes used and target those with higher counts.[10]

Case Study The Purchase class within our case study demonstrates an example of a control class.

The Collaboration, Activity, and Statechart Diagrams have added significant detail to the Class Diagram. Some of these attributes may become other classes or attributes of other classes when other Solution Areas complete.

In our case study example, the user services layer holds the forms MainFrame, PerformanceView, and OrderView. Refer to Figure 5-10—Interface Class Diagram with Implementation Specifics Added.

Figure 5-11—Control Class Diagram With Implementation Specifics Added shows some of the control classes in the business services layer that have changed. The business services layer holds the following classes:

- Performances managing Performance,
- Purchase managing PurchaseItem, and
- SeatingSummary managing Seat.

---

[9] Steve McConnell. *Code Complete: A Practical Handbook of Software Construction*. Microsoft Press, 1993.
[10] Ibid.

Build Solution

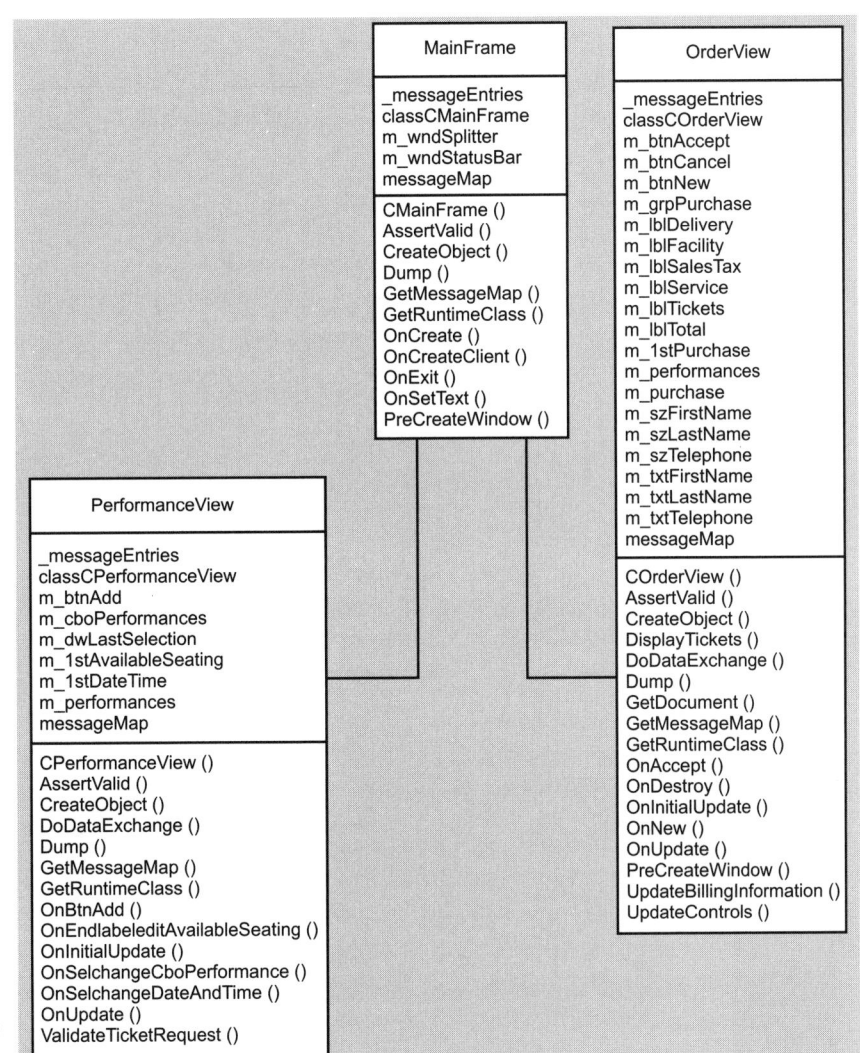

MainFrame	OrderView
_messageEntries classCMainFrame m_wndSplitter m_wndStatusBar messageMap	_messageEntries classCOrderView m_btnAccept m_btnCancel m_btnNew m_grpPurchase m_lblDelivery m_lblFacility m_lblSalesTax m_lblService m_lblTickets m_lblTotal m_1stPurchase m_performances m_purchase m_szFirstName m_szLastName m_szTelephone m_txtFirstName m_txtLastName m_txtTelephone messageMap
CMainFrame () AssertValid () CreateObject () Dump () GetMessageMap () GetRuntimeClass () OnCreate () OnCreateClient () OnExit () OnSetText () PreCreateWindow ()	COrderView () AssertValid () CreateObject () DisplayTickets () DoDataExchange () Dump () GetDocument () GetMessageMap () GetRuntimeClass () OnAccept () OnDestroy () OnInitialUpdate () OnNew () OnUpdate () PreCreateWindow () UpdateBillingInformation () UpdateControls ()

PerformanceView
_messageEntries classCPerformanceView m_btnAdd m_cboPerformances m_dwLastSelection m_1stAvailableSeating m_1stDateTime m_performances messageMap
CPerformanceView () AssertValid () CreateObject () DoDataExchange () Dump () GetMessageMap () GetRuntimeClass () OnBtnAdd () OnEndlabeleditAvailableSeating () OnInitialUpdate () OnSelchangeCboPerformance () OnSelchangeDateAndTime () OnUpdate () ValidateTicketRequest ()

Figure 5-10—Interface Class Diagram with Implementation Specifics Added

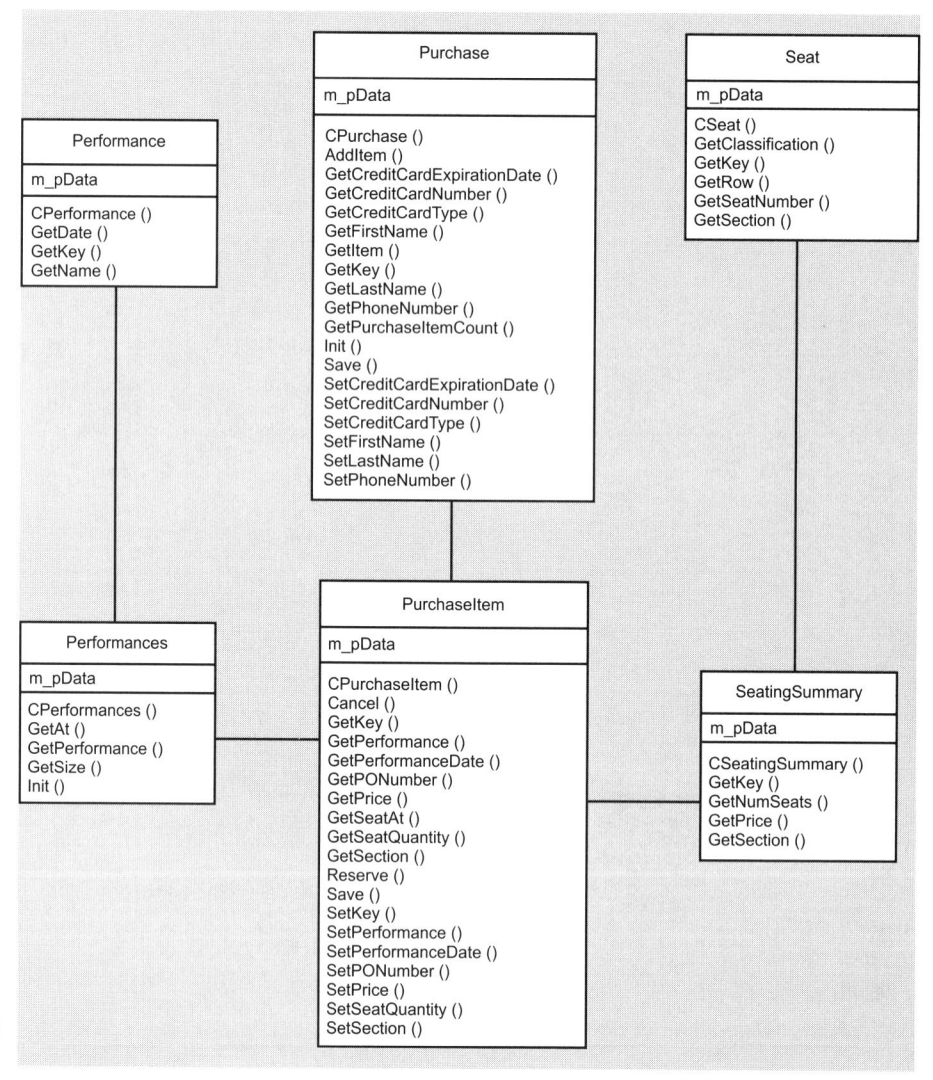

```
+-------------------+     +---------------------------------------+     +-------------------+
|   Performance     |     |              Purchase                 |     |       Seat        |
+-------------------+     +---------------------------------------+     +-------------------+
| m_pData           |     | m_pData                               |     | m_pData           |
+-------------------+     +---------------------------------------+     +-------------------+
| CPerformance ()   |     | CPurchase ()                          |     | CSeat ()          |
| GetDate ()        |     | AddItem ()                            |     | GetClassification ()|
| GetKey ()         |     | GetCreditCardExpirationDate ()        |     | GetKey ()         |
| GetName ()        |     | GetCreditCardNumber ()                |     | GetRow ()         |
+-------------------+     | GetCreditCardType ()                  |     | GetSeatNumber ()  |
                          | GetFirstName ()                       |     | GetSection ()     |
                          | GetItem ()                            |     +-------------------+
                          | GetKey ()                             |
                          | GetLastName ()                        |
                          | GetPhoneNumber ()                     |
                          | GetPurchaseItemCount ()               |
                          | Init ()                               |
                          | Save ()                               |
                          | SetCreditCardExpirationDate ()        |
                          | SetCreditCardNumber ()                |
                          | SetCreditCardType ()                  |
                          | SetFirstName ()                       |
                          | SetLastName ()                        |
                          | SetPhoneNumber ()                     |
                          +---------------------------------------+

                          +---------------------------------------+
                          |            PurchaseItem               |
+-------------------+     +---------------------------------------+
|   Performances    |     | m_pData                               |
+-------------------+     +---------------------------------------+
| m_pData           |     | CPurchaseItem ()                      |     +-------------------+
+-------------------+     | Cancel ()                             |     |  SeatingSummary   |
| CPerformances ()  |     | GetKey ()                             |     +-------------------+
| GetAt ()          |     | GetPerformance ()                     |     | m_pData           |
| GetPerformance () |     | GetPerformanceDate ()                 |     +-------------------+
| GetSize ()        |     | GetPONumber ()                        |     | CSeatingSummary ()|
| Init ()           |     | GetPrice ()                           |     | GetKey ()         |
+-------------------+     | GetSeatAt ()                          |     | GetNumSeats ()    |
                          | GetSeatQuantity ()                    |     | GetPrice ()       |
                          | GetSection ()                         |     | GetSection ()     |
                          | Reserve ()                            |     +-------------------+
                          | Save ()                               |
                          | SetKey ()                             |
                          | SetPerformance ()                     |
                          | SetPerformanceDate ()                 |
                          | SetPONumber ()                        |
                          | SetPrice ()                           |
                          | SetSeatQuantity ()                    |
                          | SetSection ()                         |
                          +---------------------------------------+
```

Figure 5-11—Control Class Diagram with Implementation Specifics Added

The data services layer classes include the ones you expect: Seat, Ticket, Purchase, and PurchaseItem. PerformanceRecord and PurchaseOrderNumber are new; their purpose is to assist the mapping to the physical database structure. Please reference the source code on the included CD-ROM for further details behind these classes. We simply created a duplicate entity class for each of the major classes from the business services layer. These become the home for the operations to map between the object and (in our example) the relational database. Note in this example each class has a GetDefaultDBName() to manage the database connection. We discuss the mapping in the activity Refine Database Structure. See Figure 5-12—Entity Class Diagram with Implementation Specifics Added.

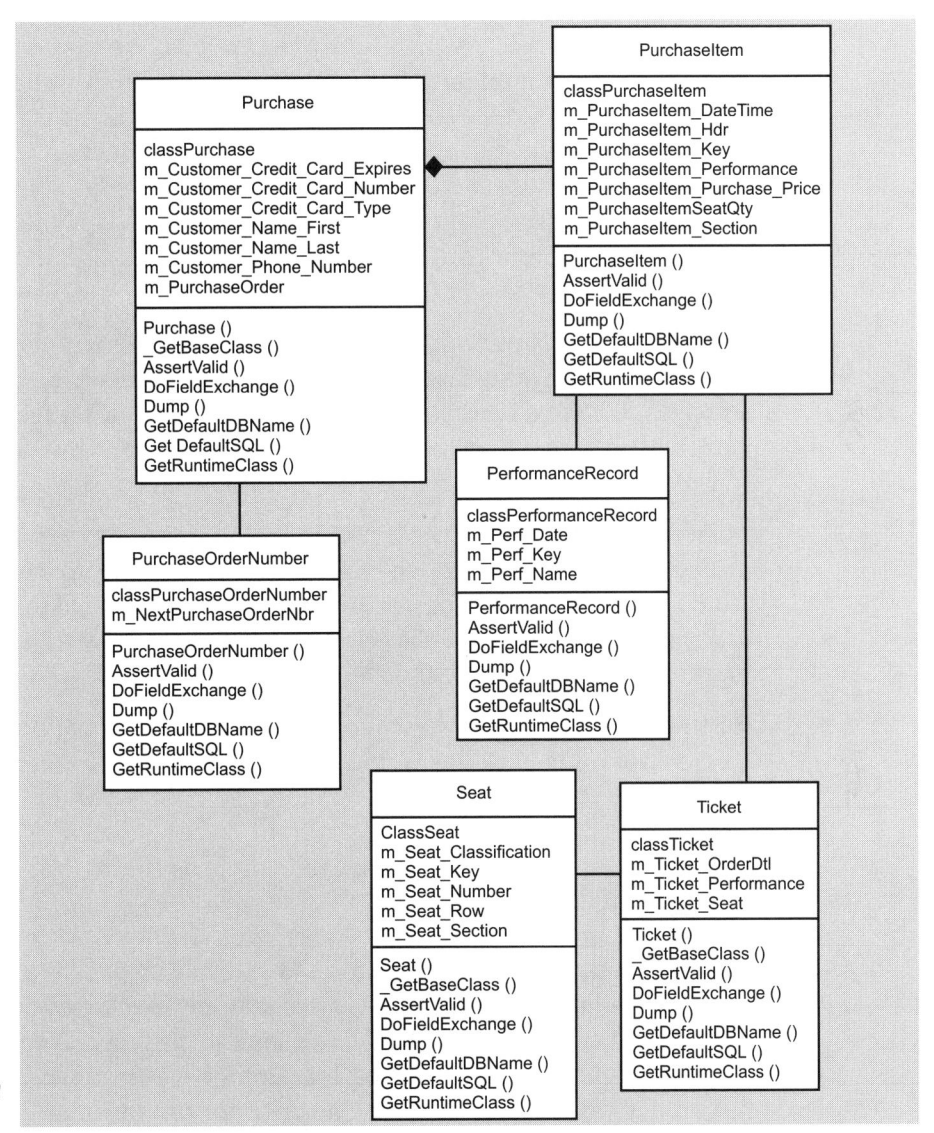

Purchase

classPurchase
m_Customer_Credit_Card_Expires
m_Customer_Credit_Card_Number
m_Customer_Credit_Card_Type
m_Customer_Name_First
m_Customer_Name_Last
m_Customer_Phone_Number
m_PurchaseOrder

Purchase ()
_GetBaseClass ()
AssertValid ()
DoFieldExchange ()
Dump ()
GetDefaultDBName ()
Get DefaultSQL ()
GetRuntimeClass ()

PurchaseItem

classPurchaseItem
m_PurchaseItem_DateTime
m_PurchaseItem_Hdr
m_PurchaseItem_Key
m_PurchaseItem_Performance
m_PurchaseItem_Purchase_Price
m_PurchaseItemSeatQty
m_PurchaseItem_Section

PurchaseItem ()
AssertValid ()
DoFieldExchange ()
Dump ()
GetDefaultDBName ()
GetDefaultSQL ()
GetRuntimeClass ()

PurchaseOrderNumber

classPurchaseOrderNumber
m_NextPurchaseOrderNbr

PurchaseOrderNumber ()
AssertValid ()
DoFieldExchange ()
Dump ()
GetDefaultDBName ()
GetDefaultSQL ()
GetRuntimeClass ()

PerformanceRecord

classPerformanceRecord
m_Perf_Date
m_Perf_Key
m_Perf_Name

PerformanceRecord ()
AssertValid ()
DoFieldExchange ()
Dump ()
GetDefaultDBName ()
GetDefaultSQL ()
GetRuntimeClass ()

Seat

ClassSeat
m_Seat_Classification
m_Seat_Key
m_Seat_Number
m_Seat_Row
m_Seat_Section

Seat ()
_GetBaseClass ()
AssertValid ()
DoFieldExchange ()
Dump ()
GetDefaultDBName ()
GetDefaultSQL ()
GetRuntimeClass ()

Ticket

classTicket
m_Ticket_OrderDtl
m_Ticket_Performance
m_Ticket_Seat

Ticket ()
_GetBaseClass ()
AssertValid ()
DoFieldExchange ()
Dump ()
GetDefaultDBName ()
GetDefaultSQL ()
GetRuntimeClass ()

Figure 5-12— Entity Class Diagram with Implementation Specifics Added

Notice that we have added Visual C++ 6.0 methods for accessing and manipulating class attributes with the SQL necessary to shuttle data in GetDefaultSQL(). We have also converted the names of the attributes and operations to follow a consistent naming convention to increase communications between developers.

Build Component Diagram

Role(s): Object Architect and Database Architect

The Object Architect works with the Database Architect to combine classes into components that become complete logical units of executables and dynamic-link libraries. A component is just a binary instantiation of a class or set of classes. Components group classes into logical units of executable work. The displayed components may be of source files or, in our preferred approach, the compiled executable and dynamic-link libraries. The Component Diagram also shows the dependencies across and between components.

The specific programming language used determines what makes up a component or what classes are parts of a component. In some languages, it is much easier to create a component. In Visual C++, for example, you create a source code file that includes the definition or reference to each class. Smalltalk does not have a concept of a component.

The UML suggests showing source code dependency on a Component Diagram. You may find accomplishing source code control better via tools specific to the programming language. The "make" files in C++ are an example of this. The view we are most interested in is the one we eventually place on the Deployment Diagram.

The Object Architect and Database Architect trace the actors in use cases from this iteration to the components created. Security restrictions flow through to identify component access permissions. To determine components for this system, we begin looking for tightly coupled classes. With larger, more complex systems, you may create components from single classes.

Case Study For the Case Study, we decide to package together the interface classes, the control classes, and entity classes each as separate components. The entity classes in the data services layer become one dynamic-link library (.DLL) with a "compiler" interface, meaning there is no calling interface. We do the same for the business services layer. We create an executable (.EXE) for the interface, or user services layer, which then loads the dynamic-link libraries for the data services layer and business services layer at run time. We diagram this with dependency relationships on the Component Diagram. For performance reasons, we may want to split the Reserve Seating classes further; for now we follow the standard three-tier client/server architecture. We also note the training Computer Skills CBT as a separate component.

Figure 5-13—Component Diagram shows how we packaged the classes into components.

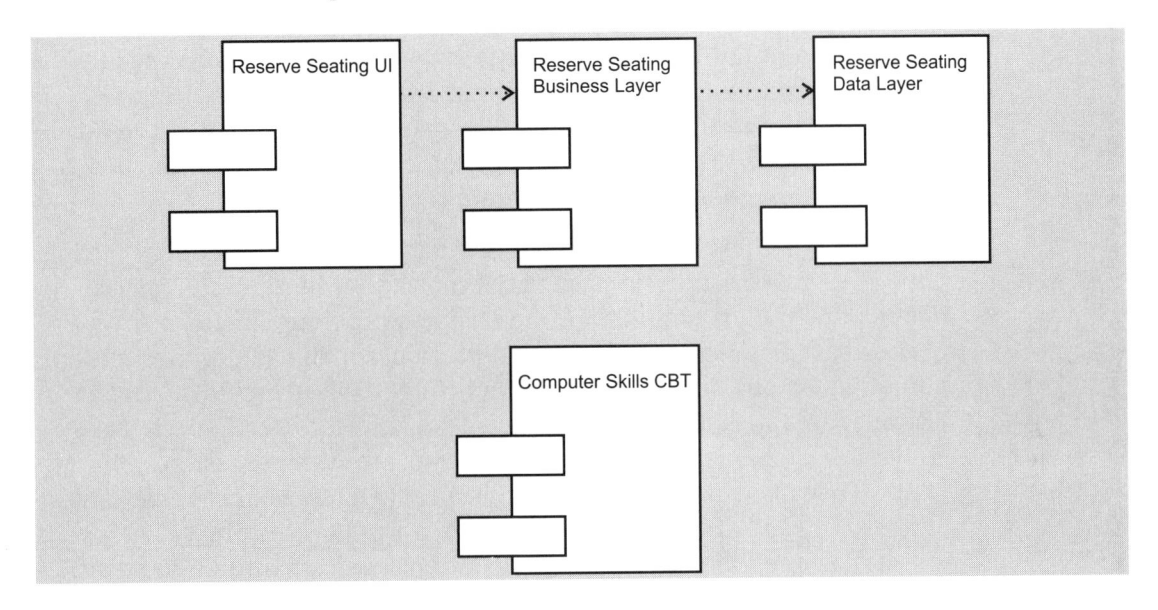

Figure 5-13—Component Diagram

Create Use Case Test Plan

Role(s): Object Architect (Facilitator), Business Area Experts, Object Developer, and Document Architect

The Object Architect, Business Area Experts, Object Developer, and Document Architect derive the Use Case Test Plan from the textual description of the newly developed Use Case Scenarios. Clear examples for the core scenario with data plus any referenced uses or extends scenarios provide the foundation for the complete testing plan.

> **Tip** Including the Trainer in this task allows a deeper understanding of the application that can be leveraged in creating the Training Support Materials.
>
> You may consider creating the Use Case Test Plan before prototyping begins for two reasons. First, it provides expected results to confirm the solution. You can also reference this during the prototype session to confirm what the user needs to see. Second, the Use Case Test Plan remains more focused on the business and less swayed by the introduction of technology.

Use case testing measures Use Case Scenario results against expected business outcomes. Testing should demonstrate that the solution meets business use requirements. You derive test cases from the textual description of the Use Case Scenarios, the breadth. You add specific criteria such as value ranges, volumes, and sequencing to measure against tested results, the depth. Clear examples of the main thread and the extends use cases with real-world sample data sets distinguishes an excellent testing plan from the ordinary.

The Use Case Test Plan forms the foundation for all subsequent testing, as you obtain the criteria primarily from the Business Area Experts who know the ins and outs of the business problem. Business Area Experts communicate exceptions, data values, behavior, and conditions that may be obvious to them, but not to the Object Architect, Object Developer, and Document Architect. The Business Area Experts have day-to-day experience with situations that the system must accommodate. They also are very clear on the specific circumstances that have a greater impact if allowed to happen. We find that this process helps flesh out exceptions which normally are just assumed to be handled. Take care to ensure that the extremely rare incidence is not included before covering the essential.

When setting up test conditions, consider class invariants. A class invariant is a condition that every object of that class must satisfy at all times.[11] For example, our test case must always have a purchase item quantity greater than zero. You should specifically include tests for class invariants.

With the Case Study, each Use Case Scenario establishes the Use Case Test Plan as illustrated in Table 5-2—Use Case Test Plan.

Table 5-2—Use Case Test Plan

Use Case Test Plan: Cash Purchase

Scope: Customer requests performance information and receives a ticket paid with cash.

Num	Test Condition	Expected Result
1.	Customer requests Performance information for a specific performer and purchases one ticket with exact amount.	Customer sees list of performances for that performer. Seat reserved.

---

11 Meilir Page-Jones. *What Every Programmer Should Know About Object-Oriented Design.* New York: Dorset House Publishing, 1995, 341.

Num	Test Condition	Expected Result
2.	Customer requests Performance information for a specific date and purchases multiple tickets.	Customer sees list of performances for that date. Multiple seats reserved.
3.	Customer requests Performance information but does not purchase.	No purchase.
4.	Customer requests Performance information but cancels purchase after seats reserved.	Reserved seats remain available. Purchase total is zero.
5.	Customer requests Performance information for a sold-out Performance.	Customer sees alternative Performances.

Test Cases 3-5 are really exceptions to be tested in future iterations. We include them here because the team identified them, and we do not want to lose the information. Nevertheless, as a project manager you want to manage the scope of each iteration. Postponing exceptions until later keeps the team focused on building a system that meets 80 percent of the events, allowing continual progress and avoiding analysis paralysis.

Refine Database Structure

The Solution Area team builds the database structure from the entity classes. With an object-oriented database, you do not need many of these tasks. With a relational database, you must decide how to model entity classes that inherit from a superclass through generalization/specialization. You need to identify primary keys and eliminate many-to-many associations by adding associative entities (also known as intersection tables). Persistent storage is the term for "saving" the contents of an object beyond the duration of the tasks in which it is used. To discuss persistence, we provide a brief background on the options for data storage.

Deliverables

Logical Data Model
Solution Area Database Structure
Solution Area Database

Today's technology supports four different types of data storage:

- "Flat" file system
- Relational database
- Object database
- Object relational database

Selecting the right data storage type depends on a combination of the data, data access need, and data security.

When your data is simple, less secure, and requires no querying, you store information in a file system.

For more secure data that requires querying, you use a relational database. A relational database allows for querying data stored in the database.

For complex data that includes graphics, images, or recorded sound with low querying, you need an object database. An object database allows for storage, querying, and processing of complex data types. Complex data types are objects that contain other objects such as pictures, movies, and sound. Most relational databases allow you to convert complex data types to a standard unformatted data type such as a BLOB (Binary Large OBject). The conversions required to store and extract from an internal version to something of use consumes both time and resources.

For example, define a mailing list as a complex data type. Then, to add two mailing lists together, you apply the principles of polymorphism and combine them with the "+" operation:

Mailing List A + Mailing List B

Complex data types translate to abstract classes that represent supertypes of specialized classes. An object database does not require you to resolve abstraction in the physical storage. Relational databases require you to decide between duplicating methods and attributes in the specialized class or moving the methods and attributes of the specialized class to the abstract class. With the latter, you need to denote class type with a code.

To query against complex data types that require high security, you need an object relational database. Should you use an object relational database? Object-oriented database management systems are faster than relational database management systems because they link the associations between objects as references rather than with real addresses. Because of this, any structural change of an object does not affect its associated objects.

Another benefit to using an object-oriented database is that it more closely matches, if not exactly, the Class Diagram. Converting a Class Diagram to a relational data model can result in poor performance and data integrity problems.[12]

You really do not need an object relational database unless you need to store and manipulate complex data types. Relational databases are more mature and reliable than object databases. Most enterprises already store and access data using relational database technology.

When new to object modeling, it is best to consider extending a relational data model with object behavior. You can make a pure object-oriented approach work with this combination. It provides significant productivity benefits and is flexible and robust. However, it requires strong object-oriented experience, experience in object to relational mapping, a good persistence framework, and a flexible approach to relational physical modeling. Do not try a pure object-oriented approach if:

1. You are inexperienced in objects,
2. The data store is shared between operational and decision support systems, or
3. You cannot find or create an object to relational persistence framework.

Instead, use an object approach for analysis, design, and application implementation. Use a relational database design only to store data. Implementing a three-tiered service model makes this much easier to do. Our case study example follows this style.

Tasks:

Create Logical Data Model

Role(s): Database Architect and Object Architect

The Database Architect creates a third normal form (3NF) data model based on entity classes from the Class Diagram. The Database Architect

---

12 Richard Winter. "Object Technology Meets VLDB." *Database Programming and Design*, December 1996.

may need to review the logical data model for mapping an existing system.

Working with the Object Architect, the Database Architect decides how to uniquely identify each entity and create primary keys. They must determine the referential integrity between entities using primary keys of one table as foreign keys in the related table. They must review generalization/specialization structures to identify the implementation of one or more physical tables. Projected volumes and primary/foreign key relationships factor into this decision. The Object Architect and Database Architect finalize all attribute characteristics. They determine where data and operations reside, either in a stored procedure or outside of the database as an entity class.

> **Tip** To determine where data and operations reside, ask if an operation could change if the class changes. If it does, that operation belongs with its entity class, not within the database.

We recommend preserving the Class Diagram as is, rather than changing it to look like an Entity/Relationship Diagram (ERD). Changing the view of the classes has a significant impact on understanding and decreases the value of the object modeling performed thus far. If an ERD is necessary, create it separately so the original intent of your Class Diagram is not lost. Then create a mapping translation layer to coordinate between the relational and object views.

Case Study Figure 5-14—Logical Data Model shows the logical data model representing the relational database.

Build Solution ■ **175**

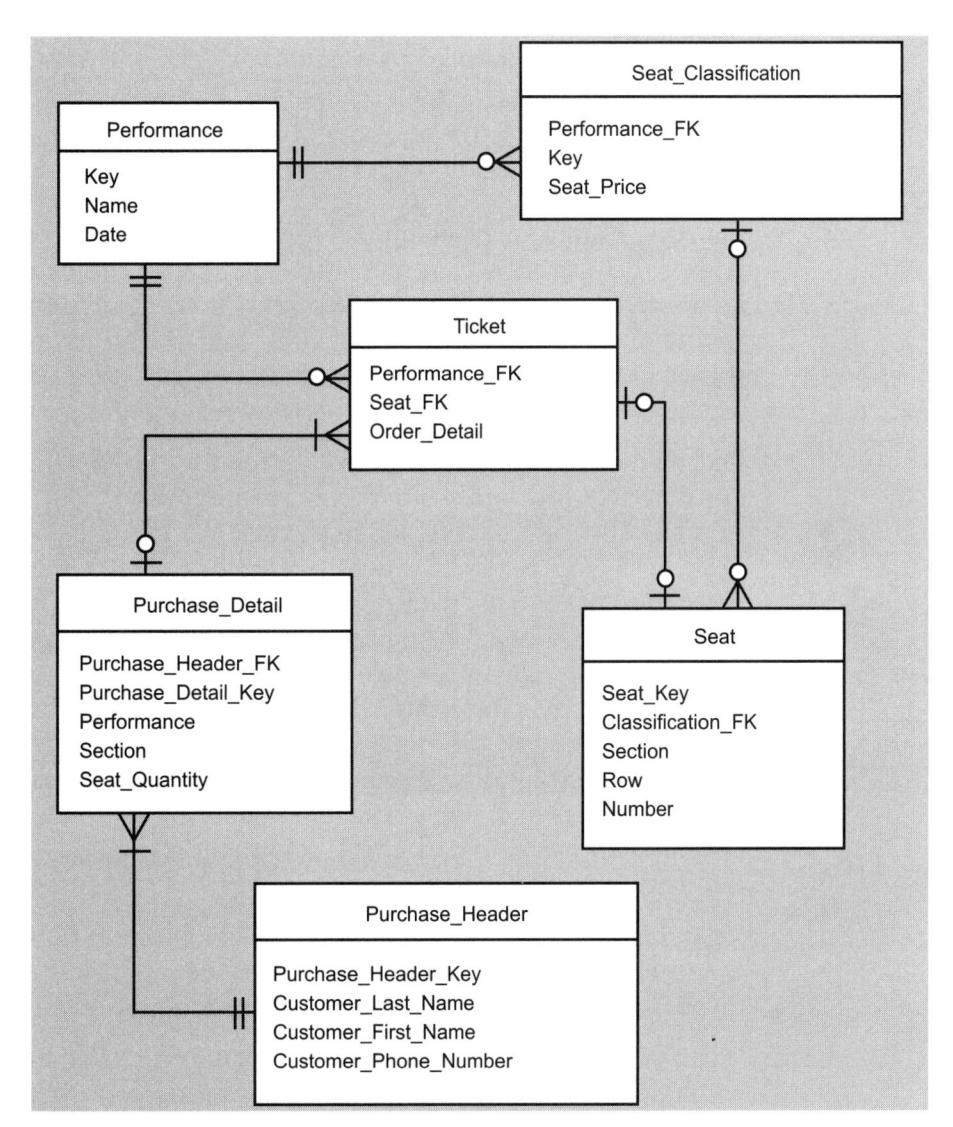

```
                        ┌─────────────────────┐
                        │ Seat_Classification │
    ┌───────────┐       ├─────────────────────┤
    │Performance│       │ Performance_FK      │
    ├───────────┤───────│ Key                 │
    │Key        │       │ Seat_Price          │
    │Name       │       └─────────────────────┘
    │Date       │              │
    └───────────┘       ┌──────────────┐
          │             │   Ticket     │
          │             ├──────────────┤
          └─────────────│Performance_FK│
                        │Seat_FK       │
                        │Order_Detail  │
                        └──────────────┘
                              │
    ┌──────────────────┐              ┌──────────────────┐
    │ Purchase_Detail  │              │      Seat        │
    ├──────────────────┤              ├──────────────────┤
    │Purchase_Header_FK│              │Seat_Key          │
    │Purchase_Detail_Key│             │Classification_FK │
    │Performance       │              │Section           │
    │Section           │              │Row               │
    │Seat_Quantity     │              │Number            │
    └──────────────────┘              └──────────────────┘
            │
            │     ┌────────────────────────┐
            │     │   Purchase_Header      │
            │     ├────────────────────────┤
            └─────│Purchase_Header_Key     │
                  │Customer_Last_Name      │
                  │Customer_First_Name     │
                  │Customer_Phone_Number   │
                  └────────────────────────┘
```

Figure 5-14—Logical Data Model

Create Solution Area Database Structure

Role(s): Database Architect

The Database Architect derives the physical structure of the database from the logical data model design.

The Database Architect converts associations with multiplicity on both ends (many-to-many) to tables that represent the relationship. When the data model is complete, the Database Architect adds reference tables and indexes.

Because Object Relational Database Management Systems (ORDBMS) are immature, this forces a translation of the persistent object data to a relational database. If your project requires a relational database, you must at least translate the entity classes to relational tables. You may also map control classes and interface classes for performance reasons. Mapping from your object model to your relational database is not straightforward. Now you must decide where to deploy the methods associated with entity objects. To minimize the translation effort, you should avoid developing unnecessarily complex object models because this creates n-way relational joins and levels of nesting. Primary- and foreign-keyed navigation are not always adequate.

Placing entity objects in the database requires more than mapping one object to one row in a relational table. An object model portrays business objects from real life, while a robust relational database model normalizes data for storage and performance. This is the crux of how object design conflicts with relational database design. A class may map to multiple tables or multiple classes may map to one relational table. Similarly, class and table attributes may not map one-to-one. For example, you may have three distinct tables that hold information about an employee: the employee personal identification information, the employee's salary and benefits, and the various employee telephone numbers and addresses. Yet in your object model, you may decide to encapsulate part of this information from the three tables into one Employee object.

Relational database and object-oriented systems have different identities. Object identity is system-wide and independent of changes in data value. Relational identity is value-based and only unique within a table.

When you add an attribute (column) to an object (table), you must either initialize the column or change code to allow for a NULL value (no value in the column). Class Diagrams explicitly implement the association that one object has with another as an attribute. Relational tables refer to these associations as foreign keys through which one table accesses the attributes of the associated table. Object associations may have one-to-one, one-to-many, or many-to-many multiplicity. Supporting this multiplicity requires you to keep a reference of the mapping paths and design for retaining the actual object associations. Translating object associations typically uses three techniques. One technique maps each class to two separate tables and adds a lookup table with foreign keys to the other two tables. Another technique collapses the two classes into one table. A third technique maps the two classes to two separate tables with one of the tables referencing the other through a foreign key. Using one table improves performance but reduces design objectives. Using lookup tables decreases performance because you must join all three tables.

Relational databases do not understand inheritance so you must decide whether to collapse or distribute the inheritance. Collapsing inheritance means the supertype and its subtypes become one table with an attribute to distinguish the type. Some attributes may have no meaning for a type and are therefore set to NULL. Distributing inheritance means each subtype becomes its own table and replicates the supertype attributes.

Now you must decide where to deploy the operations. You must decide if the operations reside in the database as stored procedures or separate from the data in the application. You deploy simple data manipulation on the database server with stored procedures and triggers. You isolate logic that is more complex or independent of the specific relational database either to the client or to the application server, applying partitioning by style of service. Following a clean, three-tiered service view and categorizing the classes into interface, entity, and control classes as you model minimizes the number of decisions when you reach this step.

Stored procedures can directly affect the response time of the database. Stored procedures are collections of SQL statements and procedural language statements in the database that control the flow of the procedure. Triggers, by contrast, are also procedures that are part of the database, and execute when there is a change to a table or column. The benefits of stored procedures are that they are compiled, reduce network load, improve consistency, reduce maintenance, and improve security. Disadvantages surround the fact that they are always proprietary to the database and sometimes incomplete in their implementation; in addition, there are the added levels of debugging, testing, and database administration. They can also create a severe database server-processing load known as a "trigger storm." SQL3 tried to standardize stored procedures; however, each vendor's compliance is still dramatically different.

It gets tricky when implementing some object operations as stored procedures. When you separate data from its operations, you move away from an object-oriented solution. Although you lose object encapsulation, you cannot easily translate all operations of entity objects as stored procedures. You only deploy simple data manipulation on the database server as stored procedures and triggers.

It is best to limit stored procedures to the operations for instantiating and destroying the object only. You parse logic that is more complex to the business services layer. It is better to use small, self-contained code objects, especially for business rules and read/update methods. Do not use stored procedures for operations that cross multiple objects, with one exception. Strong aggregates (also known as a composition) like a master/detail relationship (for example, Purchase and Purchase Item) use a stored procedure nicely. Composite aggregates are only relevant within the context of each other, since the rule of a composite is that a part only exists within its aggregation. Destroying one affects the existence of the other.

Applying good rigor to isolating object types, you place the data view of the classes in the database and access them through entity objects that coordinate the database connection. One technique, called wrapping, uses a single object-oriented application for object-to-relational translation. This application handles all database connection, storage, retrieval, and deletion. A good framework encapsulates the translation, providing a single interface to developers. Its design should provide flexibility, scalability, reliability, and fast performance. It should also know about atomic units of work and support rollback and commit.[13]

Case Study We use Microsoft Access in our case study example. Figure 5-15—Physical Database Structure shows the Microsoft Access Tools Relationships. This is the physical implementation of the database derived from the logical data model. The entity classes in the data services layer of the three-tier view control these tables.

---

13 Sunny Gupta and John Scumniotales. *Integrating Object and Relational Technologies.*, N.d.

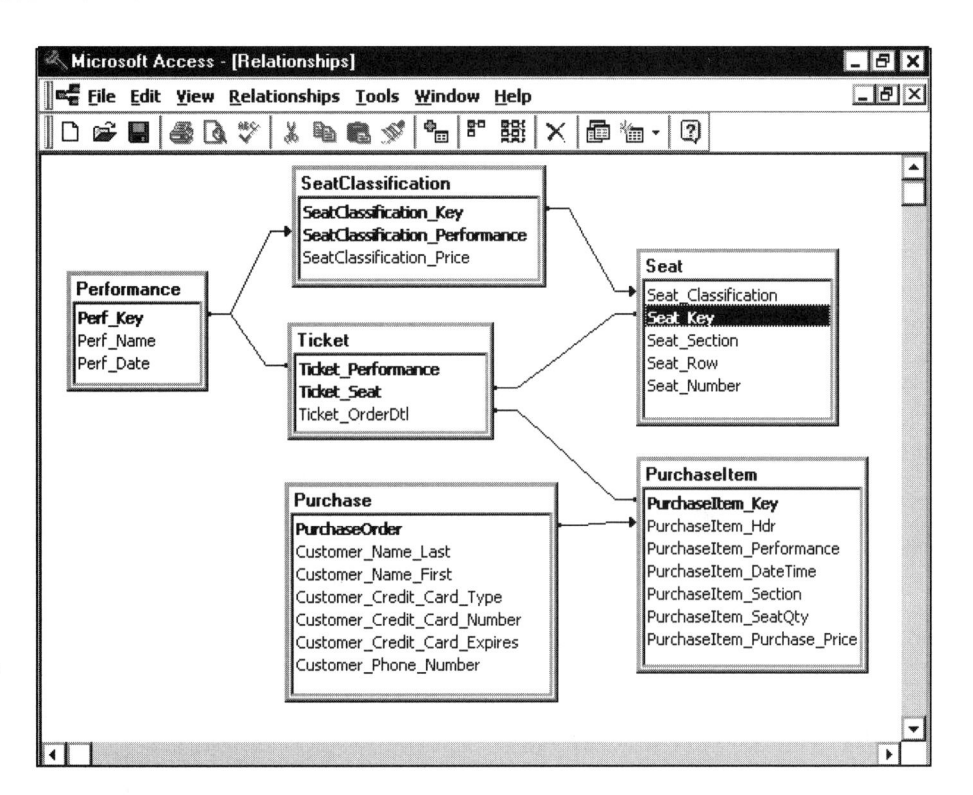

*Figure 5-15—
Physical
Database
Structure*

[Microsoft Access - Relationships window showing tables: SeatClassification (SeatClassification_Key, SeatClassification_Performance, SeatClassification_Price), Performance (Perf_Key, Perf_Name, Perf_Date), Ticket (Ticket_Performance, Ticket_Seat, Ticket_OrderDtl), Seat (Seat_Classification, Seat_Key, Seat_Section, Seat_Row, Seat_Number), Purchase (PurchaseOrder, Customer_Name_Last, Customer_Name_First, Customer_Credit_Card_Type, Customer_Credit_Card_Number, Customer_Credit_Card_Expires, Customer_Phone_Number), PurchaseItem (PurchaseItem_Key, PurchaseItem_Hdr, PurchaseItem_Performance, PurchaseItem_DateTime, PurchaseItem_Section, PurchaseItem_SeatQty, PurchaseItem_Purchase_Price)]

The partitioning of the entity classes into the data services layer makes managing the mapping to the database much more straightforward. Each entity class in the data services layer has the responsibility to shuttle the persistent data from the database to the business services layer and back again. This is the only responsibility for these classes; the business logic remains in the business services layer, not here. Ideally, the data services class follows the structure of the business services layer and not the other way around because the business design is driving the data design.

The class in the data services layer only has the responsibility to create the corresponding business service layer view of that class regardless of the underlying relational database design. This stabilizes the remainder of the application in case the database structure changes. If the database used for persistent storage changes, this structure provides the ability to make the changes in one place, thereby minimizing the impact on the rest of the application. Of course, if you add new data elements, you must accommodate their use; but a straight database conversion is a snap. The business services and user services layers are not affected.

We create a "mirror class" in the data services layer for each class in the business services layer. We do this because we use the information from each entity in the application. Sometimes, though, you do not want a mirror image. For example, say we were only working with Ticket and needed detailed performance and seating detail information. We may have chosen to map the single Ticket object to each of the Performance, Section, and Seat tables and instantiate the single object Ticket.

At this point, we just create the entity class with the same attributes as the control class. It is the responsibility of the entity class to do whatever it takes to provide that view, regardless of the underlying database structure. Each class also requires the operations for create (SQL Insert), read (SQL Select), update (SQL Update), and delete (SQL Delete) necessary to build the view of the object used by the business services layer (and indirectly the user services layer). We create the detailed methods to support this in the Build Methods task of the Build Application activity.

Build Application

The Solution Area team refines class definitions by specifying design details and building the software code. The result of this activity affects numerous associated deliverables. Testing performed here gives the Object Developer "one last chance" to make sure the solution works correctly before the walkthrough by the Solution Area team. Remember to store test cases and test beds for later reuse in future testing. Update the models as you achieve detailed definition and understanding.

Deliverables

Use Case Test Beds
Collaboration Test Plan
Collaboration Test Beds
Application

Tasks:

Create Collaboration Test Plan

Role(s): Object Developer

The Object Developer prepares to test the solution using collaboration test planning techniques. Jean Boisvert recommended a technique used in the Ericsson pilot project called gray box testing. Gray box testing combines the traditional white box testing (exercising all path segments of a unit of code) with black box testing (exercising the functionality of a component by stimulating it with various parameter values)[14]. Objects respond to messages and have state changes, inheritance, and polymorphism. Thus, testing is dynamic. This suggests that you consider both the states of an object and its collaboration with other objects in response to an event. We call this collaboration testing.

Collaboration testing resembles traditional unit or program testing. The breadth equates to a class or cluster of classes within object-oriented programming. The depth examines the object to uncover three basic things: code that produces the wrong result, code that never executes, and code that is unnecessary. For the latter two, we recommend using an object-oriented testing tool that provides "x-ray vision" into the code. This kind of a tool allows the Object Developer to step through message flows and check the state of an object at pertinent intervals. Merely looking at the test results does not provide this depth of information.

Each basic test case tests a set of items (a class or small cluster of objects), the states of those objects, and the resultant change to those objects. In other words, each test case includes required preconditions, allowable object states, and expected postconditions. Events and allowable states of the objects involved determine the test cases. Here the Collaboration Diagram in conjunction with Statechart and Activity Diagrams serve as test case specifications. The Statechart Diagram identifies the events that trigger state change and accompanying actions. The Collaboration Diagram identifies other objects that collaborate from this event. The Activity Diagram specifies the internal steps of the object methods. The goal is to obtain complete, repeatable coverage of all code.

---

14 Jean Boisvert. "OO Testing in the Ericsson Pilot Project." *Object Magazine*, July 1997.

Not only is the Collaboration Test Plan useful in validating class methods, it also helps validate the Collaboration, Statechart, and Activity Diagrams. For example, as we look for the state of Purchase during the totaling method, we see inconsistencies of the "Tallied" state with the Statechart and Activity Diagrams. Refer to Table 5-3—Collaboration Test Plan.

Table 5-3—Collaboration Test Plan

Collaboration Test Plan: Total Purchase with multiple tickets
Scope: From purchase sums multiple tickets through calculation of taxes
Precondition: Last seat selected
Postcondition: Purchase totaled
Object States: Purchase = Totaled, Purchase Item = Purchased

Num	Step	Object State
1.	User interface sends message to total purchase	Purchase Status = Tallying, Total = zero; Purchase Item = purchased
2.	Purchase sends message to each Purchase Item requesting extended price	Purchase Total = sum of Purchase Items extended prices
3.	Purchase subtracts discount	Purchase Total = Purchase Total - discount
4.	Purchase adds service charge	Purchase Total = Purchase Total + service charge
5.	Purchase adds tax	Purchase Total = Purchase Total + tax, Status = Totaled
6.	Purchase sends Purchase Total message to Customer	Customer sees Purchase Total

Create Collaboration Test Beds

Role(s): Object Developer

The Object Developer creates data in a reusable format to support the Collaboration Test Plan and fill the database with the test data. By creating a reusable Collaboration Test Bed, the database may be reloaded many times with the same values throughout the testing process.

Build Methods

Role(s): Object Developer

Code 'em up! The Object Developer builds methods with polymorphism and reusability being the foremost concerns.

A very effective way to get started is to leverage the models and the class definitions and generate the code automatically from a modeling tool, if your modeling tool supports it. This does not give you all of the necessary code, but it at least keeps the prototype structured close to the business definition. Then, simply add the classes for the visual interface elements and stub in the entity classes that eventually provide the link to your persistent storage mechanism. Some modeling tools even provide the ability to generate models from the code as well. A modeling tool that does both supports round-trip engineering, ensuring that the modeling and coding efforts synchronize. Seeing the results of this really emphasizes the difference between procedural code and object-oriented code. The latter contains all the code that acts upon one object. The former may act upon several objects similar to the Sequence Diagram.

To ease testing at this level, it is important that the Object Developer incorporates additional code to ease the testing process. This is code testability.[15] Providing testability involves supplying mechanisms for checking preconditions at the beginning and postconditions at the end of method execution. The method passes the result in its output. This contributes another clue that the test worked or failed.

Case Study We first create the methods to link the entity classes to the database. Then we detail the methods behind the operations identified in the core scenario.

We use the Purchase class from the data services layer in our example to link the entity class to the database. Figure 5-16—Full Purchase Class depicts the properties and methods for the Purchase class.

---

15 Jeffery E. Payne, Roger T. Alexander, and Charles D. Hutchinson. "Design-for-Testability For Object-Oriented Software." *Object Magazine*, July 1997.

```
                    ┌─────────────────────────────────────┐
                    │            Purchase                 │
                    ├─────────────────────────────────────┤
                    │ classPurchase                       │
                    │ m_Customer_Credit_Card_Expires      │
                    │ m_Customer_Credit_Card_Number       │
                    │ m_Customer_Credit_Card_Type         │
                    │ m_Customer_Name_First               │
                    │ m_Customer_Name_Last                │
                    │ m_Customer_Phone_Number             │
                    │ m_PurchaseOrder                     │
                    ├─────────────────────────────────────┤
                    │ Purchase ()                         │
                    │ _GetBaseClass ()                    │
                    │ AssertValid ()                      │
                    │ DoFieldExchange ()                  │
                    │ Dump ()                             │
                    │ GetDefaultDBName ()                 │
                    │ GetDefaultSQL ()                    │
                    │ GetRuntimeClass ()                  │
                    └─────────────────────────────────────┘
```

Figure 5-16— Full Purchase Class

The general structure follows this sequence:

1. Create the local variables to build the object properties. Remember that the property definitions only define the variables to use. Any logic for calculation or integrity checking is performed in either the user services layer or the business services layer to maintain partitioning by style of service.

```
class AFX_EXT_CLASS Purchase : public CDaoRecordset
{
public:
     Purchase(CDaoDatabase* pDatabase = NULL);
     DECLARE_DYNAMIC(Purchase)

// Field/Param Data
     //{{AFX_FIELD(Purchase, CDaoRecordset)
     long     m_PurchaseOrder;
     CString  m_Customer_Name_Last;
     CString  m_Customer_Name_First;
     CString  m_Customer_Credit_Card_Type;
     CString  m_Customer_Credit_Card_Number;
     CString  m_Customer_Credit_Card_Expires;
     CString  m_Customer_Phone_Number;
     //}}AFX_FIELD
```

2. Instantiate an object to hold the database values. We create the object corresponding to the database through the function Purchase::Init() via a call from OrderView::OnNew.

```
void COrderView::OnNew()
{
    m_purchase.Init();
    UpdateControls(true);
}
bool CPurchase::Init()
{
    bool bRetVal = false;
    PurchaseOrderNumber po;
    po.Open();
    if ( !po.IsEOF() )
    {
        m_pData->m_PurchaseOrder = po.m_NextPurchaseOrderNbr;
        po.Edit();
        ++po.m_NextPurchaseOrderNbr;
        po.Update();
        bRetVal = true;
    }
    m_pData->m_vPurchase.clear();
    return bRetVal;
}
```

3. Create a method for each of the properties. These are the standard methods for accessing variables in Visual C++ 6.0. Creating them now helps to maintain the class structure in the code.

```
CString CPurchase::GetCreditCardExpirationDate()
{
    return m_pData->m_Customer_Credit_Card_Expires;
}

void CPurchase::SetCreditCardExpirationDate(const CString &value)
{
    m_pData->m_Customer_Credit_Card_Expires = value;
}

CString CPurchase::GetCreditCardNumber()
{
    return m_pData->m_Customer_Credit_Card_Number;
}

void CPurchase::SetCreditCardNumber(const CString &value)
{
    m_pData->m_Customer_Credit_Card_Number = value;
}
```

```
CString CPurchase::GetCreditCardType()
{
    return m_pData->m_Customer_Credit_Card_Type;
}

void CPurchase::SetCreditCardType(const CString &value)
{
    m_pData->m_Customer_Credit_Card_Type = value;
}

CString CPurchase::GetPhoneNumber()
{
    return m_pData->m_Customer_Phone_Number;
}

void CPurchase::SetPhoneNumber(const CString &value)
{
    m_pData->m_Customer_Phone_Number = value;
}

int CPurchase::GetKey()
{
    return m_pData->m_PurchaseOrder;
}

CString CPurchase::GetFirstName()
{
    return m_pData->m_Customer_Name_First;
}

void CPurchase::SetFirstName(const CString &value)
{
    m_pData->m_Customer_Name_First = value;
}

CString CPurchase::GetLastName()
{
    return m_pData->m_Customer_Name_Last;
}

void CPurchase::SetLastName(const CString &value)
{
    m_pData->m_Customer_Name_Last = value;
}
```

4. We already illustrated the corresponding function for create using the constructor in Purchase::Init(). For a retrieve, we use the constructor based off a database record. Define the function for update with Purchase::Save() (we address the functionality for delete

using Purchase::Cancel() in the second iteration). Define these with the specific SQL necessary to get to and from the database.

```cpp
struct CPerformanceData;
class PerformanceRecord;

class AFX_EXT_CLASS CPerformance
{
public:
    // Copy constructor
    CPerformance( const CPerformance& rhs );

    // Constructor based off database record
     CPerformance( const PerformanceRecord& record );


bool CPurchase::Save()
{
   bool bRetVal = true;
   Purchase record;

   record.Open();
   record.AddNew();
      record.m_PurchaseOrder = m_pData->m_PurchaseOrder;
      record.m_Customer_Name_Last = m_pData->m_Customer_Name_Last;
      record.m_Customer_Name_First = m_pData->m_Customer_Name_First;
      record.m_Customer_Credit_Card_Type =
         m_pData->m_Customer_Credit_Card_Type;
      record.m_Customer_Credit_Card_Number =
         m_pData->m_Customer_Credit_Card_Number;
      record.m_Customer_Credit_Card_Expires =
         m_pData->m_Customer_Credit_Card_Expires;
      record.m_Customer_Phone_Number =
         m_pData->m_Customer_Phone_Number;
   record.Update();

   return bRetVal;
}
void Purchase::DoFieldExchange(CDaoFieldExchange* pFX)
{
     //{{AFX_FIELD_MAP(Purchase)
     pFX->SetFieldType(CDaoFieldExchange::outputColumn);
     DFX_Long(pFX, _T("[PurchaseOrder]"), m_PurchaseOrder);
     DFX_Text(pFX, _T("[Customer_Name_Last]"), m_Customer_Name_Last);
     DFX_Text(pFX, _T("[Customer_Name_First]"), m_Customer_Name_First);
     DFX_Text(pFX, _T("[Customer_Credit_Card_Type]"),
           m_Customer_Credit_Card_Type);
     DFX_Text(pFX, _T("[Customer_Credit_Card_Number]"),
           m_Customer_Credit_Card_Number);
     DFX_Text(pFX, _T("[Customer_Credit_Card_Expires]"),
```

```
                    m_Customer_Credit_Card_Expires);
        DFX_Text(pFX, _T("[Customer_Phone_Number]"), m_Customer_Phone_Number);
        //}}AFX_FIELD_MAP
}
```

5. Set up any other data services layer functions for specialized behavior. Notice we have extra functions for adding a purchase item AddItem() and another to retrieve items in GetItem(). The Purchase class must coordinate synchronization with its aggregate.

```
bool CPurchase::AddItem(CPurchaseItem& item)
{
    bool bRetVal = item.Reserve();
    m_pData->m_vPurchase.push_back( item );
    return bRetVal;
}
CPurchaseItem& CPurchase::GetItem(int nIndex)
{
    ASSERT( nIndex < GetPurchaseItemCount() );
    return m_pData->m_vPurchase[nIndex];
}
```

6. When called, these functions execute the SQL to build the view of the object. Note that each class has a GetDefaultDBName() function to track the database connection. For simplicity of this example, we do not worry about maintaining a constant connection. This becomes especially important when addressing a stateless connection, such as found with Internet applications.

Now we detail the methods behind the operations identified in the core scenario to purchase a ticket. The following code reveals how the process of purchasing a ticket begins. We pick up where we have the OrderView form passing the information selected including the quantity of tickets to purchase along with Performance and Purchase information to the Purchase Item object in the business services layer.

```
void COrderView::OnUpdate(CView* pSender,
                          LPARAM lHint,
                          CObject* pHint)
{
    if ( lHint )
    {
        std::auto_ptr<CPurchaseItem> pItem(
            reinterpret_cast<CPurchaseItem*>(lHint) );
        if ( !m_btnCancel.IsWindowEnabled() )
        {
            AfxMessageBox( "No open order" );
            return;
```

```cpp
            }
            pItem->SetPONumber( m_purchase.GetKey() );
            if ( m_purchase.AddItem( *pItem ) )
            {
                DisplayTickets( *pItem );
                UpdateBillingInformation();
                m_btnAccept.EnableWindow( true );
            }
        }
    }
}

void COrderView::DisplayTickets(CPurchaseItem &item)
{
    // First, update the stuff that will be common
    // for all of these
    CPerformance& performance =
        m_performances.GetPerformance( item.GetPerformance() );
    CString szPerformanceName = performance.GetName();
    CString szDate = performance.GetDate().Format(
        "%m/%d/%Y %I:%M %p" );
    CString szSection = item.GetSection();
    CString szPrice;
    szPrice.Format("$%s", item.GetPrice().Format() );
    int nSize = item.GetSeatQuantity();
    int nStartPosition = m_lstPurchase.GetItemCount();
    for ( int i = 0; i < nSize; ++i )
    {
        CString szTemp;
        CSeat& seat = item.GetSeatAt( i );
        int nRow = seat.GetRow();
        int nSeat = seat.GetSeatNumber();
        LVITEM row;
        ZeroMemory( &row, sizeof( row ) );

        row.mask = LVIF_TEXT;
        row.iItem = i + nStartPosition;
        row.iSubItem = PERFORMANCE;
        row.pszText = const_cast<LPTSTR>(
            (LPCTSTR) szPerformanceName );
        row.cchTextMax = szPerformanceName.GetLength() + 1;
        m_lstPurchase.InsertItem( &row );

        row.iSubItem = DATE_TIME;
        row.pszText = const_cast<LPTSTR>((LPCTSTR) szDate );
        row.cchTextMax = szDate.GetLength() + 1;
        m_lstPurchase.SetItem( &row );

        row.iSubItem = PRICE;
        row.pszText = const_cast<LPTSTR>((LPCTSTR) szPrice );
        row.cchTextMax = szPrice.GetLength() + 1;
```

```
            m_lstPurchase.SetItem( &row );

            row.iSubItem = SECTION;
            row.pszText = const_cast<LPTSTR>((LPCTSTR) szSection );
            row.cchTextMax = szSection.GetLength() + 1;
            m_lstPurchase.SetItem( &row );

            row.iSubItem = ROW;
            szTemp.Format( "%d", nRow );
            row.pszText = const_cast<LPTSTR>((LPCTSTR) szTemp );
            row.cchTextMax = szTemp.GetLength() + 1;
            m_lstPurchase.SetItem( &row );

            row.iSubItem = SEAT;
            szTemp.Format( "%d", nSeat );
            row.pszText = const_cast<LPTSTR>((LPCTSTR) szTemp );
            row.cchTextMax = szTemp.GetLength() + 1;
            m_lstPurchase.SetItem( &row );
      }
}
```

The Purchase object in the business services layer sends a message, Add Item, to the Purchase Item object in the data services layer.

```
bool CPurchase::AddItem(CPurchaseItem& item)
{
    bool bRetVal = item.Reserve();
    m_pData->m_vPurchase.push_back( item );
    return bRetVal;
}
```

The Purchase Item object in the data services layer inserts the purchase item to the database. If it cannot, the failure throws an exception.

```
bool CPurchaseItem::Save()
{
    PurchaseItem purchaseItem;
    purchaseItem.Open();
    purchaseItem.AddNew();
    purchaseItem.m_PurchaseItem_DateTime = GetPerformanceDate();
    purchaseItem.m_PurchaseItem_Hdr = GetPONumber();
    purchaseItem.m_PurchaseItem_Performance = GetPerformance();
    purchaseItem.m_PurchaseItem_Section = GetSection();
    purchaseItem.m_PurchaseItem_SeatQty = GetSeatQuantity();
    purchaseItem.m_PurchaseItem_Purchase_Price = GetPrice();
    purchaseItem.Update();
    return true;
}
```

The Purchase Item in the business services layer then returns the information back to the PerformanceView form that originated the functionality. After adding each purchase item for a selected Section, the PerformanceView form reserves an individual ticket by sending a message, Reserve Ticket, along with Purchase, Purchase Item, and seating information to the Ticket class in the business services layer. The Reserve() method of the Purchase Item object in the business services layer sends a Reserve Ticket message to the Ticket object in the data services layer. The data services layer Ticket then updates the Ticket availability and retrieves the Ticket from the database.

```cpp
bool CPurchaseItem::Reserve()
{
    bool bRetVal = false;
    AvailableTicket availableTicket;
    availableTicket.m_strFilter.Format(
            "Ticket_Performance = %d AND Seat_Section = '%s'",
            GetPerformance(), GetSection() );
    AvailableSeating seating;
    seating.m_strFilter.Format( "Perf_Key = %d AND"
        " Seat_Section = '%s'", GetPerformance(), GetSection() );
    seating.Open();
    if ( !seating.IsEOF() )
    {
        SetPrice( seating.m_SeatClassification_Price );
    }
    availableTicket.Open();
    int nSize = GetSeatQuantity();
    for ( int i = 0; (i < nSize) && !availableTicket.IsEOF(); ++i )
    {
        Ticket ticket;
        ticket.m_strFilter.Format( "Ticket_Performance = %d AND "
            "Ticket_Seat = %d", GetPerformance(),
                availableTicket.m_Seat_Key);
        ticket.Open();
        ticket.Edit();
        ticket.m_Ticket_OrderDtl = GetPONumber();
        ticket.Update();
        Seat seat;
        seat.m_strFilter.Format( "Seat_Key = %d",
                                availableTicket.m_Seat_Key );
        seat.Open();
        CSeat temp( seat );
        m_pData->m_vSeat.push_back( temp );

        availableTicket.MoveNext();
        bRetVal = true;
    }
```

```
        return bRetVal;
}
```

The data services layer Ticket object returns the inserted information to the Ticket object in the business services layer that returns the information back to the PerformanceView form. The PerformanceView form then builds the returned information on the OrderView form.

```
void COrderView::DisplayTickets(CPurchaseItem &item)
{
    // First, update the stuff that will be common
    // for all of these
    CPerformance& performance =
        m_performances.GetPerformance( item.GetPerformance() );
    CString szPerformanceName = performance.GetName();
    CString szDate = performance.GetDate().Format(
        "%m/%d/%Y %I:%M %p" );
    CString szSection = item.GetSection();
    CString szPrice;
    szPrice.Format("$%s", item.GetPrice().Format() );
    int nSize = item.GetSeatQuantity();
    int nStartPosition = m_lstPurchase.GetItemCount();
    for ( int i = 0; i < nSize; ++i )
    {
        CString szTemp;
        CSeat& seat = item.GetSeatAt( i );
        int nRow = seat.GetRow();
        int nSeat = seat.GetSeatNumber();
        LVITEM row;
        ZeroMemory( &row, sizeof( row ) );

        row.mask = LVIF_TEXT;
        row.iItem = i + nStartPosition;
        row.iSubItem = PERFORMANCE;
        row.pszText = const_cast<LPTSTR>(
            (LPCTSTR) szPerformanceName );
        row.cchTextMax = szPerformanceName.GetLength() + 1;
        m_lstPurchase.InsertItem( &row );

        row.iSubItem = DATE_TIME;
        row.pszText = const_cast<LPTSTR>((LPCTSTR) szDate );
        row.cchTextMax = szDate.GetLength() + 1;
        m_lstPurchase.SetItem( &row );

        row.iSubItem = PRICE;
        row.pszText = const_cast<LPTSTR>((LPCTSTR) szPrice );
        row.cchTextMax = szPrice.GetLength() + 1;
        m_lstPurchase.SetItem( &row );
```

```
        row.iSubItem = SECTION;
        row.pszText = const_cast<LPTSTR>((LPCTSTR) szSection );
        row.cchTextMax = szSection.GetLength() + 1;
        m_lstPurchase.SetItem( &row );

        row.iSubItem = ROW;
        szTemp.Format( "%d", nRow );
        row.pszText = const_cast<LPTSTR>((LPCTSTR) szTemp );
        row.cchTextMax = szTemp.GetLength() + 1;
        m_lstPurchase.SetItem( &row );

        row.iSubItem = SEAT;
        szTemp.Format( "%d", nSeat );
        row.pszText = const_cast<LPTSTR>((LPCTSTR) szTemp );
        row.cchTextMax = szTemp.GetLength() + 1;
        m_lstPurchase.SetItem( &row );
    }
}
```

This activity occurs for each row of available seats displayed on the PerformanceView form. When the current purchase completes, the PerformanceView form sums the purchased items, adds the sales tax and other charges, and displays the results on the OrderView form.

```
void COrderView::UpdateBillingInformation()
{
    int nSize = m_purchase.GetPurchaseItemCount();
    double dTicketCost = 0.0;
    double dServiceCharge = 2.5;
    double dFacilityCharge = 2.0;
    double dDeliveryCharge = 3.0;
    double dSalesTax = 0.0;
    double dSalesTaxRate = 0.055;
    double dTotal = 0.0;
    for ( int i = 0; i < nSize; ++i )
    {
        CPurchaseItem& item = m_purchase.GetItem(i);
        double dTicket = atof( item.GetPrice().Format() );
        dTicketCost += ( dTicket * item.GetSeatQuantity() );
    }
    dTotal = dTicketCost + dServiceCharge + dFacilityCharge +
            dDeliveryCharge;
    dSalesTax = dTotal * dSalesTaxRate;
    dTotal += dSalesTax;

    CString szTemp;
    szTemp.Format( "$%.02f", dTicketCost );
    m_lblTickets.SetWindowText( szTemp );
    szTemp.Format( "$%.02f", dServiceCharge );
```

```
m_lblService.SetWindowText( szTemp );
szTemp.Format( "$%.02f", dFacilityCharge );
m_lblFacility.SetWindowText( szTemp );
szTemp.Format( "$%.02f", dDeliveryCharge );
m_lblDelivery.SetWindowText( szTemp );
szTemp.Format( "$%.02f", dSalesTax );
m_lblSalesTax.SetWindowText( szTemp );
szTemp.Format( "$%.02f", dTotal );
m_lblTotal.SetWindowText( szTemp );

}
```

You can see from this traversal of messages why a Collaboration Diagram provides essential documentation outside of the application code. So many messages traveling between each of the different interface, business, and data services layers alone can confuse even the best developer! Figure 5-17—Purchase Ticket Collaboration Diagram represents this.

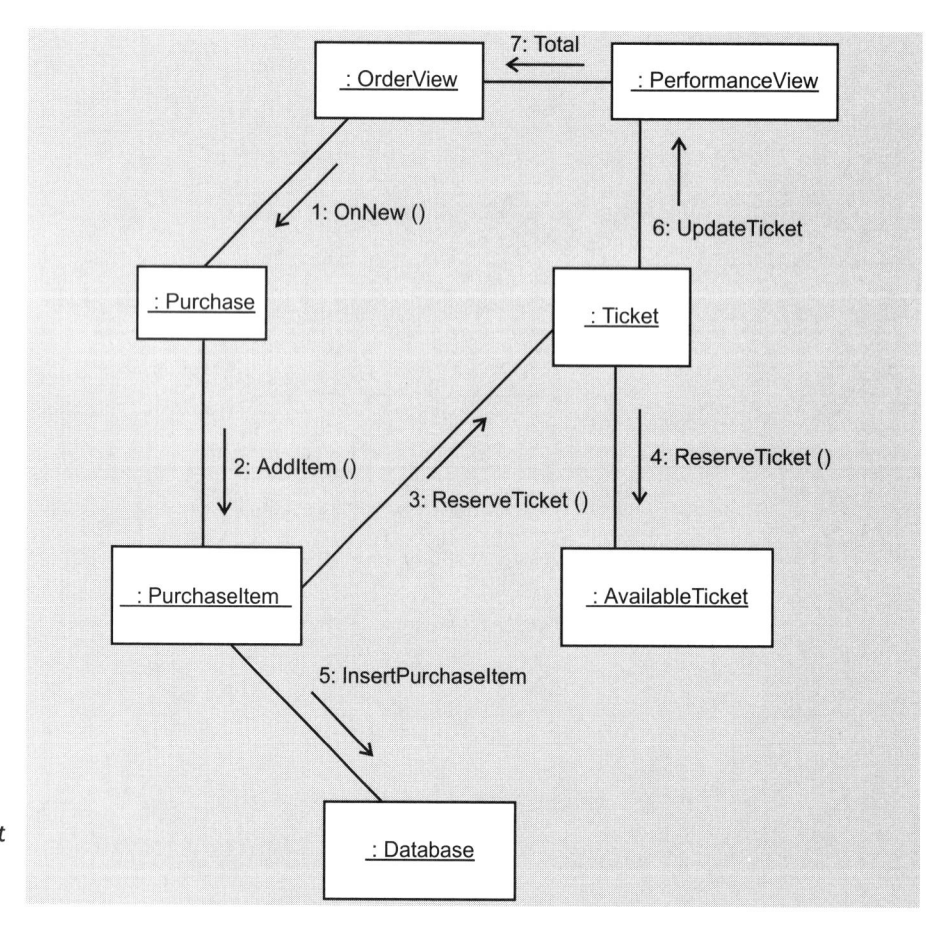

Figure 5-17— Purchase Ticket Collaboration Diagram

Execute Collaboration Test Plan

Role(s): Object Developer

The Object Developer loads the database and exercises the Collaboration Test Plan following the collaboration testing techniques and the test standards developed for this project. Consider assisting your testing with a test driver (for example, the GUI prototype).

Build Documentation

The Solution Area team begins building documentation using the Application, Use Case Test Plan, and Use Case Test Beds developed in this iteration.

Deliverables

Information Reference Guide
User Instructions Guide

Tasks:

Build Documentation Components

Role(s): Document Architect (Facilitator), Business Area Experts, and Object Developer

The Document Architect analyzes the business requirements, models, and Application developed thus far and creates the selected documentation components within the framework established in the Structure Solution phase. You can successfully accomplish this during facilitated prototyping sessions. Business Area Experts participate by developing the content "real-time" in the session to align the documentation to the Application.

Documentation development goes beyond traditional writing and paper production. Today, most applications include an Information Reference Guide within the installation package. Unfortunately, this sometimes requires using the software development tool to create the documentation. This means that the Object Developer often documents this information. We find the Document Architect must have both writing skills and knowledge of the features of the development software. An Object Developer seldom has the writing skills needed for effective communication to the user. Conversely, someone skilled in writing does not always have the skills to use the development software.

The Document Architect does not necessarily need to know the specific development tool; the Object Developer can transfer the documentation into the tool. Commercially available software packages assist in transferring documentation into an online help format. Still, it helps if they understand object-oriented concepts for building the Information Reference Guide.

The Document Architect works with the Object Developer to link any needed information references directly to the Application. The Object Developer ensures the appropriateness of the links during collaboration testing.

Case Study The first step to building the User Instructions Guide includes identifying the topics that need instructions. Generally, each use case requires a separate set of instructions. With refinement, we begin with the purpose of each use case from the initial Use Case Descriptions. Note that the structure allows for adding alternatives and exceptions as known, although they may not be part of this iteration or increment. Continuing with the Reserve Seating use case example, we have:

> Reservations Instructions
> Purpose: To sell tickets to customers for upcoming performances.
> Procedural Steps:
> 1. Show seating options and ticket prices to customer.
> 2. Get Customer Demographics.
> 3. Reserve seats requested by Customer.
> 4. Exchange money for tickets.

As the Use Case Scenarios expand the description, you detail the instructions for each procedure. You may not yet have enough detail for exception handling, but you can at least identify the exceptions. As you identify procedural sequence, you may question the order as in Get Customer Demographics. We decide to address the Customer Demographics topic immediately whether or not the customer purchases a ticket. The User Instructions Guide for Reserve Seating expands to:

> Reservations Instructions
> Purpose: To sell tickets to customers for upcoming performances.
> Procedural Steps:
> 1. Get Customer Demographics.

2. Ask Customer for which performance they want tickets. Confirm with the customer the location of the performance and show time. Show seating options and ticket prices to customer. If the performance is sold out, offer information about other similar upcoming performances.

3. Check if the requested seats are still available. If not, offer similar price and location alternatives. Reserve seats requested by Customer.

4. If customer cancels during reservation process, return seating availability.

5. When the customer finishes selecting seats, sum the total, and add the tax and any shipping charge. Inform the customer of the amount due and ask for payment.

6. If charging purchase, verify the charge account. Return the charge card to the customer. If unable to authorize, require cash from the customer.

7. Give the tickets to the Customer.

Note that although charging a purchase occurs in the second iteration, we have enough information to add instructions for handling this now.

You can either wait until the end of the Build Solution phase to create documentation or you can refine this process throughout the Build Solution phase. We recommend "build as you go." Building it throughout helps validate Use Case and Sequence Diagrams; it also minimizes deadline pressure from waiting until the end. For example, when a performance is sold out, we could have the system find and return information about other performances rather than have the ticket agent determine which performance offers the best alternative.

Information Reference Guide At the highest level of the Information Reference Guide, we list the content, which equates to the use cases. For the first incremental build, we only have Reserve Seating. Within Reserve Seating, we have the following functional windows:

1. Performance List
2. Performance Seating and Prices
3. Customer Purchase History
3.1. Purchased Tickets
3.2. Purchase Summary

We begin building the purpose of each functional window. We use function 3.2, the Purchase Summary window, to demonstrate.

3.2. Purchase Summary

The Purchase Summary window displays the total amount of the purchase, applied taxes, and payment method information for one specific customer transaction.

After the customer has selected all performance tickets, the Purchase Summary displays the total purchase and added tax. You should enter the method of payment. For cash transactions, enter the amount received.

> Within the Purchase Summary window, we define each of its fields. For example, one of the fields, Purchase Total, has the following description attached to it:
>
> Amount customer pays for all tickets purchased for this performance, including taxes.
>
> Besides using the right-down mouse button, the user can see this description when encountering any entry error.

Build Training Material

Based on the solution, the Solution Area team develops the curriculum, training support materials, and training data. Again, the Use Case Scenarios become the central reference source driving the development of the content. The Sequence Diagrams provide detailed events and examples following the core scenarios.

Deliverables
Training Curriculum

Tasks:

Refine Training Curriculum

Role(s): Trainer (Facilitator), Business Area Experts, and Document Architect

The Trainer uses information gathered during the build of the Application to refine the Training Curriculum content for the solution thus far. The Trainer leverages Use Case Scenarios from this iteration by embedding them in the Training Curriculum both as a guide to the content and as real-life samples to educate the Users. Always link training examples to Use Case Scenarios since the use cases are founded in the business view. Use Case Scenarios provide a wealth of information in the specific business area and terminology that it describes. Further detail captured on Sequence Diagrams illustrates the business events triggered and received by the actor, which in turn highlight the subject matter for training.

Case Study   We draw from the Use Case Scenarios and Sequence Diagram to create the class exercises. We use the Customer Pays With Cash Scenario as our example.

> Reserve Seating
>
> Customer purchase
>
> Customer pays with cash
>
> Purpose: By the end of this exercise, the student ticket agent has the ability to execute a cash purchase correctly.
>
> Delivery: Classroom training in a combination of lecture, demonstration, and hands-on exercises. A quiz by the Trainer and fellow students follows at the end of the section.
>
> Lesson Plan: Trainer describes terminology and concepts for this system use. Trainer shows student ticket agents where to specifically reference further information in the User Instructions Guide. Trainer demonstrates by example how to use the system to record a cash ticket purchase. Student ticket agents walk through practice exercises listed below with assistance from the Trainer as needed. At the end of the section, student ticket agents are quizzed by the Trainer and other student ticket agents using a combination of prepared and impromptu questions to verify understanding and capability. Each student ticket agent must correctly answer 90% of the questions to "pass" this section.
>
> Exercise 1:   Customer gives you, the Ticket Agent, cash in an amount more than the purchase amount. What do you do?
>
> Correct response: Ticket agent takes the cash amount from the customer and places it on the top of the cash drawer. Ticket agent must correctly enter the cash amount provided by the customer. The ticket agent takes the change amount from the cash drawer and counts it aloud for the customer, summing it from the purchase amount back to the cash amount provided by the customer. After correctly counting the change, the ticket agent must place the cash received from the customer in the sections of the cash drawer corresponding to the denominations given.
>
> Exercise 2:   Customer gives you, the Ticket Agent, cash in an amount less than the purchase amount. What do you do?
>
> Correct response: Ticket agent politely notifies the Customer of the purchase amount, and gently shows the customer that the cash amount provided is less than the purchase amount.
>
> Exercise 3:   Customer gives you, the Ticket Agent, cash in an amount equal to the purchase amount. What do you do?
>
> Correct response: Ticket agent takes the cash amount from the customer and places it on the top of the cash drawer. Ticket agent must correctly enter the cash amount provided by the customer. The ticket agent must place the cash received from the customer in the sections of the cash drawer corresponding to the denominations given.

The online tutorial follows each lesson plan, but uses different examples in an online quiz. We decide to make the tutorial topics optionally accessible from the corresponding online version of the User Instructions Guide.

Confirm Solution Build

The Solution Area team reviews the Application using use cases and the User Instructions Guide to evaluate if its functionality matches business requirements. The project team also reviews open issues, risks, and change requests.

Deliverables

Training Support Materials
Use Case Test Beds
Issues List
Change Requests
Solution Build Confirmation
Project Plan
Risk Assessment

Tasks:

Create Use Case Test Beds

Role(s): Object Developer

The Object Developer compiles test beds of the sets of actual data items for use in verifying the Use Case Scenarios from the Use Case Test Plan and any other existing data sources.

Validate Use Case Scenarios

Role(s): Object Architect (Facilitator), Project Manager, Object Developer, Business Area Experts, and Document Architect

The Solution Area team exercises the Use Case Test Plan to validate that the functionality and content of the Application meet the business solution. The Object Developer resets the database as needed with the final collection of Use Case Test Beds to assist prototyping.

Throughout this task, the Project Manager faithfully notes all issues and requests for changes. The key here is to capture all constructive comments and critiques; by now the team is usually both proud of the work and anxious to see it to fruition. Nevertheless, the entire team must acknowledge that change may occur to produce not only a system according to original requirements, but also one that meets the business value. The Object Architect measures the deliverables produced in this phase to determine stability (the stopping rule) based on the number of changes from this facilitated session. If 80 percent remains unchanged, you have achieved stability. You may decide to add another iteration if the solution is not stable.

Case Study We walked through the Use Case Test Plan for the Reserve Seating use case. The Business Area Experts feel the application appropriately supported the business functionality. The Users want a menu bar on top similar to what they see with other Microsoft® Windows applications. Other than that, the Users like the ease of use and layout.

Before the session, we counted the number of classes (15) on our Class Diagrams. After the session, changes affected only three classes significantly (PerformanceView, OrderView, and Ticket). This gives us (15-3)/15 = 80%, so we have roughly attained stability.

Confirm Usability of the Documentation Components

Role(s): Document Architect (Facilitator) and Business Area Experts

The Business Area Experts assess the documentation for usability and content. The Document Architect walks through each reference to information within the Application, and demonstrates how the documentation deliverables pertain to the Application.

Confirm Content of the Training Curriculum

Role(s): Trainer (Facilitator) and Business Area Experts

The Business Area Experts assess the Training Curriculum for correct depth of content. The Trainer demonstrates how the content aligns with the Application. Additionally, they review the measures to test understanding before, during, and after instruction. Creation of the training support materials begins.

Prepare Build Solution Change Requests

Role(s): Project Manager, Infrastructure Architect, Object Architect, Database Architect, Document Architect, and Business Area Experts

The Project Manager assembles all the issues and change requests into a coherent change document. The Project Manager then confirms the decision to proceed with each change request with the team. They reach consensus on the change requests that have business merit.

The Project Manager documents each change request in detail, writing it so that each one is understandable to those not present in the sessions.

The Business Area Experts categorize and prioritize the change requests. The Project Manager groups them according to content and order of necessity (e.g., mandatory, needed, not needed).

The Project Manager identifies the deliverables affected by the change request. The entire Solution Area team assesses the amount of work needed to implement the change request.

With all of the supporting information gathered, the team reaches agreement on how to handle each change request.

Case Study During the confirmation activity, the Users requested to have a menu bar added to the Reserve Seating application. Discussing this with the team, we agree we can easily add this change during our second iteration. We document this as a Change Request. See Table 5-4—Build Solution Change Requests.

Table 5-4—Build Solution Change Requests

Change Request Number	Change Description	Priority (High, Med., Low)	Benefit	Affected Deliverables	Disposition (Requested, Approved, Denied, Completed)
1	See related Issue 6: Print tickets at the time of purchase.	Med.	Timeliness. Keeps function at appropriate location. Reduction in mailing cost.	Use Case Diagram, Class Diagram, Reserve Seating Application	Requested
2	Move the Calculate_Total function from the user interface to its own control class.	Low	Reusability	Reserve Seating Application	Requested

Change Request Number	Change Description	Priority (High, Med., Low)	Benefit	Affected Deliverables	Disposition (Requested, Approved, Denied, Completed)
3	Add menu bar to user interface. Menu items should support same functions as the buttons in a Microsoft® Windows standard application.	Med.	Consistency	Use Case Diagram, Class Diagram	Approved

Obtain Solution Build Confirmation

Role(s): Project Manager (Facilitator), Business Area Experts, and Project Sponsor

The Solution Area team assesses the changes to judge whether the current Application is ready for immediate implementation or not. The team prioritizes each change based on complexity, severity (the impact if not addressed), and the cost to complete.

The current Application (as is, without change requests) is evaluated to see if immediate implementation provides benefit to the business. Negotiation with the Business Area Experts identifies the required change requests that enhance the Application business value for release.

The Project Manager prepares the business justification stressing the benefits for releasing the Application and includes the estimated cost to implement.

The Project Sponsor decides whether to implement based on all of the recently assembled information.

The Project Manager schedules the change requests that were not included in this release for a future release, or eliminates them altogether. The Project Manager reviews and updates the project plan to account for the actual time spent on assessing change requests and reflect any newly uncovered changes, and revises the estimates.

Assess Risk

Role(s): Project Manager

The Project Manager again updates the Risk Assessment as a checkpoint based on the results of this phase. See Table 5-5—Build Solution Risk Assessment.

Table 5-5—Build Solution Risk Assessment

Category	Item	Action
Strength	Team members understand the business.	Take the next step—get the Business Area Experts more involved in understanding OO modeling.
Weakness	Team progressing in OO skills	Watch for further progress.
	Users lack computer skills	Note: Staff had two-day training. Now they want their equipment sooner!
Opportunity	Executive management highly committed to project.	Keep in contact with regular status reporting. Involve executives in confirmation sessions.
	Accounting really likes the idea of better transaction tracking.	Give the accounting liaison query tools and suggest she mock up her five most crucial report layouts.
	Marketing was disappointed that promotions are not first (promote performance). Marketing is now on board with a full commitment from next year's budget. He will fund first increment out of this year's budget.	Threat became an opportunity. Schedule meeting to kick off Structure Solution after the first of the year.
Threat	Technology is new for the company.	President has requested that we show off the prototype at the company sales meeting.

Build Solution Iterations

This section discusses the second and third iterations of the Build Solution phase within the Case Study. We intend to show the impact of layered refinement resulting from iteration. Iteration repeats all of the Build Solution phase tasks to add detail to the pre-established content of the increment. The emerging solution begins to stabilize by including the alternatives and exceptions to the use cases. Although you generally repeat each of the tasks, we show only the alternative and exception scenarios and their impact on the Class Diagram to minimize clutter.

Second Iteration

The scope of our second iteration adds the refinement from the alternative Use Case Scenarios of the Reserve Seating use case. The alternatives include the paths for a customer canceling the purchase and a customer credit purchase. We show the changes resulting from this refinement in the Use Case Scenario, Sequence Diagram, and Class Diagram.

Cancel Purchase Scenario We consider that the customer may cancel at any time. We uncovered an operation for this in the Statechart Diagram during the life cycle analysis from the first iteration. At that time we simply captured and moved on. Now we work back to it and recognize an opportunity for reuse. We add an extends use case to the Use Case Diagram as depicted in Figure 5-18—Use Case Diagram with Cancel Purchase Extends Use Case.

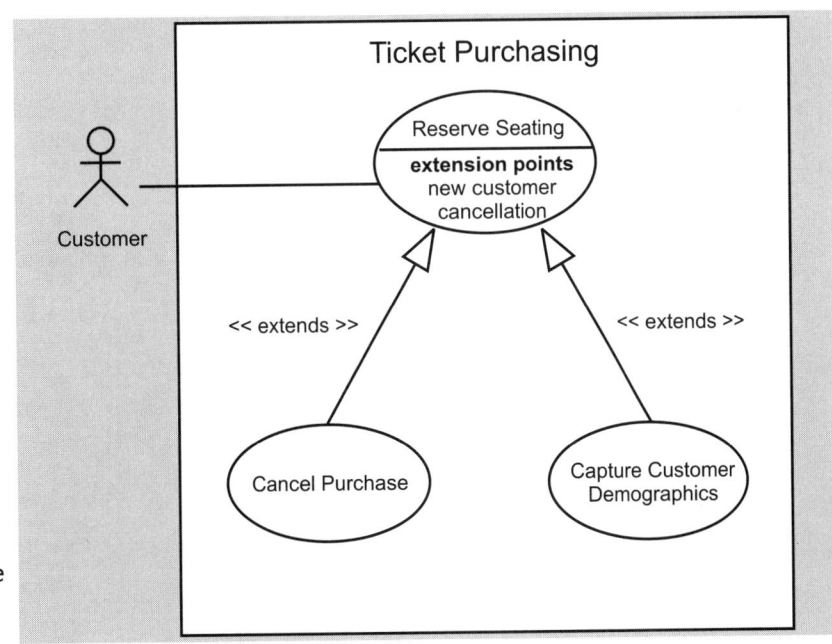

Figure 5-18—Use Case Diagram with Cancel Purchase Extends Use Case

For the Cancel Purchase Use Case Scenario, we document the distinct points where cancellation may occur. We note this by referring to the extending use case in the scenario steps. Using the Extension Points notation of the UML, we add the label "cancellation," which identifies the location within the Reserve Seating use case where the Cancel Purchase use case may occur.

We add the detail for the void transaction operation to the Purchase class. Because cancellation may occur at various times, you want to create a test case covering each situation.

Figures 5-19, 5-20, and 5-21 reflect the new methods and attributes added to handle the Cancel Purchase scenario. In the interface layer, we only add the OnCancel() operation to the OrderView form as a triggering event connected to the Purchase::Cancel() operation added previously.

MainFrame
_messageEntries classCMainFrame m_wndSplitter m_wndStatusBar messageMap
CMainFrame () AssertValid () CreateObject () Dump () GetMessageMap () GetRuntimeClass () OnCreate () OnCreateClient () OnExit () OnSetText () PreCreateWindow ()

OrderView
_messageEntries classCOrderView m_btnAccept m_btnCancel m_btnNew m_cboCreditCard m_dateCreditExpiration m_grpPurchase m_lblDelivery m_lblFacility m_lblSalesTax m_lblService m_lblTickets m_lblTotal m_1stPurchase m_nCreditCard m_performances m_purchase m_szCreditCardNumber m_szFirstName m_szLastName m_szTelephone m_txtCreditCardNumber m_txtFirstName m_txtLastName m_txtTelephone messageMap
COrderView () AssertValid () CreateObject () DisplayTickets () DoDataExchange () Dump () GetDocument () GetMessageMap () GetRuntimeClass () OnAccept () OnDestroy () OnInitialUpdate () OnNew () OnUpdate () PreCreateWindow () UpdateBillingInformation () UpdateControls () **OnCancel ()**

PerformanceView
_messageEntries classCPerformanceView m_btnAdd m_cboPerformances m_dwLastSelection m_1stAvailableSeating m_1stDateTime m_performances messageMap
CPerformanceView () AssertValid () CreateObject () DoDataExchange () Dump () GetMessageMap () GetRuntimeClass () OnBtnAdd () OnEndlabeleditAvailableSeating () OnInitialUpdate () OnSelchangeCboPerformance () OnSelchangeDateAndTime () OnUpdate ()

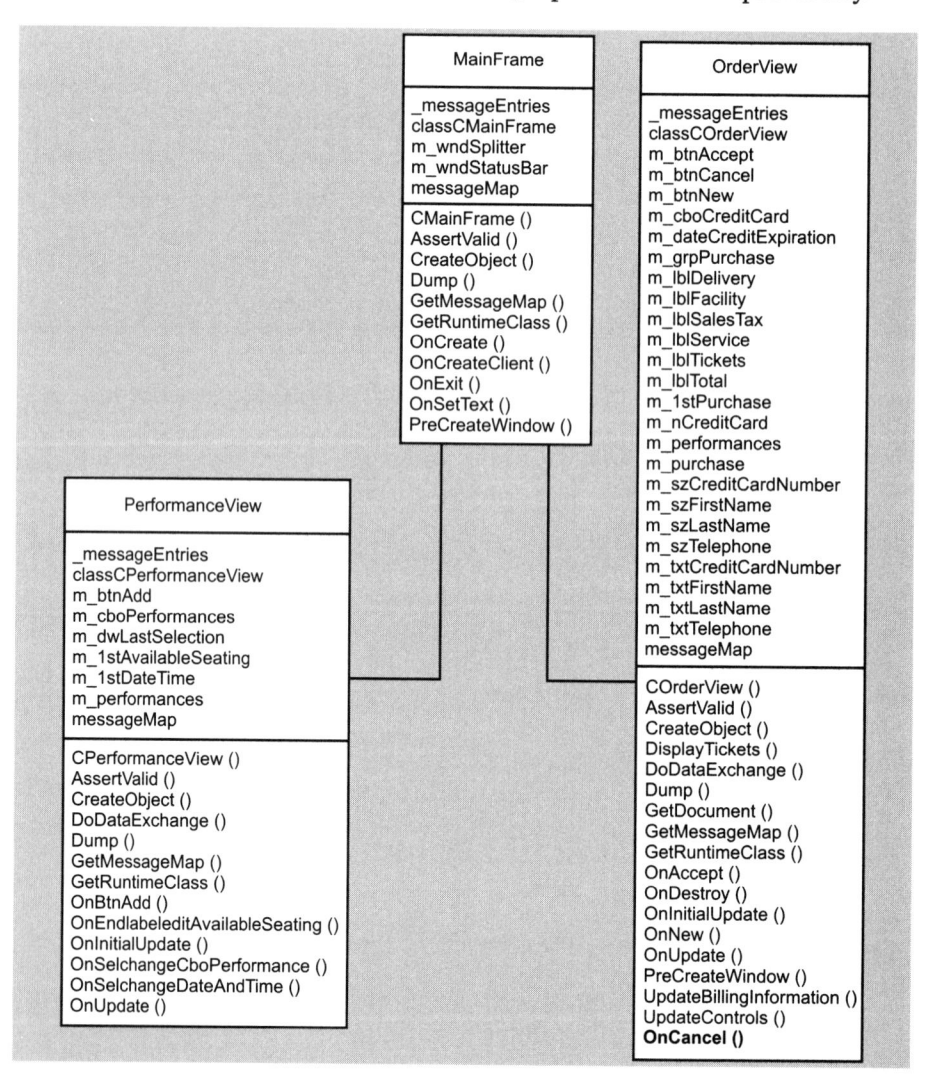

Figure 5-19—Interface Class Diagram After Iteration 2

In both the business services and data services layers, we add the related Cancel Purchase operations and methods to remove Purchase Items and unreserve Tickets.

Performance	Purchase	Seat
m_pData	m_pData	m_pData
CPerformance ()	CPurchase ()	CSeat ()
GetDate ()	AddItem ()	GetClassification ()
GetKey ()	GetCreditCardExpirationDate ()	GetKey ()
GetName ()	GetCreditCardNumber ()	GetRow ()
	GetCreditCardType ()	GetSeatNumber ()
	GetFirstName ()	GetSection ()
	GetItem ()	
	GetKey ()	
	GetLastName ()	
	GetPhoneNumber ()	
	GetPurchaseItemCount ()	
	Init ()	
	Save ()	
	SetCreditCardExpirationDate ()	
	SetCreditCardNumber ()	
	SetCreditCardType ()	
	SetFirstName ()	
	SetLastName ()	
	SetPhoneNumber ()	
	Cancel ()	

Performances	PurchaseItem	SeatingSummary
m_pData	m_pData	m_pData
CPerformances ()	CPurchaseItem ()	CSeatingSummary ()
GetAt ()	Cancel ()	GetKey ()
GetPerformance ()	GetKey ()	GetNumSeats ()
GetSize ()	GetPerformance ()	GetPrice ()
Init ()	GetPerformanceDate ()	GetSection ()
	GetPONumber ()	
	GetPrice ()	
	GetSeatAt ()	
	GetSeatQuantity ()	
	GetSection ()	
	Reserve ()	
	Save ()	
	SetKey ()	
	SetPerformance ()	
	SetPerformanceDate ()	
	SetPONumber ()	
	SetPrice ()	
	SetSeatQuantity ()	
	SetSection ()	

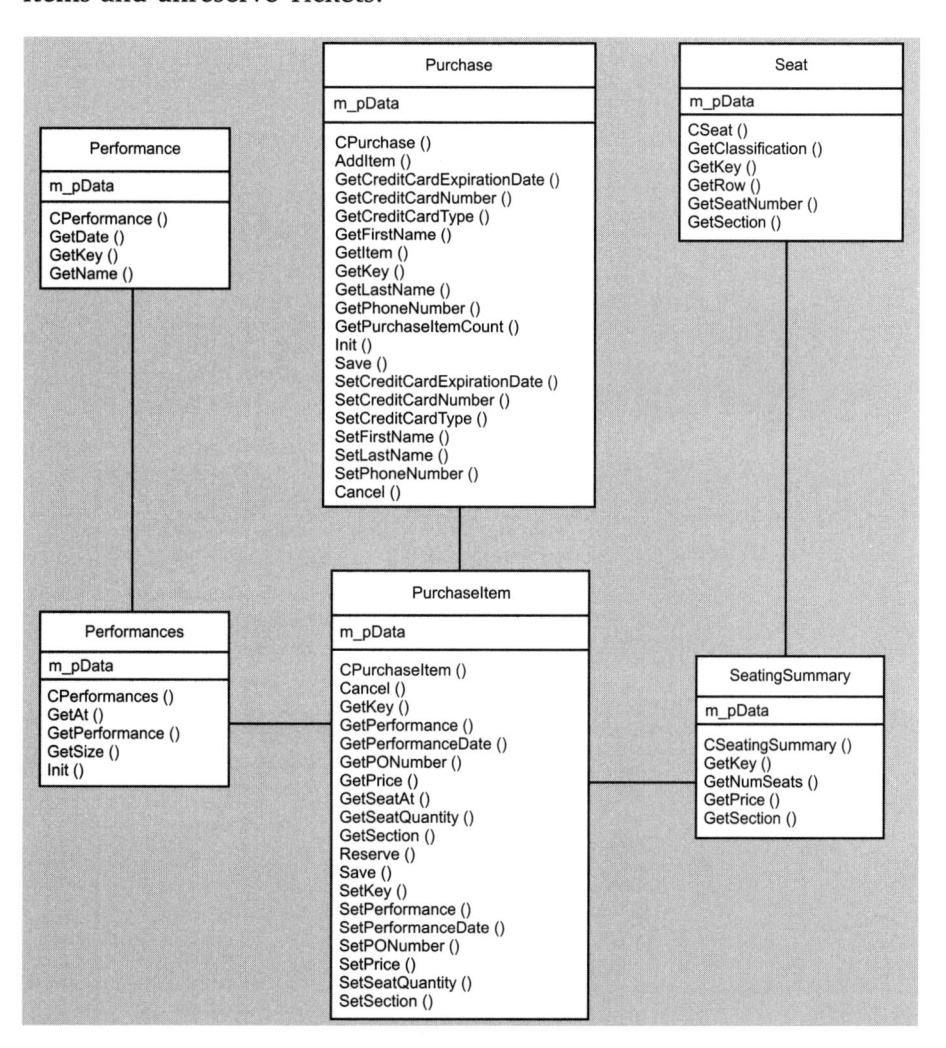

Figure 5-20—Control Class Diagram After Iteration 2

The classes must also remove the item from the data services layer. Since there is no actual delete from the database (the record has not yet been saved), the removal from the vector performed by the business layer Purchase::Cancel() is all we need. No change to the data layer is truly necessary. In the future, we may need to add the functionality to call back a purchase and then cancel it. If we were to interface to an accounting system, this is not as easy, as it requires a reversing entry. We leave the diagram unchanged for now.

```
PurchaseItem
─────────────
classPurchaseItem
m_PurchaseItem_DateTime
m_PurchaseItem_Hdr
m_PurchaseItem_Key
m_PurchaseItem_Performance
m_PurchaseItem_Purchase_Price
m_PurchaseItem_SeatQty
m_PurchaseItem_Section
─────────────
PurchaseItem ()
AssertValid ()
DoFieldExchange ()
Dump ()
GetDefaultDBName ()
GetDefaultSQL ()
GetRuntimeClass ()
```

```
Purchase
─────────────
classPurchase
m_Customer_Credit_Card_Expires
m_Customer_Credit_Card_Number
m_Customer_Credit_Card_Type
m_Customer_Name_First
m_Customer_Name_Last
m_Customer_Phone_Number
m_PurchaseOrder
─────────────
Purchase ()
_GetBaseClass ()
AssertValid ()
DoFieldExchange ()
Dump ()
GetDefaultDBName ()
Get DefaultSQL ()
GetRuntimeClass ()
```

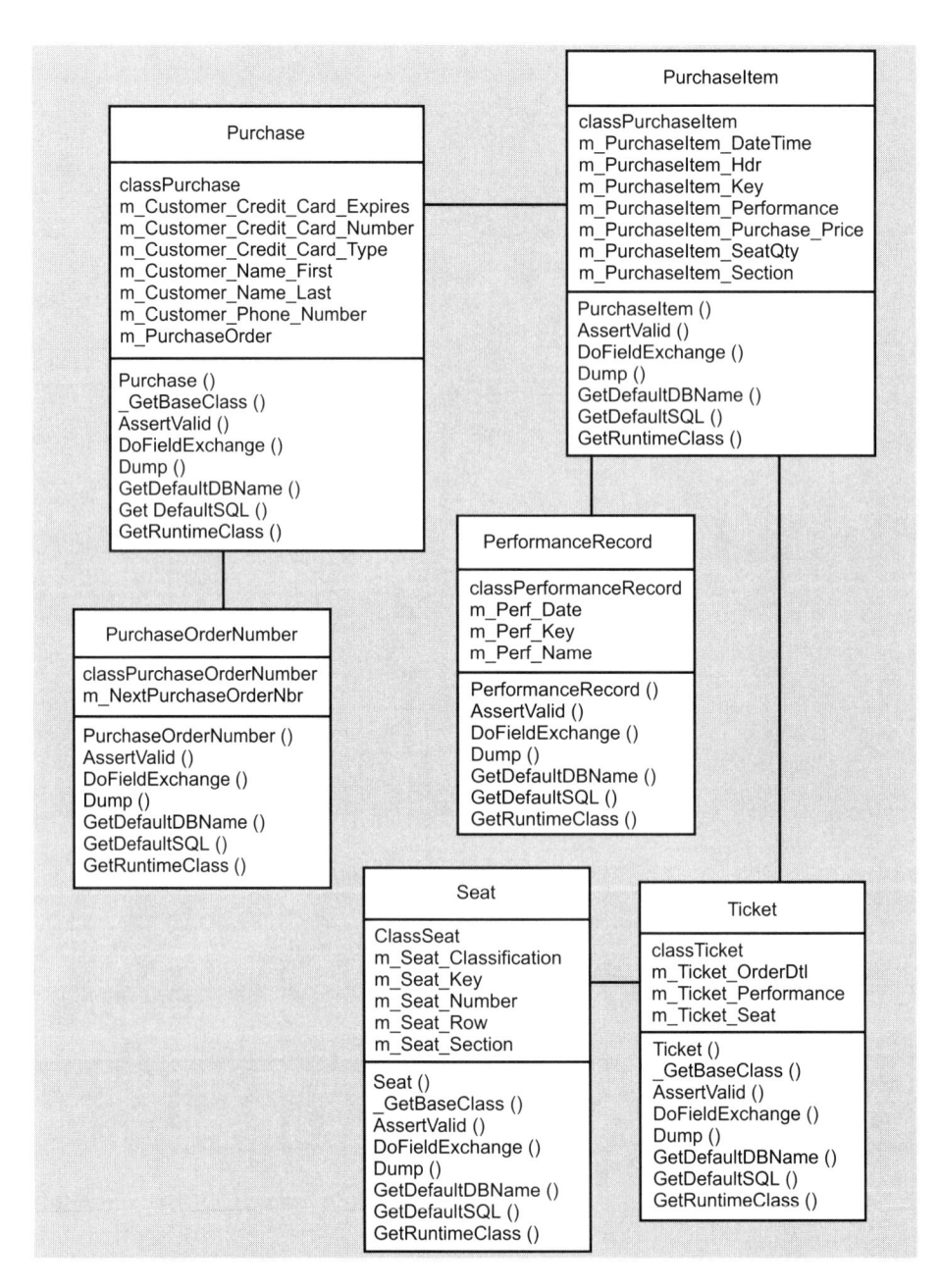

```
PurchaseOrderNumber
─────────────
classPurchaseOrderNumber
m_NextPurchaseOrderNbr
─────────────
PurchaseOrderNumber ()
AssertValid ()
DoFieldExchange ()
Dump ()
GetDefaultDBName ()
GetDefaultSQL ()
GetRuntimeClass ()
```

```
PerformanceRecord
─────────────
classPerformanceRecord
m_Perf_Date
m_Perf_Key
m_Perf_Name
─────────────
PerformanceRecord ()
AssertValid ()
DoFieldExchange ()
Dump ()
GetDefaultDBName ()
GetDefaultSQL ()
GetRuntimeClass ()
```

```
Seat
─────────────
ClassSeat
m_Seat_Classification
m_Seat_Key
m_Seat_Number
m_Seat_Row
m_Seat_Section
─────────────
Seat ()
_GetBaseClass ()
AssertValid ()
DoFieldExchange ()
Dump ()
GetDefaultDBName ()
GetDefaultSQL ()
GetRuntimeClass ()
```

```
Ticket
─────────────
classTicket
m_Ticket_OrderDtl
m_Ticket_Performance
m_Ticket_Seat
─────────────
Ticket ()
_GetBaseClass ()
AssertValid ()
DoFieldExchange ()
Dump ()
GetDefaultDBName ()
GetDefaultSQL ()
GetRuntimeClass ()
```

Figure 5-21— Entity Class Diagram After Iteration 2

The following code reveals the Cancel functionality. This activity begins when the user presses the Cancel button on the OrderView form. OrderView::OnCancel then sends the message, Cancel Purchase, to the Purchase class that in turn sends a message to delete all the purchase items. It then updates the views.

```cpp
void COrderView::OnCancel()
{
    m_purchase.Cancel();
    UpdateControls(false);
    m_lstPurchase.DeleteAllItems();
    GetDocument()->UpdateAllViews( this );
}
bool CPurchase::Cancel()
{
    bool bRetVal = false;
    int nSize = m_pData->m_vPurchase.size();
    for ( int i = 0; i < nSize; ++i )
    {
        bRetVal = m_pData->m_vPurchase[i].Cancel();
        if ( !bRetVal )
        {
            break;
        }
    }
    if ( bRetVal )
    {
        m_pData->m_vPurchase.clear();
    }
    return bRetVal;
}
```

The Purchase class unreserves each ticket and cancels the corresponding purchase item through reloading the AvailableSeating structure from the unchanged database by using the return from PerformanceListQuery (a pseudo stored procedure).

```cpp
IMPLEMENT_DYNAMIC(AvailableSeating, CDaoRecordset)

AvailableSeating::AvailableSeating(CDaoDatabase* pdb)
    : CDaoRecordset(pdb)
{
    //{{AFX_FIELD_INIT(AvailableSeating)
    m_Seat_Section = _T("");
    m_Perf_Key = 0;
    m_nFields = 3;
    //}}AFX_FIELD_INIT
    m_nDefaultType = dbOpenDynaset;
}
CString AvailableSeating::GetDefaultDBName()
{
    return _T("performance.mdb");
}

CString AvailableSeating::GetDefaultSQL()
```

```
{
    return _T("[PerformanceListQuery]");
}
void AvailableSeating::DoFieldExchange(CDaoFieldExchange* pFX)
{
    //{{AFX_FIELD_MAP(AvailableSeating)
    pFX->SetFieldType(CDaoFieldExchange::outputColumn);
    DFX_Text(pFX, _T("[Seat_Section]"), m_Seat_Section);
    DFX_Currency(pFX, _T("[SeatClassification_Price]"),
m_SeatClassification_Price);
    DFX_Long(pFX, _T("[Perf_Key]"), m_Perf_Key);
    //}}AFX_FIELD_MAP
}
```

We return to the OrderView form that sends a message to the Performances form to reload the quantities of available tickets, which reflects the removal of the PurchaseItems and Purchase.

```
void COrderView::DisplayTickets(CPurchaseItem &item)
{
    // First, update the stuff that will be common
    // for all of these
    CPerformance& performance =
        m_performances.GetPerformance( item.GetPerformance() );
    CString szPerformanceName = performance.GetName();
    CString szDate = performance.GetDate().Format(
        "%m/%d/%Y %I:%M %p" );
    CString szSection = item.GetSection();
    CString szPrice;
    szPrice.Format("$%s", item.GetPrice().Format() );
    int nSize = item.GetSeatQuantity();
    int nStartPosition = m_lstPurchase.GetItemCount();
    for ( int i = 0; i < nSize; ++i )
    {
        CString szTemp;
        CSeat& seat = item.GetSeatAt( i );
        int nRow = seat.GetRow();
        int nSeat = seat.GetSeatNumber();
        LVITEM row;
        ZeroMemory( &row, sizeof( row ) );

        row.mask = LVIF_TEXT;
        row.iItem = i + nStartPosition;
        row.iSubItem = PERFORMANCE;
        row.pszText = const_cast<LPTSTR>(
            (LPCTSTR) szPerformanceName );
        row.cchTextMax = szPerformanceName.GetLength() + 1;
        m_lstPurchase.InsertItem( &row );
```

```
        row.iSubItem = DATE_TIME;
        row.pszText = const_cast<LPTSTR>((LPCTSTR) szDate );
        row.cchTextMax = szDate.GetLength() + 1;
        m_lstPurchase.SetItem( &row );

        row.iSubItem = PRICE;
        row.pszText = const_cast<LPTSTR>((LPCTSTR) szPrice );
        row.cchTextMax = szPrice.GetLength() + 1;
        m_lstPurchase.SetItem( &row );

        row.iSubItem = SECTION;
        row.pszText = const_cast<LPTSTR>((LPCTSTR) szSection );
        row.cchTextMax = szSection.GetLength() + 1;
        m_lstPurchase.SetItem( &row );

        row.iSubItem = ROW;
        szTemp.Format( "%d", nRow );
        row.pszText = const_cast<LPTSTR>((LPCTSTR) szTemp );
        row.cchTextMax = szTemp.GetLength() + 1;
        m_lstPurchase.SetItem( &row );

        row.iSubItem = SEAT;
        szTemp.Format( "%d", nSeat );
        row.pszText = const_cast<LPTSTR>((LPCTSTR) szTemp );
        row.cchTextMax = szTemp.GetLength() + 1;
        m_lstPurchase.SetItem( &row );
    }
}
```

Figure 5-22—Cancel Purchase Collaboration Diagram provides a roadmap of this discussion.

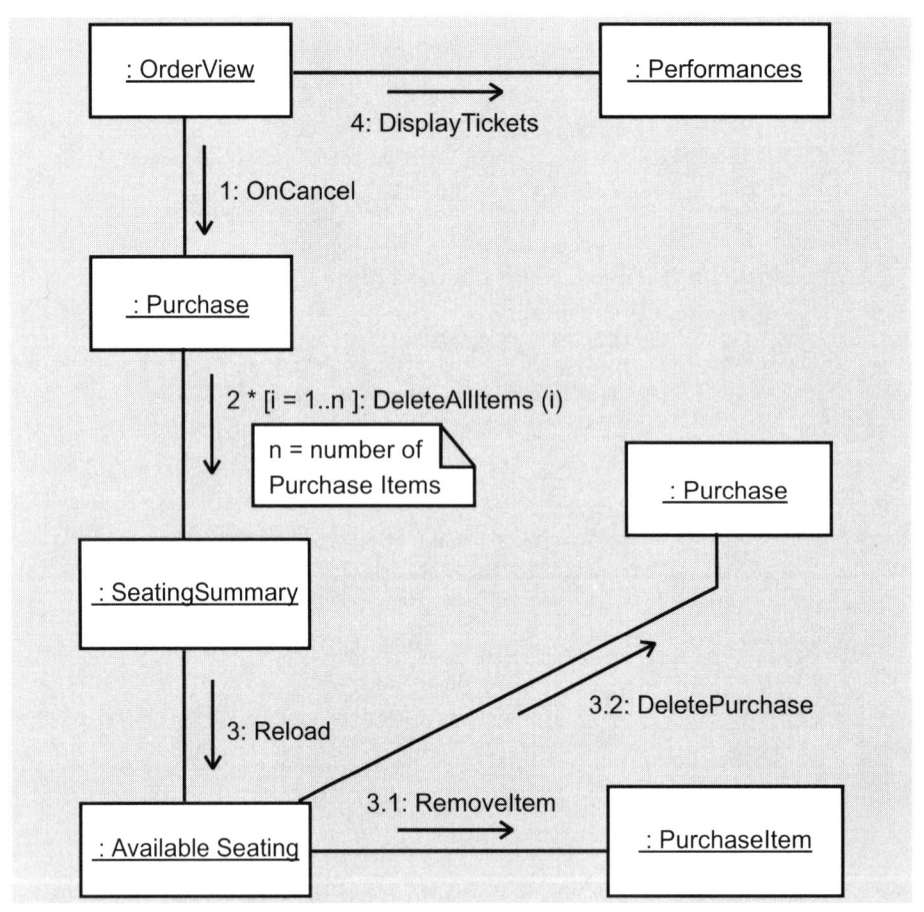

Figure 5-22—
Cancel Purchase
Collaboration
Diagram

Credit Purchase Scenario The additional steps created for the Credit Purchase Use Case Scenario replace only the cash purchase steps. The remainder of the scenario (and the corresponding Sequence Diagram) stays the same. Recall the original Problem Assessment allowed for credit checking to take up to 24 hours; nevertheless, this does not impact the scenario.

Credit Authorization Passes Scenario We pick up with the relevant text from the Use Case Description to derive the scenario steps:

> The customer provides payment (credit) amount.

We first change the Use Case Description to clearer phrasing—"available credit is more than the total" becomes "the purchase amount does not exceed the available credit."

If payment is by credit card, the system calls for credit authorization. The system collects credit card issuer, number, and expiration date to verify that the purchase amount does not exceed the available credit.

Purchase requests credit information from Customer.

Customer provides credit information to Purchase.

Purchase requests authorization from Credit.

There are only two possible options: the credit authorization either passes or fails.

If credit card authorization passes, the seats are reserved.

Credit returns authorization (passed) to Purchase.

If authorization passes, the remainder of the scenario is unchanged.

Credit Authorization Fails Scenario It is a different case altogether when authorization fails. The system asks the customer for an alternate payment method. This can either be a different credit card (in which case repeat this scenario) or cash (proceed to the cash scenario).

If authorization fails, the customer has the option to pay with any other payment method.

Credit returns authorization (failed) to Purchase.

Purchase requests alternate payment from Customer.

Customer provides payment amount.

(Proceed to appropriate scenario)

This use case ends when the customer leaves.

We need to add the credit attributes to the Purchase class along with their corresponding Let and Get properties. We show only the additions and changes.

```
CString    m_Customer_Credit_Card_Type;
CString    m_Customer_Credit_Card_Number;
CString    m_Customer_Credit_Card_Expires;
CString    m_Customer_Phone_Number;

// Sets the phone number of the purchaser
void SetPhoneNumber( const CString& value );
```

```
// Returns the phone number of the purchaser
  CString GetPhoneNumber();

// Sets the credit card type for the purchaser
  void SetCreditCardType( const CString& value );

// Returns the credit card type for the purchaser
  CString GetCreditCardType();

// Sets the purchaser's credit card number
  void SetCreditCardNumber( const CString& value );

// Returns the purchaser's credit card number
  CString GetCreditCardNumber();

// Sets the expiration date of the credit card
  void SetCreditCardExpirationDate( const CString& value );

// Returns the expiration date of the credit card
  CString GetCreditCardExpirationDate();
```

We then update the SQL in the corresponding functions of the Purchase class to reflect the new properties. Note that only the Purchase::Save function addresses the detail of each property. The other functions work with more streamlined SQL by using the full row definition with the SQL "*" wildcard operator.

```
record.m_Customer_Credit_Card_Type =
   m_pData->m_Customer_Credit_Card_Type;
record.m_Customer_Credit_Card_Number =
   m_pData->m_Customer_Credit_Card_Number;
record.m_Customer_Credit_Card_Expires =
   m_pData->m_Customer_Credit_Card_Expires;
record.m_Customer_Phone_Number =
   m_pData->m_Customer_Phone_Number;
record.Update();
```

Third Iteration

We postpone the exceptions for the Reserve Seating use case to the third iteration. We build the exceptions only after building the core and alternative scenarios in the previous two iterations. For this illustration, we select the sold-out performance and the event when a customer selects more tickets from a section than available.

Performance Sold Out Scenario For the Performance Sold Out Scenario, we pick up from the "Customer requests availability..." step and add one more step:

> The Customer selects a Performance from the Interface.
>
> The Interface requests all available Tickets for that Performance.
>
> Ticket returns "Performance is Sold Out" to Customer (via the user interface).

The only change is an additional operation to send a message to the customer. The remainder of the use case is unchanged.

Selected Number of Tickets Greater Than Available by Section Scenario Likewise, for this scenario, the "Customer requests availability..." step is the start. In this path, we check to ensure that the number of tickets selected in the section is less than or equal to the number of tickets available.

> The customer selects seating area and number of seats.
>
> Ticket returns "Purchase quantity is greater than available tickets" to Customer (via the user interface)

For this particular iteration, we have minimal change to the Class Diagram. We merely add code to handle exceptions in the interface class PerformanceView form. The exception handles when the User wants to purchase more tickets than available.

```
bool CPerformanceView::ValidateTicketRequest()
{
    int nCount = m_lstAvailableSeating.GetItemCount();

    // Not necessary in this compiler, but I don't want
    // this code to break when the ANSI/ISO standard gets
    // implemented correctly.
    int i = 0;
    for ( ; i < nCount; ++i )
    {
        const int KnBufferSize = 256;
        LVITEM item;
        int nRequestedQuantity = 0;
        int nAvailableQuantity = 0;
        TCHAR buffer[KnBufferSize];
        ZeroMemory( &item, sizeof( item ) );
        item.mask = LVIF_TEXT;
        item.iItem = i;
        item.iSubItem = QTY_COL;
        item.pszText = buffer;
```

```
            item.cchTextMax = KnBufferSize;
            m_lstAvailableSeating.GetItem( &item );
            nRequestedQuantity = atoi( buffer );

            // User didn't request any tickets, keep going.
            if ( nRequestedQuantity <= 0 )
            {
                continue;
            }

            item.iSubItem = SEATS;
            m_lstAvailableSeating.GetItem( &item );
            nAvailableQuantity = atoi( buffer );

            // If they asked for more than what we have, let
            // them know.  We only need one failure to say the request
            // is bad.
            if ( nRequestedQuantity > nAvailableQuantity )
            {
                AfxMessageBox( "Purchase quantity is greater"
                               " than available tickets" );
                break;
            }
        }

        // If the loop variable is equal to the number of items in
        // the list box, then all items must have been valid.
        return ( i == nCount );
    }
```

Second Increment

The changes for the second increment of the Reserve Seating solution area are rather trivial. We discuss the change here rather than in the Integrate Solution phase to simplify that discussion.

The second increment added the Customer class as a distinct class, whereas in the first increment we simply stored customer information with the Purchase. The reason for this change is to eliminate redundant entry of customer information for each purchase. We can then track multiple purchases for a single customer easily. Although keeping the customer information in the Purchase class was not a preferred approach, at the time it followed our rule to deliver a system as soon as possible. We are building the solution in a structured manner, only adding and refining responsibility as necessary. One of the most difficult challenges to face as an experienced professional is the temptation to "just throw it in there, we know we'll need it later." This is how many systems fail; they have fallen prey to scope creep. Putting the customer information in the Purchase class does break the rule that each class should do one thing—carry out its responsibility—and do that one thing well. Sometimes the most responsible thing is not to do too much when it really is not necessary. In this case, we had only stubbed in what was necessary to deliver the first increment, knowing that we would come back to it in the second increment.

The creation of the Customer class is rather straightforward. Within the context of what we need, we simply pull the customer information out of the Purchase class, create the association back to Purchase, and create its mapping class in the data services layer to accommodate its persistent storage needs. The interface class, the OrderView form, does not change in appearance; however, the underlying code structures have to change to incorporate the new class. The two main points here are first, that we were able to leverage entirely the prototyping session from the first increment, and second, that the remainder of the solution does not change. The stability of a well-thought-out approach is already showing benefits. We have localized the change to just the OrderView form class, the Purchase class, and the new Customer class. All other classes remain unchanged. The solution, though malleable, still maintains its integrity.

See Figures 5-23, 5-24, and 5-25.

MainFrame

_messageEntries
classCMainFrame
m_wndSplitter
m_wndStatusBar
messageMap

CMainFrame ()
AssertValid ()
CreateObject ()
Dump ()
GetMessageMap ()
GetRuntimeClass ()
OnCreate ()
OnCreateClient ()
OnExit ()
OnSetText ()
PreCreateWindow ()

OrderView

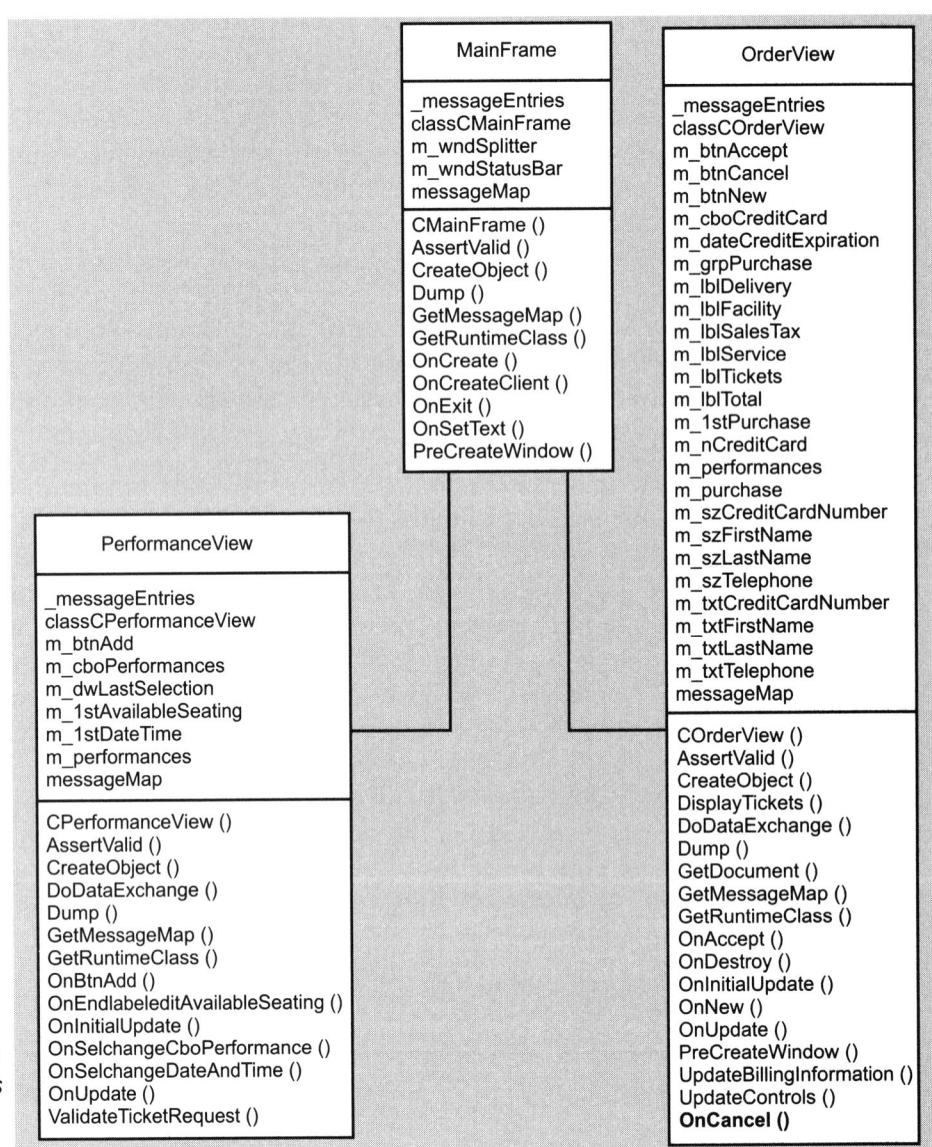

_messageEntries
classCOrderView
m_btnAccept
m_btnCancel
m_btnNew
m_cboCreditCard
m_dateCreditExpiration
m_grpPurchase
m_lblDelivery
m_lblFacility
m_lblSalesTax
m_lblService
m_lblTickets
m_lblTotal
m_1stPurchase
m_nCreditCard
m_performances
m_purchase
m_szCreditCardNumber
m_szFirstName
m_szLastName
m_szTelephone
m_txtCreditCardNumber
m_txtFirstName
m_txtLastName
m_txtTelephone
messageMap

COrderView ()
AssertValid ()
CreateObject ()
DisplayTickets ()
DoDataExchange ()
Dump ()
GetDocument ()
GetMessageMap ()
GetRuntimeClass ()
OnAccept ()
OnDestroy ()
OnInitialUpdate ()
OnNew ()
OnUpdate ()
PreCreateWindow ()
UpdateBillingInformation ()
UpdateControls ()
OnCancel ()

PerformanceView

_messageEntries
classCPerformanceView
m_btnAdd
m_cboPerformances
m_dwLastSelection
m_1stAvailableSeating
m_1stDateTime
m_performances
messageMap

CPerformanceView ()
AssertValid ()
CreateObject ()
DoDataExchange ()
Dump ()
GetMessageMap ()
GetRuntimeClass ()
OnBtnAdd ()
OnEndlabeleditAvailableSeating ()
OnInitialUpdate ()
OnSelchangeCboPerformance ()
OnSelchangeDateAndTime ()
OnUpdate ()
ValidateTicketRequest ()

Figure 5-23—Interface Class Diagram After Increment 2

Customer

m_pData

GetCreditCardExpirationDate ()
GetCreditCardNumber ()
GetCreditCardType ()
GetFirstName ()
GetLastName ()
GetPhoneNumber ()
SetCreditCardExpirationDate ()
SetCreditCardNumber ()
SetCreditCardType ()
SetFirstName ()
SetLastName ()
SetPhoneNumber ()

Purchase

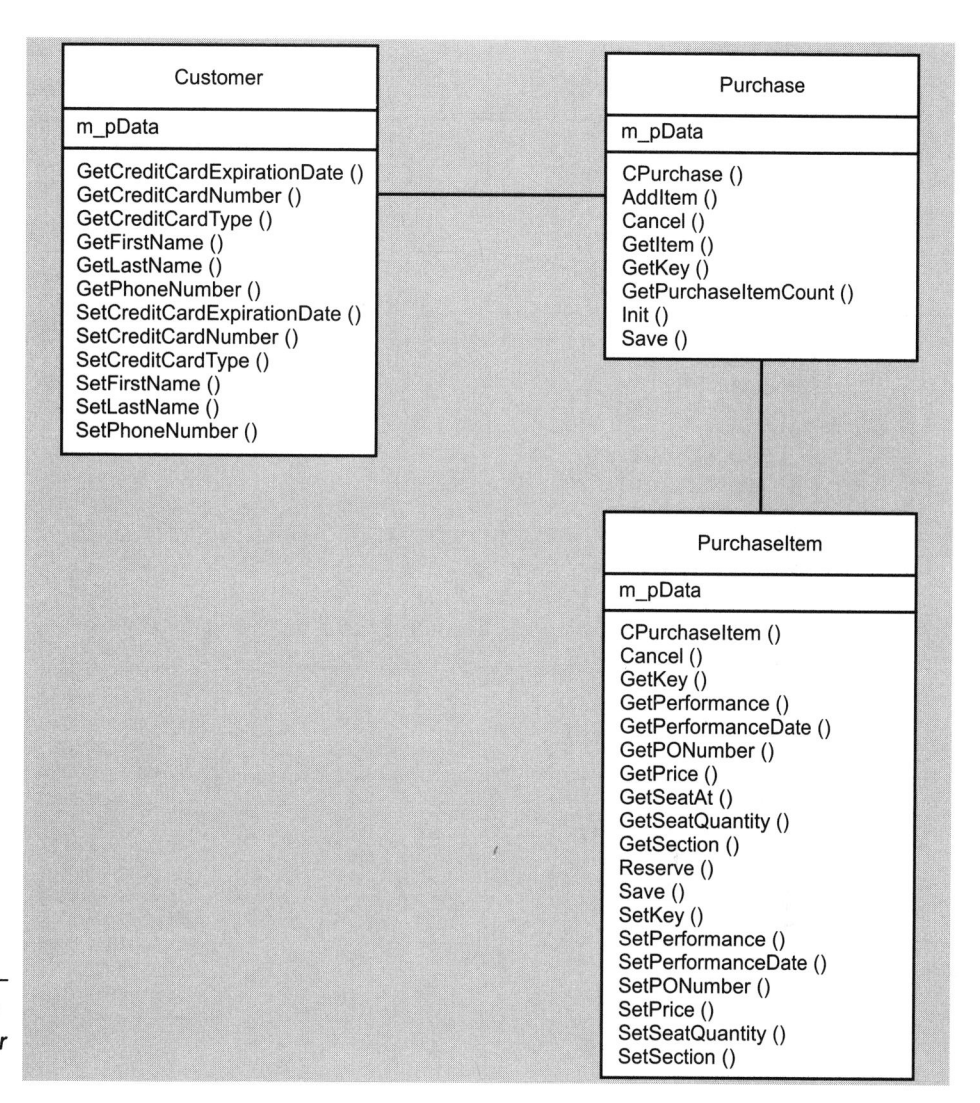

m_pData

CPurchase ()
AddItem ()
Cancel ()
GetItem ()
GetKey ()
GetPurchaseItemCount ()
Init ()
Save ()

PurchaseItem

m_pData

CPurchaseItem ()
Cancel ()
GetKey ()
GetPerformance ()
GetPerformanceDate ()
GetPONumber ()
GetPrice ()
GetSeatAt ()
GetSeatQuantity ()
GetSection ()
Reserve ()
Save ()
SetKey ()
SetPerformance ()
SetPerformanceDate ()
SetPONumber ()
SetPrice ()
SetSeatQuantity ()
SetSection ()

Figure 5-24—Control Class Diagram After Increment 2

220 ■ Chapter 5

Customer

classCustomer
m_Customer_Credit_Card_Expires
m_Customer_Credit_Card_Number
m_Customer_Credit_Card_Type
m_Customer_Name_First
m_Customer_Name_Last
m_Customer_Phone_Number

Customer ()
_GetBaseClass ()
AssertValid ()
DoFieldExchange ()
Dump ()
GetDefaultDBName ()
GetDefaultSQL ()
GetRuntimeClass ()

Purchase

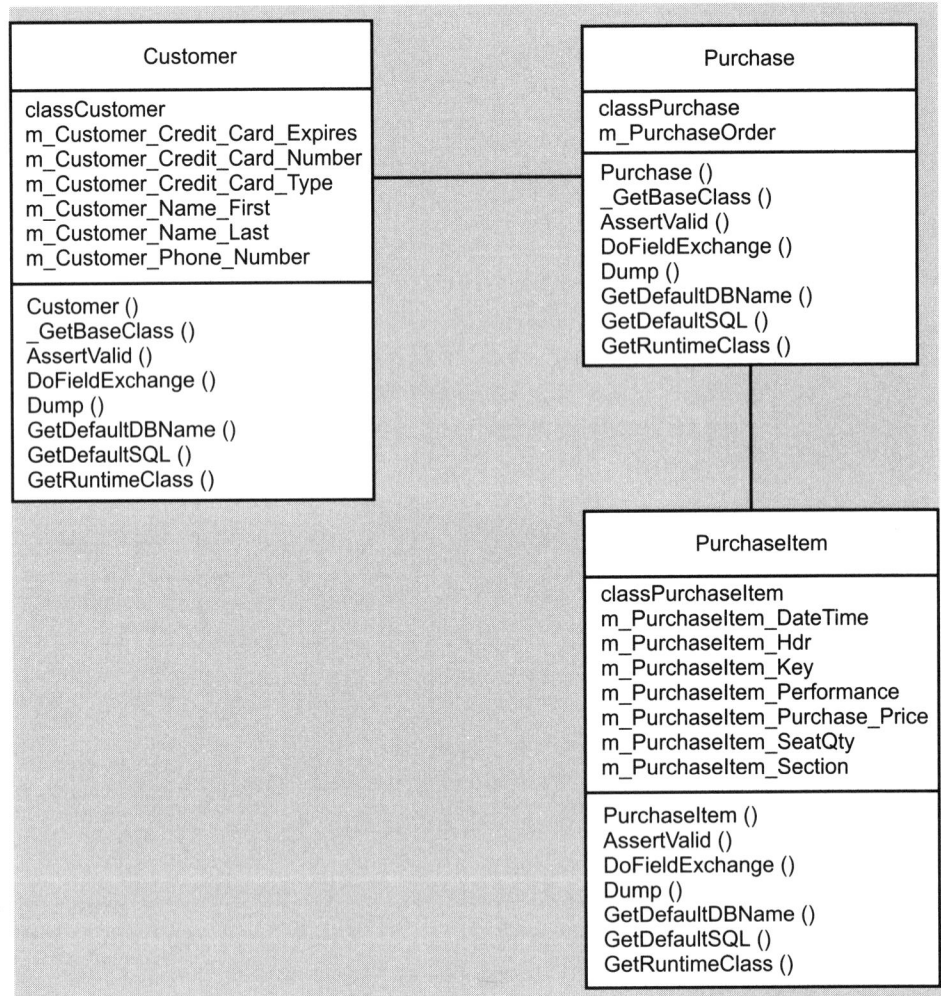

classPurchase
m_PurchaseOrder

Purchase ()
_GetBaseClass ()
AssertValid ()
DoFieldExchange ()
Dump ()
GetDefaultDBName ()
GetDefaultSQL ()
GetRuntimeClass ()

PurchaseItem

classPurchaseItem
m_PurchaseItem_DateTime
m_PurchaseItem_Hdr
m_PurchaseItem_Key
m_PurchaseItem_Performance
m_PurchaseItem_Purchase_Price
m_PurchaseItem_SeatQty
m_PurchaseItem_Section

PurchaseItem ()
AssertValid ()
DoFieldExchange ()
Dump ()
GetDefaultDBName ()
GetDefaultSQL ()
GetRuntimeClass ()

*Figure 5-25—
Entity Class
Diagram After
Increment 2*

Chapter Summary

In this chapter, we demonstrated the traceability of the Use Case Diagram to other object models, the application code, the database, and other supporting materials. We showed how textual descriptions of Use Case Scenarios define scope, functionality, and information for a specific use of the system. The Use Case Scenario identifies information and behavior that the Sequence Diagram then translates into objects and sequential messages that connect them. The Sequence Diagram identifies busy objects that the State Diagram organizes to depict object life cycles. For complex activity within an object state, the Activity Diagram details the procedural steps to complete the activity. The Sequence Diagram easily translates into a Collaboration Diagram that provides a view of the object as it participates in a specific interaction. The Use Case Diagram identifies likely user interfaces to prototype. Prototyping adds further detail to object information and interaction. Use Case Scenarios also drive user documentation and training materials.

We showed how each of these deliverables provides distinct views for refining and validating the Class Diagram. We extended the Class Diagram operations to specify the application code as methods. We discussed how the classes then package into well-contained components for anticipated deployment on the appropriate processor. The Class Diagram also provides direction to the definition of the database. We discussed how the differing purposes of the Class Diagram and the database cause translation difficulties between classes and relational database tables.

The deliverables discussed in this chapter are the building blocks that must eventually communicate with classes developed by other Solution Areas. We integrate these Solution Area deliverables in the next chapter.

Chapter 6
Integrate Solution

Overview

The Integrate Solution phase synthesizes the new work with the old and with the other Solution Areas. During integration, you want to leverage existing or concurrent work. This reduces replicated effort while providing the foundation to build reusable objects. This is the convergence point for multiple Solution Area teams to align their work with each other. The timing of when a Solution Area is ready for integration rarely coincides with the other Solution Areas. Still, integration must occur with the "best view" of the other Solution Areas to keep progressing to the final solution.

Larger organizations may have the luxury of an Object Administration group to oversee consistency and manage meaning. This group likely evolved from what was once a Data Administration group. If such a group does not exist within your organization, the responsibility rests with the Object Architects from all of the Solution Areas. Be sure to

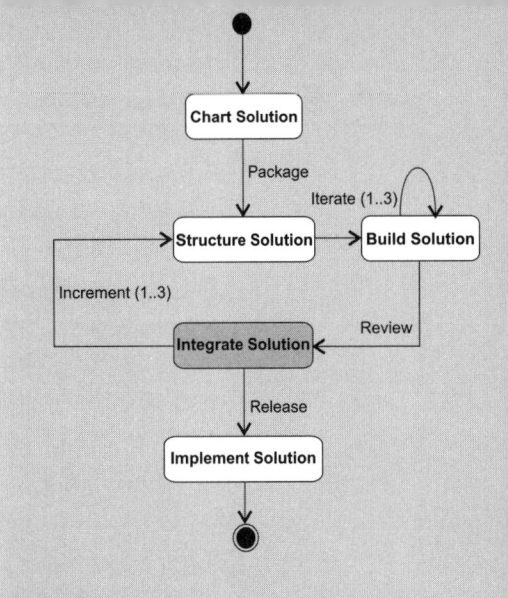

Deliverables:

Application
Change Requests
Class Diagram
Component Diagram
Deployment Diagram
Documentation Distribution Procedure
Information Reference Guide
Integration Test Beds
Integration Test Plan
Issues List
Logical Data Model
Operations Guide
Project Plan
Risk Assessment
Solution Area Classes/ Implementation Classes Matrix
Solution Area Database
Solution Area Database Structure
Solution Integration Confirmation
Training Support Materials
User Instructions Guide

plan for the availability of the Object Architect to allow participation when needed.

Some of the developed solution may be ready to implement as is. Look for "quick hits" that benefit the business, even if the full solution is not yet complete.

Although we require this phase to occur here as a convergence point, we recommend frequent informal integration of deliverables throughout development. Doing so minimizes the pain of the design ownership wars that may occur.

At the end of this phase, you loop back to the Structure Solution phase, establish the content for the next increment, and again spin through the Build Solution phase and its iterations before returning here. The final solution, or a partial solution ready for implementation, takes you to the Implement Solution phase; otherwise, you again loop back to the Structure Solution phase to take on the next content to develop.

The Case Study describes the integration of the Reserve Seating Solution Area with the Contract Performance Solution Area and its effect on the Class and Component Diagrams. We also illustrate the Deployment Diagram, readying it for implementation. We assume the integration of the second increment customer demographics and address standardization from the first increment of the Reserve Seating Solution Area has already occurred.

Activities

Integrate Solution Areas

The Solution Area team reviews all deliverables from the Build Solution phase and integrates all additions and changes.

> **Deliverables**
>
> Solution Area Classes/ Implementation Classes Matrix
> Class Diagram
> Logical Data Model
> Change Requests
> Project Plan
> Solution Area Database Structure
> Solution Area Database
> Application

Tasks:

Integrate Class Diagrams

Role(s): Project Manager (Facilitator), Object Architect, and Database Architect

The Object Architect assesses the current view of the solution against any existing implementation to incorporate changes and additions from integration needed to implement. The Object Architect and the Database Architect document changes to classes previously implemented in the class library and production database using a Solution Area Classes/Implementation Classes Matrix. This matrix identifies the classes and databases affected by the forthcoming implementation.

This task is a cross-Solution Area working session to reconcile classes for common naming, definition, content, and structure. Classes are reconciled with the implemented class library and other Solution Areas to enhance the enterprise understanding of the developed classes. The goal is to identify reusability of the common class structures.

The Solution Area team addresses the portions of their Application deemed ready for immediate implementation with a higher priority and urgency. They only apply those changes that affect their Solution Area. Other Solution Areas may not be ready for implementing their solution pieces. It becomes important to recognize the change early, though, so that these changes do not wait until the other Solution Area becomes ready for implementation.

These people also meet with their Solution Area counterparts to remove redundancies in classes shared by multiple Solution Areas and to maintain clear custodianship of each class to minimize replicated work. This is the last check that everything planned has ownership responsibility assigned for each iteration. Note this task may encompass all deliverables created or changed thus far.

After the integration sessions, the Object Architect and the Infrastructure Architect create a Solution Area Classes/Implementation Classes Matrix. They use the information from the integration session and the Change Requests from the Build Solution phase as a reference to organize any remaining enhancements to make the solution ready for implementation. They assemble all of this into the Integration Change Document.

The Project Manager captures any additional work stemming from this task back into the Change Requests. The Project Manager assesses the impact and changes the Project Plan as needed.

Case Study Recall that the Contract Performance Solution Area defines performance and establishes ticket prices. We assumed early on that pricing changes in the Reserve Seating use case are the responsibility of the Ticket class. Originally, the Contract Performances Solution Area had planned to define prices by Ticket. Recall, though, that we suggested to the Contract Performances Solution Area team to consider a simpler means—pricing by Section rather than by Ticket. The solution the Contract Performance Solution Area arrived at was the Classification class, which they own. Because we anticipated this early on and the entire project team considered this the right solution, we forestalled a painful integration that could have occurred had we waited.

The Contract Performance Solution Area establishes initial performance information and ticket prices. Figure 6-1—Contract Performance Solution Area Class Diagram provides a view of the Class Diagram that we reference for integration.

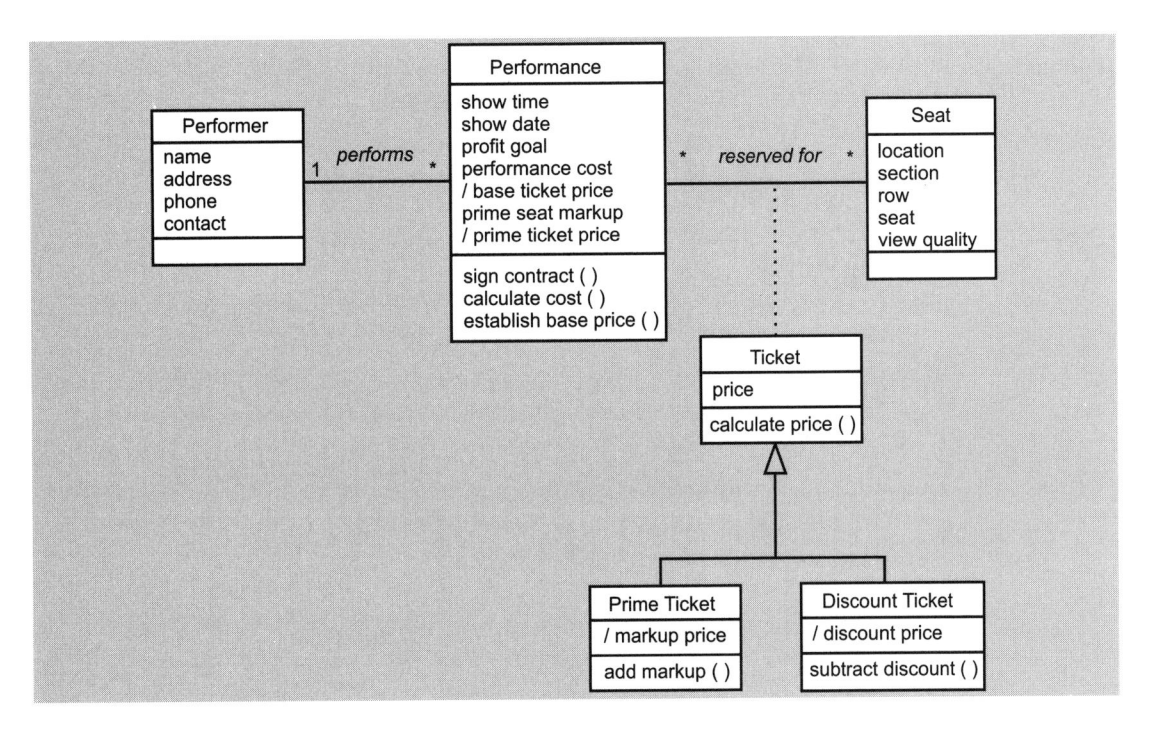

Figure 6-1—Contract Performance Solution Area Class Diagram

The Performances form built during the Reserve Seating Build Solution iterations shows performance information. Since Contract Performances has the responsibility to define a performance, we need to integrate this information. Figure 6-2—Reserve Seating Class Diagram of Performance shows how the Reserve Seating Solution Area defined Performance.

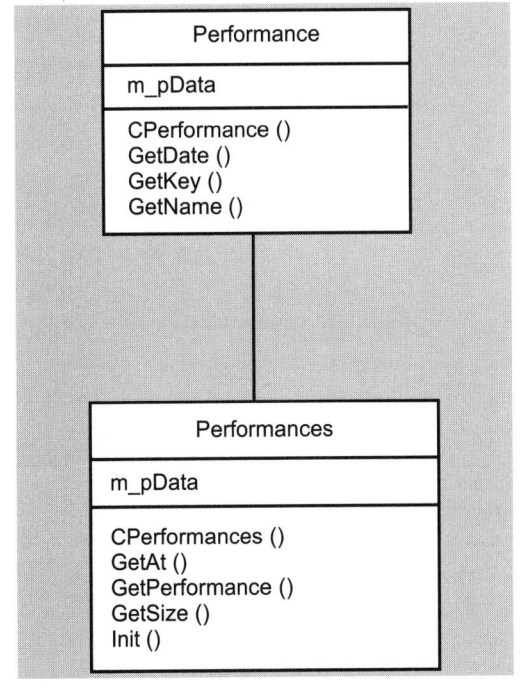

Figure 6-2—Reserve Seating Class Diagram of Performance

When determining base ticket price, the business includes the cost of the performance plus the standard markup per ticket. A "prime" seating location adds an additional markup to the base price of the ticket. The Contract Performance Solution Area has a more refined view of pricing. We incorporate the attributes and methods of Performance needed by the Reserve Seating Solution Area into that of the Contract Performance Solution Area. Figure 6-3—Integrated Reserve Seating and Contract Performance Class Diagram shows the integrated view.

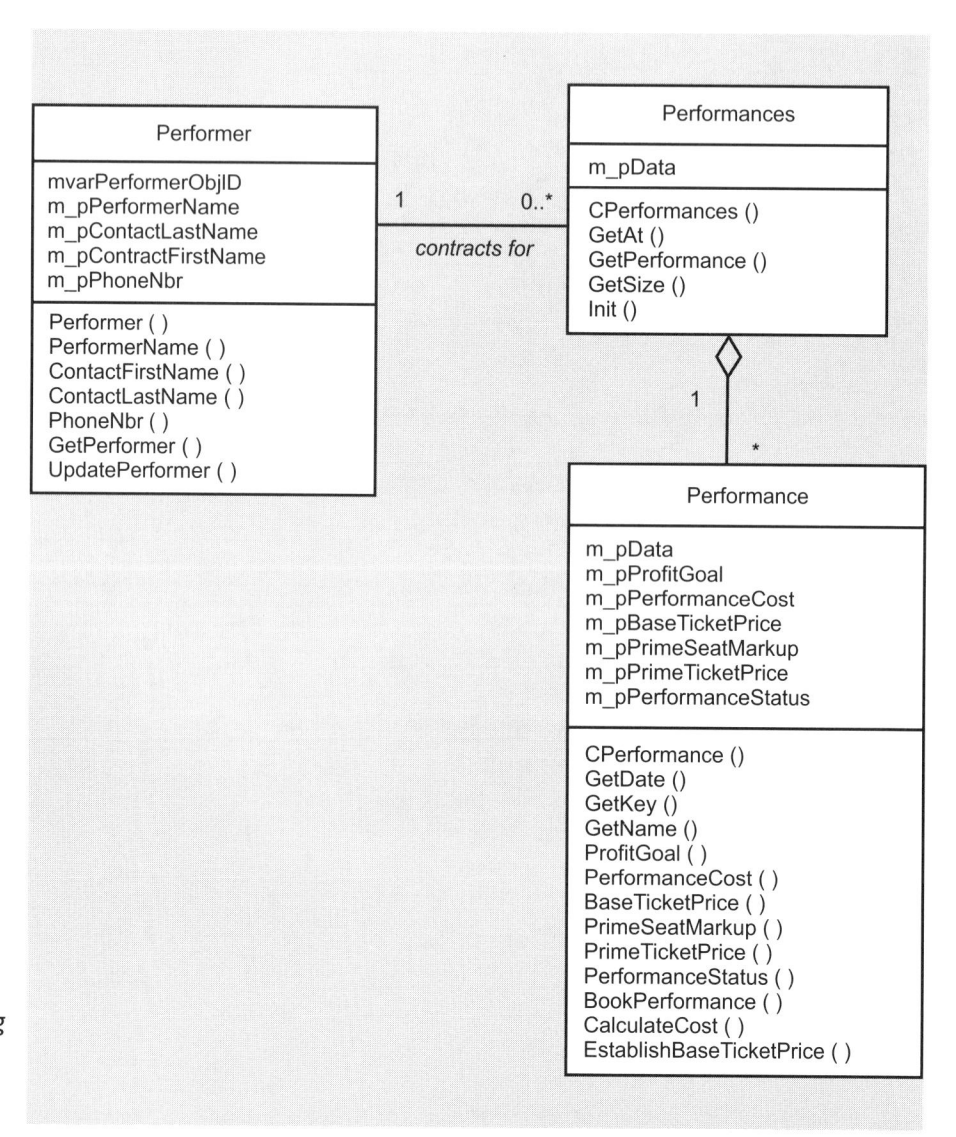

Performer
mvarPerformerObjID
m_pPerformerName
m_pContactLastName
m_pContractFirstName
m_pPhoneNbr
Performer ( )
PerformerName ( )
ContactFirstName ( )
ContactLastName ( )
PhoneNbr ( )
GetPerformer ( )
UpdatePerformer ( )

1   contracts for   0..*

Performances
m_pData
CPerformances ( )
GetAt ( )
GetPerformance ( )
GetSize ( )
Init ( )

Performance
m_pData
m_pProfitGoal
m_pPerformanceCost
m_pBaseTicketPrice
m_pPrimeSeatMarkup
m_pPrimeTicketPrice
m_pPerformanceStatus
CPerformance ( )
GetDate ( )
GetKey ( )
GetName ( )
ProfitGoal ( )
PerformanceCost ( )
BaseTicketPrice ( )
PrimeSeatMarkup ( )
PrimeTicketPrice ( )
PerformanceStatus ( )
BookPerformance ( )
CalculateCost ( )
EstablishBaseTicketPrice ( )

Figure 6-3—
Integrated
Reserve Seating
and Contract
Performance
Class Diagram

The Reserve Seating Solution Area team notices that Ticket does not have a "print" operation. The Contract Performance team did not include the actual printing of tickets within the scope of their solution since the business currently pays a print shop to handle printing. This answers the outstanding Issue 6, to have tickets printed at the time of purchase. For the current solution, the team decides that purchases for tickets reserved at other locations will continue to be mailed to the customer or shipped to the purchasing location. Refer to Table 6-1 for the updated Issues List.

Table 6-1—Issues List

Num	Issue Description	Resolution
1.	What content belongs on the Internet? Options include schedules, performers, concert dates, and locations, with query capability for any of the above.	The Promote Performance Solution Area will use the Internet to broaden the target market. The Reserve Seating Solution Area also offers potential where the customer directly purchases tickets through the Internet. Postpone Reserve Seating Internet development until after deployment of the core solution.
2.	Does purchase information need to interface to the accounting system?	Not for the first release. Reconsider in next year's budget.
3.	Will we support payment by check?	No. Checks present too much of a credit risk. Reconsider automated check verification as an enhancement after first release.
4.	What is the difference between reservation and purchase?	No difference. We will use the term purchase, since the customer does not reserve a ticket; the customer purchases a ticket.
5.	What is the difference between a seat and a ticket?	The seat is part of a location. The ticket, in the real world, represents a seat. A customer purchases a ticket to attend a performance in that seat.
6.	Can we have tickets printed at the time of purchase? Are purchases allowed for tickets at other locations? (Currently, tickets are preprinted, so the ticket has to be mailed to the customer or shipped to the purchase location.)	Because the business currently pays a print shop to handle printing, tickets cannot be printed at the time of purchase. Purchases for tickets reserved at other locations will continue to be mailed to the customer or shipped to the purchasing location.

Integrate Database Structures

Role(s): Project Manager (Facilitator) and Database Architect

The Database Architect assesses the current view of the solution against any existing implementation to incorporate changes and additions from integration needed to implement. The Database Architect documents changes to the database structure previously implemented in the production database.

Case Study The Contract Performance Solution Area needs integration of the database similar to the integration in the Class Diagram. Note in Figure 6-4—Integrated Logical Data Model that the Performance class retains the status as an attribute. Yet in the database, status has its own table. The status of Performance is mapped to the Performance object in the data layer object that builds the individual Performance object.

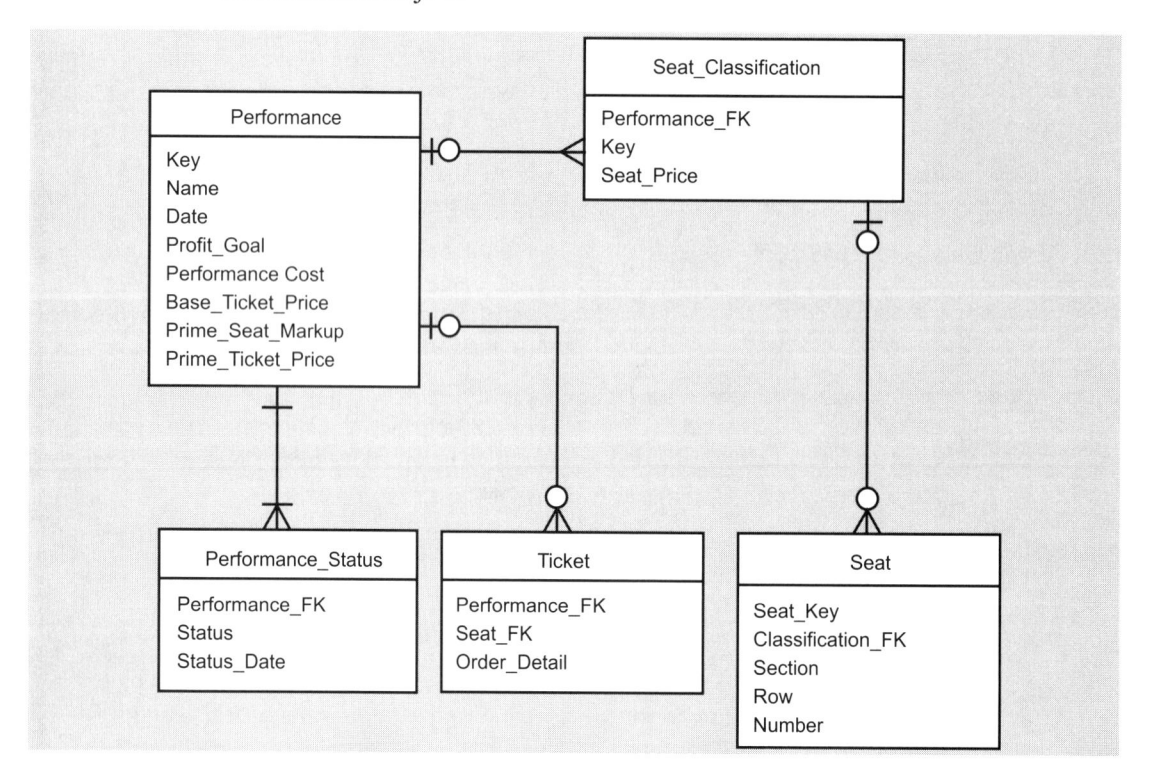

Performance
- Key
- Name
- Date
- Profit_Goal
- Performance Cost
- Base_Ticket_Price
- Prime_Seat_Markup
- Prime_Ticket_Price

Seat_Classification
- Performance_FK
- Key
- Seat_Price

Performance_Status
- Performance_FK
- Status
- Status_Date

Ticket
- Performance_FK
- Seat_FK
- Order_Detail

Seat
- Seat_Key
- Classification_FK
- Section
- Row
- Number

Figure 6-4—Integrated Logical Data Model

Modify Application for Integration

Role(s): Object Architect, Object Developer, and Document Architect

The group develops the interfaces required to communicate between Solution Areas and external systems. This includes remote access considerations. They create the code for the methods that communicate across Solution Areas.

The Object Developer makes the changes to the Application identified in the Integration Change Document. The Object Developer gives special attention to finalizing the Application to fit the implementation environment and standards.

The Database Architect applies any implementation-specific changes to the database structure including performance and capacity adjustments.

Note that we integrate the code from two Solution Areas, but we also must apply any coding standards that have evolved since the beginning of the project. Three possible situations may have occurred since beginning the project. One, the project team did not know all the standards. Two, the project team did not know all the standards needed at the start of the project. Three, the team knew the standards, but the standards changed since the project began—not the best situation, but it happens. You should allow time to respond to these kinds of changes. This also plans contingency for the unforeseen. For example, when you began building the Solution Area, the Information Technology department may have built a utility class that gives all applications the same look and feel. You may decide that it greatly enhances your Application and should incorporate it now. Sometimes, you do not have the choice. If you do not use the utility, the Information Technology department may not support your Application!

Case Study Since the Contract Performance solution area "owns" Performance, we merge the Reserve Seating Solution Area Performance class methods and attributes into theirs. Testing of the Performance class should include both the integration points and full regression testing.

Refine Implementation Diagrams

We begin looking for tightly coupled classes to determine the components for this system. Once defined, you place the components on the Deployment Diagram to show potential installation on processors.

Deliverables

Component Diagram
Deployment Diagram
Operations Guide

Tasks:

Enhance Component Diagram

Role(s): Object Architect

The Object Architect reviews the individual Component Diagrams developed within each Solution Area to combine or further decompose components.

Case Study For the Case Study, we add the Customer Demographics business services layer and data services layer as separate components. Note that the Reserve Seating user interface acts as the user interface component for accessing the Customer Demographics components. We also add the purchased address standardization package and access it only through the Customer Demographics business component. The Contract Performance Solution Area also has three components following the three-tier structure. Figure 6-5—Integrated Component Diagram shows the component packaging after integration.

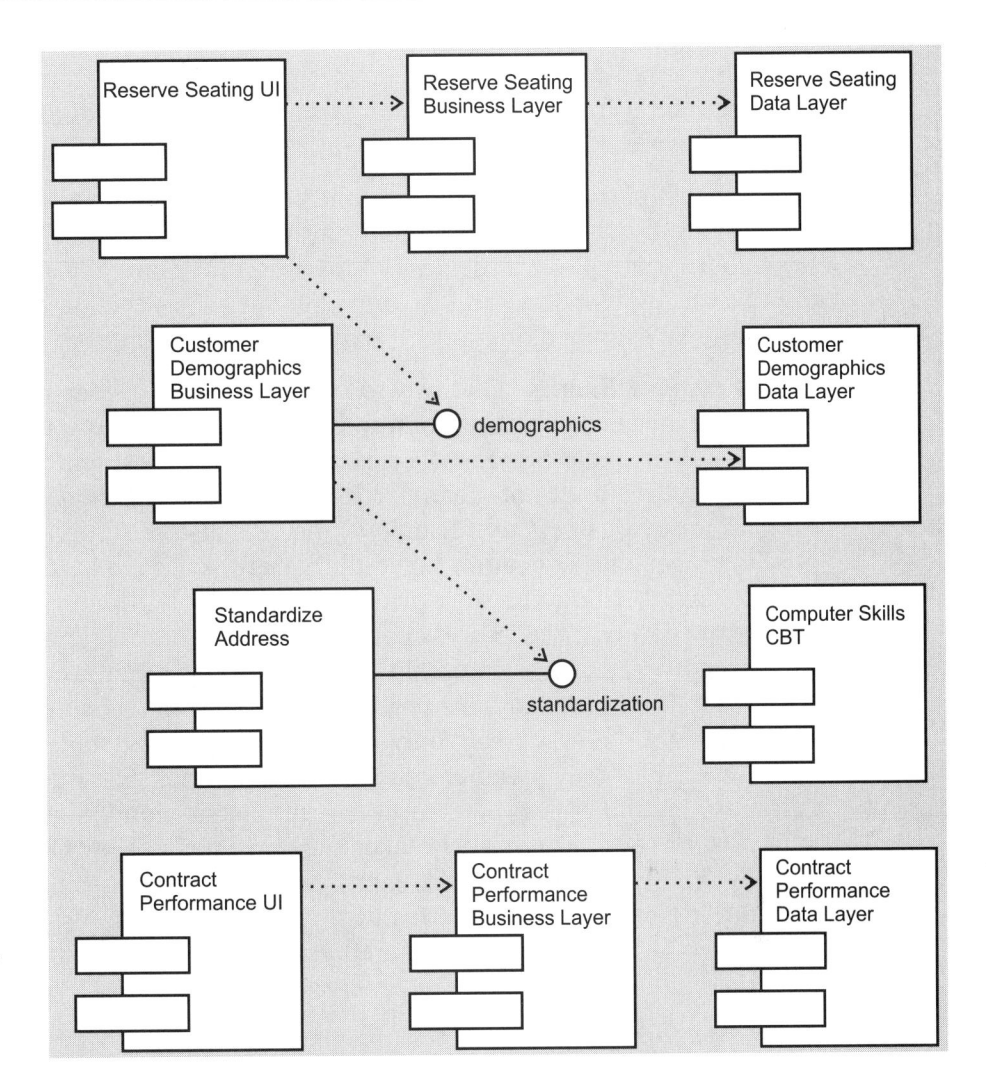

Figure 6-5—
Integrated
Component
Diagram

Create and Integrate Deployment Diagram

Role(s): Object Architect, Database Architect, and Infrastructure Architect

The Object Architect and Infrastructure Architect discuss the proper partitioning and placement of the components on the processors. They address partitioning issues such as data distribution, processor load balancing, and *n*-tier architecture decisions. They place these components on an individual Deployment Diagram for each Solution Area.

After establishing the needs for each Solution Area, the Object Architect and Infrastructure Architect integrate the individual Solution Area Deployment Diagrams to arrive at the enterprise view.

What is partitioning? It is the splitting and combining of packages to represent where objects should physically reside and execute on the appropriate physical device. We partition for many reasons, including balancing workload and isolating changes. This section discusses the influences on making a good partitioning decision.

Business Events One way to partition is to consider what organizations in the business respond to business events. You group together the objects that provide the services needed to respond to the business event. This does not mean partitioning by organization structure, but rather by business use. Examples include customer services, resource management, education scheduling. Here you have an opportunity to re-engineer how the software currently supports the business. Today many corporations process data by functional areas, known as vertical or stovepipe processing. This leads to solutions that are difficult to reuse. It is better to have processing respond to a business event and complete the processing only when it has provided value to the customer. This may mean crossing functional areas. For example, a business today may have three distinct departments that handle a customer's order. Order Entry takes the customer's order, Credit verifies the ability to pay, and Customer Delivery informs the customer that the order is ready for pickup. Instead, you could design a single system that takes the order, verifies credit immediately, and estimates pickup time all during the initial contact with the customer.

Geography Some business events may occur at specific geographic locations, for example, providing Customer Services in Milwaukee, Chicago, and Detroit. Resource Management may occur only in Milwaukee. You want to distribute objects to the appropriate geographic locations. Knowing which locations use objects is important because you do not want to access data from a remote site unnecessarily. Objects with a high degree of coupling (i.e., objects that exchange messaging frequently) should be kept together geographically.

Processor Types Knowing geographically where you intend to deploy a system dictates the kinds of processors needed at each geographic site. For distributed systems, you may need to support intersite communication through a network or replicate objects.

Volume and size of transactions may dictate how many tiers you need. When designing the infrastructure architecture, a major decision is whether to implement a two-tier, three-tier, or *n*-tier architecture. Two-tier architecture is typically well suited for tactical operations when traffic is low (for example, less than 100 users), response is quick, volume is small, and interactions are isolated.

You should deploy an object on the hardware device appropriate to its processing needs. Generally, you deploy business logic as packaged components of control objects on the application server. Business logic involves calculations or accessing multiple objects. Through object-oriented deployment, your business is able to adapt more quickly to a business need with less pain. To ensure security, you may want a separate processor. Creating separate control classes to manage security makes this transition smoother.

You typically deploy user interface objects on the client. If you factor in the Internet, the user interface object may be deployed on the web server, be passed to the browser, and run components on the client.

You normally deploy entity objects on the database server. Placing methods directly in a database encapsulates entity objects but affects scalability if the database management system changes. As the number of users outgrow the database server, you can install a larger processor and isolate the upgrade to entity objects. This, then, achieves scalability and stability. When the business rules change, this may only affect control objects, thus achieving stability and localizing change. If you need to upgrade the database server because of the increase in transaction activity, and if the upgrade requires a software change, you can easily isolate that change to objects on the database server. Having the control object retain the code for accessing entity objects thereby separates the access logic from the storage physicality.

Distributing physical data has its advantages and disadvantages. Central storage avoids issues of inconsistency. Because it is the central processor, it must be able to scale up as access increases. However, when the database fails with this design, the whole system is unusable. Storing data on a client processor increases availability, but it limits data sharing or requires synchronization if data is to appear consistent among users. Additionally, it may be necessary to replicate data across several hundred client processors. For more information, see the discussion on Data Replication below.

Performance You may need to repartition based on current and projected network traffic. This means moving objects from one processor to another to improve performance. The level of concurrent use, the occurrences of events, transaction size and duration, network transmission speed and sequential processing all affect performance. Performance includes not only the speed of execution, but also the quality of execution, that is, doing it the right way. Speed alone is not enough.

Adding applications to the network affects response time and network traffic. This addition can be quite significant, degrading the performance of all previously installed applications.

Monitoring performance begins during development and continues throughout the life of a system. Persistent monitoring helps prevent bottlenecks from occurring during critical business production.

Other factors to consider include:

1. How large is the complete database if there is only one database?
2. How many tables are in a typical join? The more complex the table interconnectivity, the more resource consumption.
3. How many data sources are there and of what variety?

Data Replication Replicating data means physically storing the same data in multiple databases. Replication introduces data redundancy to improve access performance or data recoverability, but at a cost of storage, network use, and maintainability. This design decreases the impact of failure but increases the potential number of failure points. Replication also requires synchronization. Some guidelines for replication are:

1. Use a central database if you need to see all changes to data immediately, as there is always a lack of tools, personnel, and support infrastructure to manage distributed data.
2. Partition data if distributed users need different cuts of data, horizontally or vertically.
3. Replicate the database if distributed access need is for read only or distributed users need the same data but not immediate access to all updates.

Data Availability Data availability refers to the perceived need to have instantaneous information. However, it may be acceptable to refresh the data every 24 hours or longer. You may ask yourself if users are satisfied with weekly refreshes of replicated data.

Availability also includes backup and disaster recovery. Consider contingency for a "crashed" application or system and the manual business processes required to operate until the system is up and running again. Strive to solidify the application to guard against this. Recognize, though, that the shorter the required downtime, the higher the cost to design failsafe mechanisms and build them into the system. Placing this cost in the proper perspective, you ask the budget planners "what is the cost to your business if the system is down for 'x' hours?"

Economics The bottom line always determines what you do. Provide alternatives for both a low-cost architecture and one that the business can grow into when funds become available. This may even mean falling back to a two-tier architectural design that significantly affects object partitioning. Understand this may simply delay cost, and the net present value could be better to do it now. Refer to the Prepare the Cost/Benefit Analysis task in the Chart Solution phase.

Maintenance Support Do you have the personnel to support a remote database considering maintenance, security management, backup, and recovery? If unable to administer it locally, you may not want a processor located at that site unless you have distributed management tools. Choose the tools based on the requirements, not the other way around.

Legacy Systems Of course, you may have an existing system or legacy system. It is best to interface with these systems in a very contained fashion so that if you change or remove those systems, you minimize the effect on the new system. In fact, treat the system interface as just that—an interface object (recall that external systems are actors on the Use Case Diagram). Resist the temptation to spread your architecture across these systems in a way that forever ties your fortunes to the existence of that processor. It is much more prudent to put in a separate processor to deal with the other processor on a messaging basis. Then, you do not compromise the new system by removing the interfacing system. With luck, you may only have to update the shared messages.

We do suggest reviewing a partitioning strategy to meet future growth. For example, if our brave little company experiences massive growth, we want to simply redeploy the components, as is, to multiple remote locations. Confirm an overall view of which components are possible to deploy this way (within a five-year planning horizon), as it has a great impact on how to code the specific methods. Therefore, always write components as standalone as possible to prevent rewriting the application later.

Case Study The Manage Location Solution Area deployed its components similar to Figure 6-6—Manage Location Deployment Diagram.

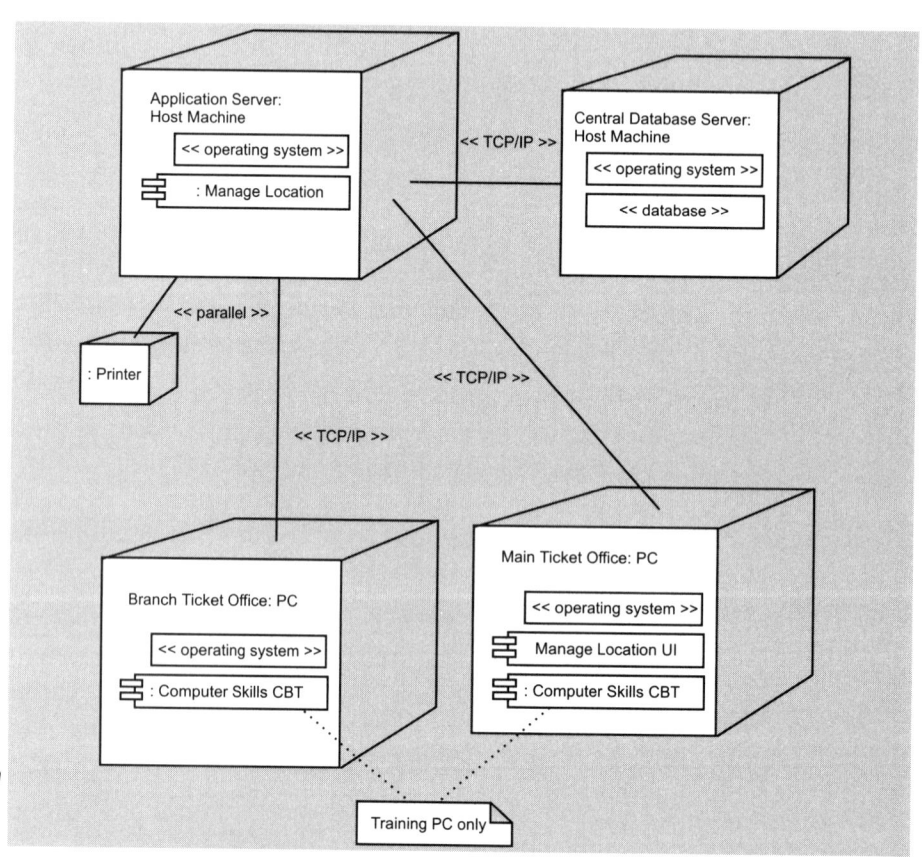

Figure 6-6—Manage Location Deployment Diagram

The deployment diagram created for the Reserve Seating Solution Area is shown in Figure 6-7—Reserve Seating Deployment Diagram. The Contract Performance Solution Area created a similar view.

Integrating the Reserve Seating and Contract Performance Solution Areas with the Manage Location Solution Area produces a new deployment diagram as depicted in Figure 6-8—Integrated Manage Location, Reserve Seating, and Contract Performance Deployment Diagram.

Integrate Solution ■ **239**

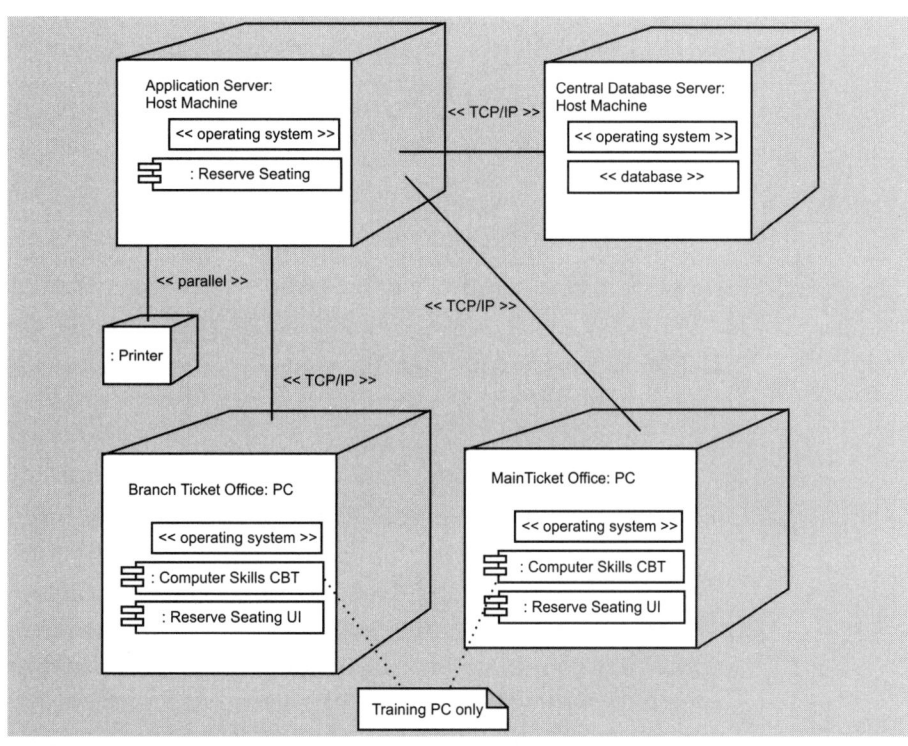

Figure 6-7— Reserve Seating Deployment Diagram

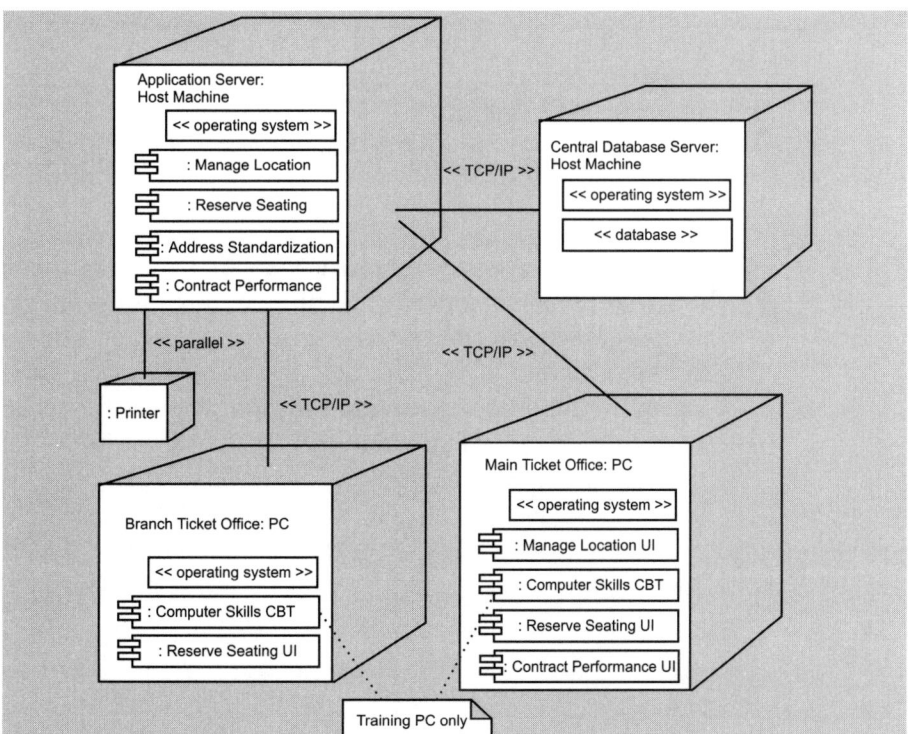

Figure 6-8— Integrated Manage Location, Reserve Seating, and Contract Performance Deployment Diagram

We add the Reserve Seating user interface to both the branch and main ticket office PCs. We also add the Reserve Seating business and data layer components and Address Standardization to the local application servers. For performance reasons, the data layer components reside on local servers and access the central database server. We only need to add the Contract Performance user interface to the main ticket office PCs because we perform this function centrally. We can easily transport these classes to another node to improve performance later.

Build Operations Guide

Role(s): Infrastructure Architect and Document Architect

The Infrastructure Architect identifies how the system operator should keep the system functioning properly. The Document Architect documents the procedures to support the Application including security, backup, and disaster recovery.

The Operations Guide includes schedules of when to back up the system, when to initiate any hardcopy reports, and when to start any time-initiated events. The Infrastructure Architect creates the initial Operations Guide with help from the Document Architect.

Note that we would have liked to work on this task earlier in the approach; however, this cannot happen until after completing the decisions for deployment.

You must test the Operations Guide in a non-critical setting to verify coverage of as many contingencies as possible.

Case Study The system must be available during normal business hours. Support personnel back up incremental updates of personal computers weekly through the application server. The application and database servers incrementally back up every night during non-peak hours; the database transaction journal suffices for recovery between the incremental backups. The Infrastructure Architect schedules full monthly backups of all servers for the first week of the month. All monthly backups are stored off-site. The Operations Guide to accompany these instructions looks similar to Table 6-2—Excerpt from Operations Guide.

Table 6-2—Excerpt from Operations Guide

Normal Backup Schedule

Day	Time	Task
Friday	11:00 PM	Run client PC backups to tape.
All	12:00 AM	Run incremental application and database server backups to tape.
End of Month	12:00 AM	Run full database and application server backups to tape. Duplicate tape and store off-site.

Recovery Run Procedures
1. Restore the full backup from the previous month to the appropriate database or application server.
2. Restore all incremental backups since the full backup to same server as in step 1.
3. Restore the database from the transaction journal.

In our Case Study, the operator that supports the system assumes responsibility for future maintenance.

Integrate Documentation

The Documentation Architect assembles and combines all documentation components for this increment. Unlike integrating the solution by merging content, this task only assembles the various pieces to validate completion. It may not make sense to create one big set of documentation when the various Solution Areas have dramatically different Users.

Deliverables

User Instructions Guide
Information Reference Guide
Documentation Distribution Procedure

Tasks:

Standardize User Instructions Guide

Role(s): Document Architect and Object Developer

The Document Architect assembles and edits all of the User Instructions Guide components for comprehension, flow, and usability. The Document Architect works with the Object Developer to link any needed information references directly to the Application.

Standardize Information Reference Guide

Role(s): Document Architect

The Document Architect assembles and edits all of the Information Reference Guide components for comprehension, flow, and usability.

Standardize Documentation Distribution Procedure

Role(s): Document Architect

The Document Architect creates the procedure steps for distributing updated documentation to Users according to project or enterprise-wide standards.

Integrate Training

The Trainer merges all curriculum content for this increment into a cohesive package of training support materials. Again, this is much like documentation; it only assembles the various components to create a complete package. Any merging of content between Solution Areas exists solely for reusability.

Deliverables

Training Support Materials

Modify Training for Integration

Role(s): Trainer

The Trainer makes the changes to the Training Support Materials identified in the Integration Change Document. The Trainer gives special attention to finalizing the Training Support Materials to fit the implementation environment and standards.

Transform Training Curriculum into Training Support Materials

Role(s): Trainer and Object Developer

The Trainer assembles the entire curriculum content created for this increment and transforms it into training support materials in the style of the selected training delivery vehicle. This may entail a great amount of work! For example, coordinating video shoots or the development of CBT software (if not purchased) has a logistical component that may seem to supersede the effort to create the content. The Trainer works with the Object Developer to link any training support materials directly to the Application.

Integration Test the Solution

During this activity, the Solution Area team makes sure that the current version of the incremental area correctly communicates with existing software to which it interfaces and correctly performs all functionality.

Deliverables

Integration Test Plan
Integration Test Beds

Tasks:

Create Integration Test Plan

Role(s): Object Architect

The Object Architect assembles the separate Solution Area test plans into one cohesive Integration Test Plan. The Object Architect adds tests specific to the integrated changes.

The breadth of integration testing includes all concurrently developed Solution Areas. The depth tests inter-Solution Area messaging, core scenarios, alternative paths, and exceptions that alter inter-Solution Area conditions. Integration testing begins with confirming the appropriateness and correctness of new and enhanced inter-solution messaging. This moves into a full test of the system. This test combines requirements testing, stress testing, and regression testing. Requirements testing includes other system-specific needs such as distribution and response. For regression testing, you exercise the reusable test cases saved from previous implementations (that is, previous versions of the solution). Stress testing determines the limits on the system in terms of concurrent use and data volume.

Case Study For the Case Study, we specifically pay attention to the Performance class. Not only do we test the conditions affected by the integration, but we thoroughly regression test. Table 6-3—Integration Test Plan illustrates an example of the Integration Test Plan as well as some regression test cases. Note that most of the regression test cases came directly from the use case and collaboration test cases established during the Solution Area builds.

Table 6-3—Integration Test Plan

Integration Test Plan: Purchase

Scope: New performance establishes ticket pricing and customer purchases a ticket.

Num	Test Condition	Expected Result
1.	New performance contracted. Customer purchases a single ticket.	New Performance information defined. Performance cost is accurately calculated. Ticket prices are established for each section. Performance is booked. Customer's order accurately reflects Ticket price. Ticket becomes unavailable.
2.	New date and time contracted for a previously contracted Performance. Customer requests Performance information for the new date and purchases multiple tickets.	New date and time setup for a similar Performance. Performance cost is accurately calculated. Ticket prices are established for each section. Performance is booked. Customer sees list of performances for that date. Multiple seats reserved.
3.	New date and time established for a Performance previously contracted. Performance entered but not booked. Customer requests Performance information.	Newest date and time not shown.
4.	Customer requests Performance information but does not purchase.	No purchase.

Num	Test Condition	Expected Result
5.	Customer requests Performance information but cancels purchase after seats reserved.	Reserved tickets remain available. Purchase total is zero.
6.	Customer requests Performance information for a sold-out Performance.	Customer sees alternative Performances.
7.	Multiple locations attempt to reserve tickets for the same performance at the same location.	Ticket reserved only once in a first come, first serve order. Other locations know of the potential for the reservation without waiting for the entire transaction to complete.

Build Integration Test Beds

Role(s): Object Developer

The Object Developer assembles the current increment's Use Case Test Beds into the regression and stress test beds to create one cohesive Integration Test Bed.

Prepare Integration Environment for Testing

Role(s): Infrastructure Architect, Database Architect, and Object Architect

The Infrastructure Architect installs hardware and configures software for the network and all other processors, including client machines. The integration test environment should mimic the final implementation environment as closely as possible to support the planned testing.

The Database Architect installs and configures the database management system. Then, the Database Architect creates an Integration Database incorporating the current Solution Area Database Structure with the previous release. The Object Developer, with assistance from the Database Architect, loads the Integration Test Bed into a separate test area and reloads it as needed to support the integration test.

The Object Architect distributes the recent version of source components on the appropriate processors following the Deployment Diagram.

Integration Test the Application

Role(s): Object Architect, Object Developer, Document Architect, Database Architect, Trainer, and Project Manager

The Object Architect exercises the Integration Test Plan. The Project Manager faithfully records all variances from the expected results on the Change Requests. The Object Developer, Document Architect, Trainer, and Database Architect enhance their deliverables to address identified variances.

Confirm Solution Integration

The Solution Area team reviews deliverables produced thus far and confirms that the team has accurately integrated the solution with the previous version and other Solution Areas.

Deliverables

Solution Integration Confirmation
Project Plan
Issues List
Change Requests
Risk Assessment

Tasks:

Obtain Solution Integration Confirmation

Role(s): Project Manager (Facilitator) and Business Area Expert

The Project Manager reviews validation results of the Integrate Solution phase with the Business Area Experts and obtains confirmation to proceed to the Implement Solution phase. The project team also reviews open issues, risks, and change requests.

Assess Risk

Role(s): Project Manager

The Project Manager updates the Risk Assessment, having addressed all threats and weaknesses. The Project Manager reviews and updates the project plan to accommodate the actual time spent, any uncovered changes, and revisions to the estimates.

Case Study Refer to Table 6-4—Integrate Solution Risk Assessment.

Table 6-4—Integrate Solution Risk Assessment

Category	Item	Action
Strength	Infrastructure discussions went well.	Post the final diagram in a common area for everyone to see.
Weakness	It seemed that too much time was spent discussing the definition of Ticket between the two solution areas. The teams did not sound like they were part of the same business.	Look for ways to get the groups together ahead of time, informally if possible, in order to create common ground.
	Response time is a concern.	Determine benchmarking statistics. Explore distributing some of the objects to branch ticket office servers.
Opportunity	Prototype session at the company sales meeting was a hit.	Good publicity.
Threat	Scheduling the integration meetings took longer than anticipated, although it was on the project plan. This caused a delay in holding a Contract Performance facilitated session and irritated the Business Area Experts.	Be sure to send out meeting notices at least two weeks in advance and request an RSVP.
	Performer cancellation affects customers extra hard with the non-refund policy on purchases.	Implement the solution as is. Add another increment to effectively "back out" purchases by providing new use case for managing refunds.

Chapter Summary

In this chapter, we discussed how all deliverables developed thus far integrate with deliverables developed by other Solution Areas and the current released version of the solution. We discussed techniques for validating the integrated solution.

The next chapter discusses how to deploy the integrated solution, train Users and support staff on the appropriate uses and needs of the integrated solution, and provide ongoing support.

Chapter 7
Implement Solution

Overview

Now that we have built and integrated a solution using iterative and incremental development, we make the solution available to Users.

Implementing the solution means installing the infrastructure architecture and application components, training the final Users, and measuring the effectiveness of the solution against anticipated business value.

This phase occurs once for the final solution and once for every partial solution that is ready to implement. When this phase completes for a partial solution, you either loop back to the Structure Solution phase to structure, build, and integrate another increment, or complete the remaining work for the final solution. If this is the final implementation, you are done! You may loop back to the Chart Solution phase to begin another project, version release, or major enhancement.

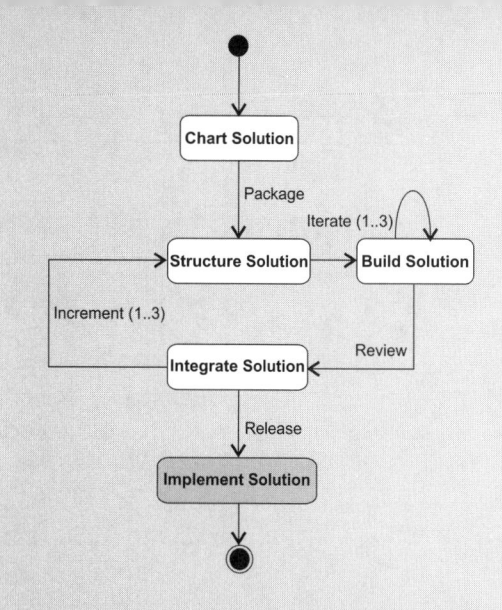

Deliverables:

Application
Change Requests
Implementation Database
Implementation Database Backup Files
Implementation Database Structure
Implementation Environment
Implementation Schedule
Issues List
Post-Implementation Review Document
Project Plan
Risk Assessment
Solution Implementation Confirmation
Training Environment
Training Schedule
Training Test Beds

Activities

Prepare Implementation Environment

During this activity, the project team prioritizes the order of installing the solution components. The project team plans the rollout schedule for incrementally releasing the Application.

Deliverables
Implementation Schedule

Tasks:

Plan Implementation Schedule

Role(s): *Project Manager and Solution Area Managers*

The Project Manager and the Solution Area Managers determine the functionality to release and in which order. They consider geographic location, exposure, business cycle duration, and informational dependency.

> **Tip** Although our approach installs the infrastructure architecture before training, these activities may be reversed. It depends upon the project. If you install the infrastructure architecture before training, you can overcome problems that often occur with new infrastructure architecture. Sometimes, though, you cannot install without affecting the current applications. In that case, you need to train before installing an upgrade to the infrastructure architecture.

Case Study We implemented the first increment of the Manage Location Solution Area immediately after we built it. This enabled the business to begin the cumbersome task of identifying seating structures. Only one location still needs its seating structures defined. Users should complete that definition within one month. Nevertheless, we can still implement the Contract Performance and Reserve Seating solution at the other locations. We just need to plan our

Implementation Schedule to accommodate the definition of the final seating structure for the remaining location.

We want to minimize exposure of problems that may occur with the installation. Since we installed Manage Location at the main ticket office, we again plan to begin the installation there, progressively rolling out the solution to the branch ticket offices.

To ensure quality before rollout, we plan to "test" the solution through one full cycle of a performance beginning with the contract and ending with the actual concert performance. We will install the solution at a branch ticket office only after the business feels comfortable that the solution performs properly.

We do not need to install additional hardware at the main ticket office because this occurred when we installed the Manage Location Solution Area components. We only need to install the Contract Performance Solution Area components following the implementation Deployment Diagram. We will install the Reserve Seating Solution Area components after the Concert Coordinator completes the contract with one performer and establishes ticket prices. Unfortunately, during this time only the main ticket office will have the ability to reserve a seat. Other branches will temporarily need to telephone or fax any purchases made at the remote locations to the main ticket office. Ticket Agents at the main ticket office must enter the purchase for the branch ticket offices.

To minimize the risk of having multiple requests for the same seats, the business allocates seating sections to each location before "opening the doors" for purchasing. This cycle from contract entry to concert performance lasts two weeks.

The day following the performance, we will install the Contract Performance Solution Area and Reserve Seating Solution Area components at the first branch ticket office. To do this, though, we must first install the infrastructure architecture. This installation will "test" the cross-location access of performance information. The main ticket office will set up the second performance so that both the main ticket office and the branch can reserve seating directly. During this cycle, the branch ticket office will set up the third performance, the first at its location. Both offices can reserve seating for performances at each of the two locations. This cycle lasts another three weeks.

When the business feels comfortable with cross-location purchasing, we will roll out the solution to the other locations. Because the last branch will have completed the seating structure definitions by that time, we can add the three remaining branches in succession, one every week.

We allow for one week of training at each location. Training will coincide with the installation of the infrastructure architecture.

Implement Infrastructure Architecture

The Infrastructure Architect implements the planned Implementation Environment and authorizes access to the network for all Users.

Deliverables

Implementation Environment

Tasks:

Implement Supporting Architecture

Role(s): Infrastructure Architect and Database Architect

The Infrastructure Architect installs the hardware and configures system and network software for the Implementation Environment. The Database Architect installs and configures the database management system.

The Infrastructure Architect distributes documentation for operating the system and trains the support staff in troubleshooting. The Infrastructure Architect sets up any automated scheduling and network access permissions.

Case Study We have already installed the hardware, database management system, and operating system at the main ticket office to support the Manage Location Solution.

For the remaining locations, we upgrade the application servers, install the operating system, and upgrade the client machines. For each application server, we verify the connection to the database server at the main ticket office.

Train Users

This is a flurry of activity for the Trainer. Everything the Trainer has prepared since the beginning of the project culminates now. The Trainer prepares the training environment, schedules the participants, and conducts the training sessions.

Deliverables

Training Test Beds
Training Schedule
Training Environment

Tasks:

Schedule Training Participants

Role(s): Project Sponsor, Trainer, and Users

If not already done, the Project Sponsor provides the vision of how this project fits into the enterprise to the Users. The Project Sponsor explains the strategic or tactical plans for the project, explains the overall plans for training and implementation, and obtains User commitment.

The Trainer coordinates the Training Schedule with the Implementation Schedule so that training does not occur too soon or, worse, too late. The Trainer then schedules the Users for the appropriate training session. This begins with a letter to the participant (and their manager) inviting the User to the training session including the location, dress code, and date.

After the Users are scheduled, the Project Sponsor distributes a confirmation letter with any materials to review before the training session. After all of the work putting together the curriculum, this is somehow easily forgotten!

Presenting the course at the right time does wonders for retaining and applying the skills learned. This also enhances job satisfaction by reducing stress associated with changing job content. The increased comfort level gained through practice smooths the cultural transition resulting from technology change. Plan to provide the training within a week or two before the Users begin using the system on a regular basis. This allows Users to apply what they have learned soon after training but allows you time to make ease-of-use improvements that trainees may have found cumbersome.

Case Study We schedule the training to coincide with the Implementation Schedule. The Implementation Schedule allows for one week of training. After refining the training schedule, we find this is excessive. We will begin with one half day at the main ticket offices to train System Operations on support for the two new solutions, Contract Performance and Reserve Seating.

Then, we plan one day for Concert Coordinators to learn how to use the Contract Performance application followed by another day for the Ticket Agents to learn the Reserve Seating application.

At the first branch ticket office, we plan one day for System Operations training followed by one day for Reserve Seating. We then plan to repeat this schedule for the remaining three branch ticket offices.

We mail the schedules and make adjustments based on participant replies. After the final commitment, we distribute the Operations Guide to support staff and user training materials to Ticket Agents and Concert Coordinators.

Implement Deployment Diagram for Training

Role(s): Infrastructure Architect and Database Architect

The Infrastructure Architect installs the network software, database management systems, and middleware software for training. The Infrastructure Architect uniformly configures all software to meet training needs.

The Database Architect installs the training database.

Tip When training at multiple sites, wait until completion of the first training session before installing the infrastructure architecture at the remaining sites. This way, if any changes occur during the initial training session, you do not have to re-install (and retrain!) at the other sites.

Case Study For the Case Study, we have already installed the training machine for CBT use. We connect the training machine to the application server. We install the Contract Performance and Reserve Seating user interface on each of the training machines at the main ticket office. We ensure LAN connection to the application server, connection to the training database, and access to each of the applications and the database.

Prepare for Training Sessions

Role(s): Trainer, Infrastructure Architect, Database Architect, and Object Architect

The Infrastructure Architect clears out the training User accounts and resets passwords. Then the Infrastructure Architect assigns security access permissions for the Trainer and the training class participants, usually a reserved set of User accounts reused for each class session.

The Trainer reviews the planned Training Curriculum with the Database Architect to identify specific data needed before each training session. The Database Architect then creates the reusable test beds and loads the reusable Training Test Beds as needed for training sessions. The Object Architect distributes the correct version of components on the appropriate processors. The Trainer tests the installation by running through the Training Curriculum.

> **Tip** Wait until completing the first training session before distributing training materials to remaining classes.

Case Study We begin by installing the training database on the central database server at the main ticket office. Next, we install the business services layer and data services layer components on the application server and database server, respectively. We assign Ticket Agents access permissions to Reserve Seating components and Concert Coordinators access to Contract Performance components using the operating system file permissions. We install the Training Test Beds and validate the training scenarios to ensure full functionality.

The branch ticket offices requires the same installation excluding the Contract Performance components.

Train Users

Role(s): Trainer and Users

For an instructor-led training session, the Trainer distributes training support materials and other user documentation such as the User

Instructions Guide. Then the Trainer conducts the training session, demonstrates the system, and encourages hands-on participation from the Users.

Alternative styles of training may require different means to conduct the training. The common thread is to ensure that the participants have access to the proper training support materials and a chance to discuss what they have learned with someone knowledgeable in the solution. Conduct measurement of the training before, during, and after to assess comprehension and retention.

Case Study Before beginning training, we distribute the updated Operations Guide to the operations staff. We walk through the Operations Guide, demonstrating instructions on the training machine.

We also distribute updated materials, including the skill assessment, to the Ticket Agents and Concert Coordinators and have these Users perform the curriculum scenarios. These Users also confirm the usability and content of the Information Reference and the User Instructions Guide. The Users also complete the training measurement materials.

Implement Application

The purpose of this activity is to deploy the Application after installing the Implementation Environment using the Deployment Diagram as a guide. One challenge is to maintain the integrity of the current database during implementation.

Deliverables

Implementation Database Backup Files
Implementation Database Structure
Implementation Database
Application

Tasks:

Back Up Implementation Database

Role(s): Database Architect

The Database Architect copies the current structure and content of the database in case the entire installation needs to be backed out.

Case Study We back up the one table, Seat, which we installed with Manage Location. Seat has two new relationships, one with SeatClassification and one with Ticket. Although Seat has no major changes, we take no chances!

Implement Database and Application Components

Role(s): Database Architect, Object Architect, and Infrastructure Architect

The Database Architect updates the current structure and content of the database to support the Application. The Object Architect installs the recent version of Application components. The Infrastructure Architect grants applications access permissions to the appropriate roles.

Case Study We apply the new database structure including Performance, SeatClassification, Purchase, PurchaseItem, and Ticket to the database. We also have a small table, PurchaseOrderNumber, which assigns the next sequential purchase order number. We initialize the sequential number to 100 on this table.

We install the Contract Performance Solution Area components (business service and data service layers) on the proper servers. Then, we install the user interface on one of the user machines. We test that the installation functions properly. After completing a performance contract, we install the Reserve Seating Solution Area components (business service and data service layers) on the servers and its user interface on one user machine. We test one ticket reservation before installing the user interface on the remaining Users' machines. Finally, we assign Ticket Agents access permissions to Reserve Seating components and Concert Coordinators access to Contract Performance components.

We install Reserve Seating components similarly at the other branch locations following the Implementation Schedule.

Back Up Converted Database

Role(s): Database Architect

The Database Architect copies the recently installed structure and content of the database in case updates applied by the recent version of software are working improperly.

> **Case Study** We back up all the tables after the initial database installation at the main ticket office to include those recently installed, as well as Seat.

Confirm Solution Implementation

The project team assesses the effectiveness of the installation against expectations. Users always find bugs and the project team destroys them. Final implementation tuning occurs and the Project Sponsor confirms acceptance of the solution.

Deliverables

Post-Implementation Review Document
Project Plan
Solution Implementation Confirmation
Issues List
Change Requests
Risk Assessment

Tasks:

Support Implementation

Role(s): Project Manager, Database Architect, Object Developer, and Infrastructure Architect

Providing ongoing support is, in itself, an ongoing task. Nevertheless, especially soon after implementation, the Project Manager takes an active role in assuring that the system functions properly. Specifically scheduling a time for dedicated support directly after implementation commits the entire project team to remain on the project to address problems. The Project Manager directs User requests for assistance to the appropriate person for resolution. Once assistance becomes routine, the Project Manager transitions the process to a help desk function.

The Project Manager disposes of system problems as they occur or as Users reveal them. The team prepares for adjustments to ease usage, correct errors, and meet newly discovered business needs.

The Infrastructure Architect monitors the network directly after implementation and periodically thereafter to verify that the recently implemented version is not adversely affecting network communications. The Infrastructure Architect may repartition components to another processor.

The Database Architect monitors the database directly after implementation and periodically thereafter to verify that the database is being accessed as efficiently as possible. The Database Architect adds any necessary indices to improve performance or recommends changes to the source code to reduce data access time.

The Object Architect and the Object Developer apply changes to the Object Models and the Application to enhance performance and quality.

> **Tip** Sometimes the support team includes members that were not part of the development effort. To minimize transition gaps, have the support team actively participate in the final testing tasks.

The ability to repartition your components easily ties directly to the quality of your Class and Component diagrams. If you have modeled discrete, contained objects, you see enormous payoff here! Moving the components around should not force any serious programming changes.

You want to control the release of changes, of course, by prioritizing them with other development. One of the best ways to control this is to measure the change request against the business objectives. The breadth should not stray from the original scope boundaries identified at the start of the project and as refined throughout development. The depth should focus on business value, for example, meeting customer satisfaction and increasing profit.

Obtain Feedback for the Post-Implementation Document

Role(s): Project Manager and Users

The Project Manager interviews the User community to obtain responses on how easy the system is to use, if it includes all required functionality, and if it correctly performs all functions. Additionally, the Project Manager obtains feedback on the quality of support provided when learning to use the system, keeping it operational, and addressing any functional problems. Next, the Project Manager assesses the development process for improvements in quality and reduction in development expense.

A more common name for this task is a "postmortem." However negative that may sound, this is the chance to not only look at what went wrong objectively, but to also look at what went right. Ideally, you conduct this within one month of "completion." Time delays beyond one month make the facts cloudy; doing this earlier makes objectivity difficult.

Do not tie the results of the analysis to someone's performance review. This is not a "witch hunt" but rather an assessment of the process. The goal is to uncover good and bad, not to execute someone for a mistake. Otherwise, after the first public execution, you may find the remaining citizens clam up.

The biggest benefit from conducting this consistently after each project is that you can take what worked and use it on the next project. How else can you expect to get better than by at least recognizing and preventing the same mistakes?

A proper assessment can show many items overlooked in the heat of the battle. For example, someone may have discovered that simply adding a few extra gigabytes of disk space one month earlier would have greatly improved database load testing. Accommodate this on the next project.

Case Study The Ticket Agents like the Application ease of use but find response time slow. The Database Architect determines the database access that builds Performances in Reserve Seating causes the slow response. The Object Developer discovers that the Reserve Seating application retrieves all performances in the function GetPerformances, even after the performance date has passed. The Object Developer adjusts the Application by adding a WHERE PERFORMANCE.PERF_DATE >= DATE() clause to the SQL statement in the entity object and response time improves. Note that the remainder of the Application is unchanged. The object-oriented solution built in the stability to make the change quickly and in only one small place.

Obtain Solution Implementation Confirmation

Role(s): Project Manager and Project Sponsor

The Project Manager and the Project Sponsor measure the success and business value of the implemented solution against the Problem Assessment business objectives identified during the Chart Solution phase. Testing continues even after releasing the version of the solution. The testers, though, are the Users themselves. This becomes the final acceptance of the solution. The project team also finalizes the Issues List, Risk Assessment, and Change Requests.

The Project Sponsor formally acknowledges acceptance of the solution.

Assess Risk

Role(s): Project Manager

The Project Manager summarizes any remaining topics from the final Risk Assessment, as shown in Table 7-1—Implement Solution Risk Assessment, and closes down the project. The Project Manager updates the project plan with final costs.

Table 7-1—Implement Solution Risk Assessment

Category	Item	Action
Strength	The group has truly gelled. The experience of making it (almost) through the first project has them fired up to take on the next one.	Maintain and try to keep the team together; not likely. Discuss with each team member the roles he or she would like to have in future projects. Talk to team about strengths of working together as a team that takes on the next project, reusing the approach learned from this project.
		When the project is officially over, celebrate the achievement with lunch or an after-work gathering.
Weakness	The team has a lot of stress from all of the minor changes. They want to move on to a new project and disown this one.	Keep them involved by having a mini-contest to see who can correct the most application bug fixes in a day. The winner gets to have lunch catered in the next day.

Category	Item	Action
Opportunity	New projects are in the works. Other departments want to participate given the success of this one.	Discuss upcoming project possibilities with executive management. Highlight the team's experience and use this project as a showcase. Use the process assessment as an information source.
Threat	One of the ticket offices is busy with higher than average number of performances; the manager of that office states that her office did not adequately learn the application during formal training. She cannot allow her staff any more time for training right now.	Consider providing one of the more proficient Users as a direct "help line" to this office. If possible, this User could also provide on-site assistance.

Chapter Summary

This chapter presented the final tasks for deploying an object-oriented solution. In this phase, we delivered the developed and purchased products to the enterprise, trained the Users, and transitioned the system to the support staff. We conducted a Post-Implementation Review to use in improving the approach, and managed an orderly shutdown of the project.

Conclusion

Highlights of This Approach

You may discover that this approach provides more information about your system than many others, yet none of the information is superfluous to creating the solution! The consistent focus on deliverables, the application of best practices such as the UML, and the use of an iterative style all contribute to your success. The payoff in terms of reuse and reduced maintenance, though, will not be seen until after the second or third project, as you must first build the foundations of stability and the enterprise view of the business model.

We demonstrated that the Chart Solution phase established the scope and began the initial planning of the project. The Structure Solution phase then packaged the solution into smaller, more manageable Solution Areas that allow for concurrent development. We completed the planning by specifying delivery content with increments, estimating duration, and applying layered refinement using timeboxed iterations. The Build Solution phase used UML object modeling to construct the software applications and created the supporting deliverables for those applications. The Integrate Solution phase merged the Solution Area deliverables with the current released version of the solution and with other Solution Areas. The Implement Solution phase deployed all software and hardware for version release. At the end of each phase, we assessed risk and obtained confirmation that the solution met expectations and continued to provide business value.

We presented our approach to iterative UML development that naturally progresses from a business problem to a technology solution that supports it. The approach included not only the specific object-oriented deliverables in UML notation, but also the major deliverables of the supporting vocations of project management, documentation, training, testing, and infrastructure architecture. The approach required that you base all of these deliverables on the business needs as expressed by the Business Area Experts and the Project Sponsor. We believe this comprehensive team approach will work for you, too.

Selling This Approach to Your Enterprise

What if your enterprise has never heard of iterative development? What if your enterprise has tried but has not succeeded with iterative development? What could you say to encourage your enterprise to try the approach we have outlined in this book? We suggest you attempt this approach with a small proof of concept. Test it with a non-mission-critical project, minimize scope, begin with a non-complex area, and select a team of talented, enthusiastic people.

To test the approach, manage the delivery of the estimated effort using three three-week iterations. Allow at least one week between iterations to assess the outcome of the previous iteration. Identify what worked and what you could do to improve the process. Gather information from the entire team, including the Project Sponsor and Users. This should demonstrate enough proof that this approach produces successful results so that you can continue with another increment of three three-week iterations. Run the proof of concept using sequential increments your first time out. Save concurrent increments and the greater integration challenge after you have gained experience.

It takes time to learn how to contain development breadth and how to focus on the correct level of depth within an iteration. It may take until the third iteration before the team learns how to postpone the less essential until the appropriate iteration. Developers may need to learn how to "stub in" code and refine that code as the team acquires more information. All of this must balance with an understanding of the vision for the entire solution. Do not build a solution "with blinders on." Integrate frequently with other Solution Areas, validate the solution early and often with technical and business people, and consistently respond to risk.

We have found great rewards applying this approach to application development. We encourage you to explore the ideas in this book and remain absolutely inspired and committed to make it happen for you!

Deliverables Glossary

Activity Diagram

The Activity Diagram is a type of Statechart Diagram. It describes a decomposition of action states and transitions within a specific state of the object.

Application

The Application is the software used to run the system that supports the business solution.

Change Requests

The Change Request documents the key elements to manage change. Each change is measured against the potential business value. Typical items to include in a change request are:

1. Description
2. Priority (high, med., low)
3. Benefit
4. Affected deliverables
5. Disposition—identifies the current state of the change request such as Requested, Approved, Denied, or Completed

Class Diagram

The Class Diagram models the business. A Class Diagram contains classes and the relationships between the classes. A class is a template for objects with similar structure, behavior, and relationships. Each class has a name, attributes, and operations. Some object modeling tools use the Class Diagram to generate programming code and database structures.

Class Library Cross Reference

The Class Library is a list of reusable software components. A cross-reference to this library identifies which specific classes within the library a project or Solution Area will use.

Collaboration Diagram

The Collaboration Diagram shows the implementation of a Use Case Scenario or an operation. The Collaboration Diagram filters out the timing or sequential view of the Use Case Scenario to look at the static structure of objects involved in the interaction.

Collaboration Test Beds

Collaboration Test Beds are reusable data for initially loading a database for collaboration testing.

Collaboration Test Plan

The Collaboration Test Plan identifies conditions and expected results for specification, state-based, and structural testing of objects involved in a collaboration. It verifies every path of inter-object behavior, the various combinations of method parameters, and any resulting state transitions.

Component Diagram

The Component Diagram models the software component dependencies including source code, binary code, and executable components. It shows the bundling of software (the packaging) meaningful at compile time.

Cost/Benefit Analysis

The Cost/Benefit Analysis identifies capital expenditures and expenses that the project expects to incur. It also identifies measurable and non-measurable benefits of the project. Costs and measurable benefits provide a quantitative result, the Return On Investment (ROI).

Typical capital expenditures include hardware and software needed. This includes implementation, development, and training environments. Expenses include wages, travel, materials, training, and maintenance fees.

Deployment Diagram

The Deployment Diagram models physical processors and devices, security, and the executable programs that reside on the physical processors. The Deployment Diagram represents the partitioning of packages to their physical location. It details where to allot classes within the system's infrastructure.

Development Environment

The actual hardware, software, and network needed to develop the solution.

Documentation Approach

The Documentation Approach is an overall statement of specific document deliverables produced during the project, their delivery vehicle (for example, hardcopy or online), and the strategy for producing them. It specifies responsibility for documentation changes and ongoing distribution. It also specifies how the distribution of the documentation takes place.

Documentation Distribution Procedure

The Document Distribution Procedure documents steps for distributing online and hardcopy instructions and information references to Users.

Implementation Database

The Implementation Database is the data plus the storage and retrieval mechanism for the implemented application.

Implementation Database Backup Files

Implementation Database Backup Files are archived copies of the Implementation Database. Backup copies generally occur both before and after changes to either the Implementation Database Structure or a mass reload of data.

Implementation Database Structure

The schemas used to create the Implementation Database. They identify standard access paths and ensure integrity of the data.

Implementation Environment

The hardware, software, and network needed to deploy the solution.

Implementation Schedule

The Implementation Schedule provides a plan for deploying the solution to various Users considering geography, security, priority, and dependency. The Implementation Schedule indicates specific dates to deploy the various solution components such as infrastructure architecture, purchased software, developed software, training, and documentation.

Information Reference Guide

The Information Reference Guide guides the User while using the application. It may comprise window- and field-level descriptions, tutorials, and wizards. In addition, the Information Reference Guide assists Users in resolving input errors.

Infrastructure Acquisition Timeline

The Infrastructure Acquisition Timeline establishes dates for purchasing hardware, software, and network resources for development, training, and deployment.

Infrastructure Requirements

The Infrastructure Requirements identifies capacity, concurrency, complexity, and disaster recovery needs that will impact hardware, software, and network resources for development, training, and deployment.

Integration Test Beds

Integration Test Beds contain the reusable data for initially loading a database for integration testing.

Integration Test Plan

The Integration Test Plan identifies conditions and expected results for testing inter-solution messaging and dependencies. Additionally, it applies this plan in a normal operation mode and in an overload mode.

Issues List

The Issues List captures topics that prevent the team from making progress and require resolution from someone outside of the team. Typical items to assist the resolution of an issue include:

1. A statement of the issue in terms of a question asking for resolution
2. The date issue was raised
3. Who raised it
4. The affected deliverables
5. Whom the team feels "owns" the problem (the decision-maker)
6. Who should assist in obtaining the answer
7. A due date
8. Resolution of the issue

Logical Data Model

The Logical Data Model is a normalized view of the database. Typically, this view occurs as a graphical depiction of entities and their relationships derived with data modeling techniques.

Operations Guide

The Operations Guide provides procedures for keeping the system running. This includes system backups, scheduling, and upgrade procedures. It details how to make an archive of the data and components for recovering from disaster.

Post-Implementation Review Document

The Post-Implementation Review Document assesses the quality of the implemented solution.

Problem Assessment

The Problem Assessment is a statement identifying business objectives, business processes, operational problems, and current environment. This represents the intent of the desired business solution, not just the project that builds the technology solution. It provides a boundary for the solution scope and measurement for success.

Project Plan

The Project Plan consists of tasks, roles, time estimates, and deliverables needed to produce a solution.

Project Standards

Project Standards define guidelines for design, development, and communications among a project team. Guidelines include a strategy for documenting object models, coding, testing, error handling, and security.

Risk Assessment

The Risk Assessment is a statement of project challenges categorized into strengths, weaknesses, opportunities, and threats. The risk elements are prioritized based on severity, probability, and time frame. This deliverable is a living document throughout the life of the project.

Security Restrictions

Security Restrictions define the proper levels of access to the system. Security evolves defined by departments and individual Users.

Sequence Diagram

The Sequence Diagram depicts object interaction ordered in time. It identifies the messages exchanged between objects in response to an event and the messaging sequence.

Software Distribution Procedure

The Software Distribution Procedure details how to install software components. This includes version enhancements of both developed and purchased software.

Solution Area Classes/Implementation Classes Matrix

The Solution Area Classes/Implementation Classes Matrix cross-references change from the Solution Area Classes to the Implementation Classes. It identifies enhancements and extensions to the Implementation Classes.

Solution Area Database

The Solution Area Database is the data used to develop a Solution Area. It controls the data content and isolates this Solution Area from others.

Solution Area Database Structure

The schemas used to create the Solution Area Database. They identify standard access paths and ensure integrity of the data.

Solution Area Scope Statement

The Solution Area Scope Statement delimits the boundaries of the Solution Area derived from the Use Case Diagram and Class Diagram. It uses both in conjunction to prevent functional decomposition and minimize coupling between classes. It specifies the content of each increment and the sequence of development of all the increments. After the Structure Solution phase, it contains the scope and strategy for building an increment through iteration.

Solution Build Confirmation

The Solution Build Confirmation determines the decision to proceed to the next iteration of the Build Solution phase when the solution meets acceptable validation requirements.

Solution Implementation Confirmation

The Solution Implementation Confirmation is the agreement that the solution meets expectations and provides business value.

Solution Integration Confirmation

The Solution Integration Confirmation determines if the integrated solution meets acceptable validation requirements and development can proceed to the Implement Solution phase. It signifies that the project team may release the current version of the solution for implementation.

Solution Strategy Confirmation

The Solution Strategy Confirmation determines the decision to proceed to the Structure Solution phase. The decision rests on whether the project has the appropriate strategy in terms of scope, use, and support.

Solution Structure Confirmation

The Solution Structure Confirmation determines the decision to proceed to the Build Solution phase. It confirms the content of each Solution Area as well as the strategy for development within the Solution Areas.

Statechart Diagram

The Statechart Diagram models the dynamic state of an object. The Statechart Diagram consists of states, actions, activities, and transitions within one specific object. It identifies the events that cause an object to transition from one state to another.

Third-Party Product Evaluation

Third-Party Product Evaluation documents the formal findings of third-party product offerings. It includes required functionality, a listing of strengths and weaknesses of each product evaluated, and a recommendation for purchase.

Training Approach

The Training Approach identifies the types and number of users, any previous or in-process training efforts, and the potential number of geographic locations. It also outlines the measurement style of training success.

Training Curriculum

The Training Curriculum details the courseware or syllabus for training Users. It identifies the level of training required and the factors for focusing training to the type of Users who will access the system.

Training Delivery Mechanism

The Training Delivery Mechanism defines the training method for using the system. This includes the type and style of information to present, presentation dynamics, the "levels" of User comfort with computing tools, and the potential cultural impact caused by the new environment. It also specifies the means of presenting the instruction (such as video, computer-based training, instructor-led, and lab exercises).

Training Environment

The Training Environment consists of all hardware and software dedicated to training. Software typically includes the current release of the solution and accompanying database.

Training Schedule

The Training Schedule specifies dates, times, and participants requiring training for the current release of the solution.

Training Support Materials

Training Support Materials include all software, data, and workbooks needed for training. Training Support Materials support the curriculum's delivery requirements.

Training Test Beds

Training Test Beds contain reusable sample data used to load a training database.

Use Case Diagram

The Use Case Diagram documents external interactions with the system to show its "use." It graphically depicts use cases and the actors that participate in them with an accompanying textual description.

Use Case Scenarios

A Use Case Scenario is a description of the sequential steps detailing the path of events through a use case instance. There is at least one core scenario for each use case. The core scenario details the most commonly traversed path through the use case. Additional scenarios may also represent exceptions and alternative paths that are relatively minor in complexity.

Use Case Test Beds

Use Case Test Beds contain reusable sample data for testing Use Case Scenarios.

Use Case Test Plan

The Use Case Test Plan identifies conditions and expected results for verifying Use Case Scenarios. The purpose of a Use Case Test Plan is two-fold. First, it provides a framework for recognizing simple measures to test use case validity and completeness by considering ranges of values, volumes, and sequencing. It establishes the solution's tie to the business throughout development. It forms the basis for the other testing mechanisms (collaboration, integration, etc.). Second, the Use Case Test Plan assists in identifying missing scenarios, a completeness check all by itself. Business Area Experts are the primary source as they know the ins and outs of the business problem and have day-to-day experience with situations to accommodate.

User Instructions Guide

The User Instructions Guide is a reference document for understanding the common functions and workflow within the Application.

Bibliography

Advanced Concepts Center of Lockheed Martin Corporation. *Object-Oriented Analysis Using UML,* Volume 1 of 1, N.p., n.d.

Boehm, Barry W. "A Spiral Model of Software Development and Enhancement." *IEEE Comp. 21 (5)*, May 1988.

Boisvert, Jean. "OO Testing in the Ericsson Pilot Project." *Object Magazine*, July 1997.

Booch, Grady, James Rumbaugh, Ivar Jacobson. *The Unified Modeling Language User Guide.* Reading, MA: Addison Wesley Longman, 1999.

Chidamber and Kemerer, as cited in Keyes, J. "New Metrics Needed For Software Generation." *Software Magazine*, May 1992.

Coad, Peter, and Edward Yourdon. *Object-Oriented Analysis*. Englewood Cliffs, NJ: Yourdon Press, 1991.

Cusack, Sally. "Dev Trends: Snapshots from the Web front—developers find performance counts." *Application Development Trends*, September 1997.

Gupta, Sunny, and John Scumniotales. *Integrating Object and Relational Technologies*. http://www.vigortech.com/white/htm, N.d.

Harel, David. "Statecharts: A Visual Formalism for Complex Systems." *Science of Computer Programming* Vol. 8, 1987.

Jacobson, Ivar, Magnus Christerson, Patrik Jonsson, and Gunnar Övergaard. *Object-Oriented Software Engineering: A Use Case Driven Approach*. Wokingham, England: Addison Wesley, 1992.

Martin, James. *Cybercorp: The New Business Revolution*. New York: Amacom, 1996.

_____. *Information Engineering: A Trilogy*. Englewood Cliffs, NJ: Prentice Hall, 1989.

_____. *Information Engineering Book I: Introduction*. Englewood Cliffs, NJ: Prentice Hall, 1989.

_____. *Information Engineering Book II: Planning and Analysis*. Englewood Cliffs, NJ: Prentice Hall, 1990.

McConnell, Steve. *Code Complete: A Practical Handbook of Software Construction*. Microsoft Press, 1993.

Meyer, Bertrand. *Object-Oriented Software Construction*. Upper Saddle River, NJ: Prentice Hall PTR, 1997.

Page-Jones, Meilir. *What Every Programmer Should Know About Object-Oriented Design*. New York: Dorset House Publishing, 1995.

Patel, Ameet. "Internet Development: Web-object middleware integration and architecture." *Application Development Trends*, June 1997.

Payne, Jeffery E., Roger T. Alexander, and Charles D. Hutchinson. "Design-for-Testability For Object-Oriented Software." *Object Magazine*, July 1997.

Putnam, Lawrence H., and Ware Myers. *Measures for Excellence: Reliable Software On Time, Within Budget*. Englewood Cliffs, NJ: Yourdon Press, 1992.

Rational Software Corporation, et al. *UML Notation Guide version 1.1*. N.p. September 1, 1997.

_____, et al. *UML Semantics version 1.1*. N.p. September 1, 1997.

_____, et al. *UML Summary version 1.1*. N.p. September 1, 1997.

Rumbaugh, James, Ivar Jacobson, Grady Booch. *The Unified Modeling Language Reference Manual*. Reading, MA: Addison Wesley Longman, 1999.

Stonebraker, Michael. "Architectures for Object-Relational DBMSs: The Good, the Bad, and the Ugly." In *DCI's Database & Client/Server World Conference Proceedings*, Vol. II, Chicago, IL, December 11, 1996.

Taylor, David A. *Object-Oriented Technology: A Manager's Guide.* Reading, Massachusetts: Addison Wesley, 1992.

The American Heritage® Dictionary of the English Language, Third Edition. Houghton Mifflin Company, 1992.

Winter, Richard. "Object Technology Meets VLDB." *Database Programming and Design*, December 1996.

Index

360 guideline, 40
80 percent rule, 38, 101

A

abstraction, 8, 31, 33
access permissions, 128
action state, 22-23, 159
activity, 23
Activity Diagram, 22, 59
    building, 158-160
aggregation, 9, 16-17, 104
    composite, 17
aggregation class, 104
application, 34
Application,
    building, 180-195
    implementing, 256-258
    modifying, 231
    testing, 246
approach, tailoring, 84-85
architecture, 3-4
    implementing, 252
association class, 16
associations, 14, 16, 68
associations multiplicity, 102-103
assumptions, 97
asynchronous implementation, 4
asynchronous message, 18
attribute properties, 16
attributes, 101-102

B

backup, 116
black box testing, 181
Build Solution phase, 58-59
    overview, 135-136
Business Area Expert, 53-54
business services layer, 160, 179

C

calling dependency, 25
case study summary, 63-65

change control management, 46-47
change requests,
    example, 106, 202
    preparing, 201-203
Chart Solution phase, 58-59
    overview, 61
class, 8, 16
    aggregation, 104
    association, 16
    control, 161
    entity, 152, 179-180
    inherited, 104
    interface, 148
Class Diagram, 15-17, 59
    assessing, 160-167
    creating, 72-74
    integrating, 225-230
    structuring, 100-108
class invariant, 170
class library, using, 108-109
classes,
    defining, 101-102
    identifying, 101
    leveraging, 145
    structuring, 96-109
client/server architecture, 3
cohesion, 79, 162-163
    measuring, 163-164
Collaboration Diagram, 20-22, 59
    building, 156-158
Collaboration Test Bed, creating, 182
Collaboration Test Plan,
    creating, 181-182
    example, 182
    executing, 195
collaboration testing, 181
comments, 13
communicates association, 14
compiler dependency, 25
Component Diagram, 24-25, 59, 118
    building, 168-169
    enhancing, 232-233

components, 24
composite aggregation, 17
constraints, 13
control class, 161
control object, 6, 11
controlling object, 143
cost/benefit analysis, 90
    models, 89-90
    preparing, 88-90
coupling, 79, 162
    measuring, 163
Critical Path Method, 84

D

data replication, 236
data services layer, 160, 179-180
data storage, 172
database, 172
    backing up, 256-257
    object, 172
    object relational, 172-173
    relational, 172, 176
Database Architect, 54
database components, implementing, 257
database structure,
    integrating, 230
    refining, 171-180
deliverables, 34-35
    characteristics of, 34
    validating, 49
dependencies, 25
Deployment Diagram, 25-26, 60
    creating, 233-240
    developing, 118-122
    implementing, 128, 254-255
    integrating, 233-240
development,
    incremental, 35
    iterative, 35-41
    object-oriented, 29-34
development tasks, 58
diagrams, refining, 232-241
Document Architect, 54
documentation, 48
    assessing, 200
    building, 195-198
    integrating, 241-242
    standardizing, 242
    structuring, 109-111
documentation approach, establishing, 74-75
documentation components, building, 195-198
domain objects, 72

E

e-commerce, 4
encapsulation, 8-9, 31
Enterprise Agent, 52
entity class, 152, 179-180
entity object, 6, 10, 152
Entity/Relationship Diagram, *see* ERD
ERD, 174
exception handling, 214
exceptions, 137-138
extends association, 14
extends relationship, 68
extends use case, 68, 97-98

F

facilitation, 42-44
Facilitator, 43
feedback, obtaining, 259-260

G

generalization, 103
gray box testing, 181
grouping, 148

I

identity, 176
Implement Solution phase, 58, 60
    overview, 249
implementation
    environment, 250-252
    schedule, 250-252
    support, 258-259
incremental development, 35
increment, 35, 38-40, 80-81, 130
    second, 216-220
infrastructure, 48-49
    requirements, 115-117
infrastructure acquisition timeline,
    establishing, 125-126

Infrastructure Architect, 54-55
infrastructure architecture,
    implementing, 252
    options, 76-78
    structuring, 113-129
inheritance, 9, 31, 103-104, 177
inheritance association, 17
inherited class, 104
instance, 8
Integrate Solution phase, 58, 60
    overview, 223-224
integration environment, preparing, 245
Integration Test Beds, building, 245
Integration Test Plan,
    creating, 243-245
    example, 244-245
integration testing, 243-244
interface class, 148
interface object, 6, 10
Internet, 4-6
issues, 47
issues list example, 66, 105, 131-132, 141-142, 229
iteration, 19, 35, 204-205
    refining, 129-130
    second, 205-214
    sizing, 130
    third, 214-216
iterative approach, 35-41, 87, 136 *see also* iterative development
    advantages of, 36
iterative development, 37, 264 *see also* iterative approach

L

legacy systems, 237
link associations, 103
link attribute, 16
logical data model, creating, 173-175

M

message, 139
    types, 18
method, 139
methods, building, 183-194
multiplicity, 16, 176

associations, 102-103

N

needs test, 34
normal forms, 162-163
n-tier architecture, 5

O

object, 8
    identity, 176
    modeling, 6-7
    state, 3-4
    types, 10-11
Object Architect, 55
object database, 172
Object Developer, 55
object relational database, 172-173
object-oriented concepts, 8-11
object-oriented database, advantages of, 172-173
object-oriented development, 29-34
objects,
    control, 6, 11
    controlling, 143
    entity, 6, 10, 152
    interface, 6, 10
    source, 143
    system interface, 10
    target, 143
    user interface, 10
operation, 139
    properties, 16
Operations Guide, building, 240-241

P

Package Diagram, 26-27
packaging, 26
partitioning, 4, 234
    strategy, 234-237
performance, 236
    improving, 162
persistence, 171
PERT scheduling, 84
polymorphism, 9-10, 31
postconditions, 97
preconditions, 97

problem assessment, defining, 62-66
project, 34
    management, 44-46
Project Manager, 44, 55
project scope, 62
    establishing, 62-78
Project Sponsor, 55
project standards, establishing, 78
project team roles, 52-56
properties, 16
prototyping, 146-148

R
recovery, 116
recursion, 18
refinement, 97, 129-130
regression testing, 244
relational database, 172, 176
relational identity, 176
relationships, 16, 68
replication, 236
requirements testing, 244
resources, allocating, 86-88
Return On Investment, 88-90
reuse, 8, 33
risk, assessing, 91-93, 132, 204, 246-247, 261-262
risk assessment example, 93, 133, 204, 247, 261-262
ROI, *see* Return On Investment
roles, 52-56
    assigning, 86-88

S
scheduling, 40-41, 85-87
scope, 62
    establishing, 62-78
    testing, 50
second increment, 216-220
second iteration, 205-214
security, 127
    restrictions, 127-128
Sequence Diagram, 17-19, 59
    building, 142-145
simple aggregation, 16

software distribution procedure, establishing, 126-127
solution,
    confirming, 200-204
    modeling, 136-171
    packaging, 78-90
    testing, 243-246
Solution Area
    database structure, 175-180
    scope statement, 79-83
Solution Areas, 44
    integrating, 225-231
solution implementation, confirming, 258-262
solution integration, confirming, 246-247
solution iterations, building, 204-220
solution strategy, confirming, 90-93
solution structure, confirming, 131-133
source object, 143
specialization, 103
spiral approach, 36
stability, 38
    achieving, 38-39, 200-201
state, 19, 154
    action, 22-23, 159
    maintaining, 3-5
    wait, 159
Statechart Diagram, 19-20, 59, 104
    building, 153-156
STEM approach, 50-51
stereotypes, 13
stopping rules, 39
stored procedures, 177-178
stress testing, 244
Structure Solution phase, 58-59
    overview, 95-96
SWOT analysis, 91-93
synchronous implementation, 3
synchronous message, 18
system, 34
system interface object, 10

T
target object, 143
tasks, estimating, 85-86
test case, 181

testability, 183
testing, 33, 49-51, 181
    black box, 181
    collaboration, 181
    gray box, 181
    integration, 243-244
    regression, 244
    requirements, 244
    scope, 50
    STEM approach, 50-51
    stress, 244
    white box, 181
thin client/fat server, 4
third iteration, 214-216
third-party software, evaluating, 122-125
three-tier architecture, 4
three-tier partitioning, 6
timebox, 37
timeboxing, 37-38, 40
traceability, 11
Trainer, 47-48, 55-56
training, 47-48, 129, 253-256
    integrating, 242-243
    scheduling, 253-254
    structuring, 111-113
training approach, establishing, 75-76
training curriculum, 198-199
    example, 199
training sessions, preparing for, 255
transition, 20
triggers, 177-178
two-tier architecture, 3

U

UML, 11
Unified Modeling Language, *see* UML
use case, 14
    example, 98, 100, 196-197
    structuring, 96-109
    testing, 169
Use Case Description, 59
    example, 98, 100
    refining, 97-100
Use Case Diagram, 13-15, 59
    creating, 66-72
Use Case Scenario, 14-15, 49, 59
    building, 137-142
    validating, 200-201
use case summaries, example, 70-71
Use Case Test Beds, creating, 200
Use Case Test Plan,
    creating, 169-171
    example, 170-171
User, 56
user interface applications, prototyping, 146-153
user interface object, 10
user services layer, 160
uses association, 14
uses relationship, 68

V

Visual C++ 6.0 code, 184-194, 209-211, 213-216

W

wait state, 159
waterfall approach, 36
white box testing, 181
wrapping, 178

Other Books from Wordware Publishing, Inc.

Communications/General

The Complete Communications Handbook
Demystifying ATM/ADSL
Demystifying EDI
Demystifying ISDN
Demystifying TCP/IP (3rd Ed.)
Demystifying Virtual Private Networks
Developing Internet Information Services
Digital Imaging in C and the World Wide Web
Learn Advanced Internet Relay Chat
Learn Internet Relay Chat (2nd Ed.)
Learn Microsoft Exchange Server 5.5 Core Technologies
Writing and Publishing with Your PC

Applications/Operating Systems

Learn ACT! 3.0 for Windows 95
Learn ACT! 3.0-4.0 for the Advanced User
Learn AutoCAD in a Day
Learn AutoCAD 12 in a Day 
Learn AutoCAD LT 97 for Windows 95/NT
Learn AutoCAD LT 98
Learn Linux 3-D Graphics Programming
Learn Lotus 1-2-3 Rel. 5 for Windows in a Day
Learn Microsoft Access 2.0 for Windows in a Day
Learn Microsoft Access 7.0 for Windows 95 in a Day
Learn Microsoft Access 97/2000 Programming for the Advanced User
Learn Microsoft Excel 7.0 for Windows 95 in a Day
Learn Microsoft Excel 2000 VBA Programming
Learn Microsoft FrontPage 97
Learn Microsoft Office 95
Learn Microsoft Office 97
Learn Microsoft Office 2000
Learn Microsoft PowerPoint 7.0 for Windows 95 in a Day

Applications/Operating Systems

Learn Microsoft Publisher 2000 for the Advanced User
Learn Microsoft Word 6.0 for Windows in a Day
Learn Microsoft Word 7.0 for Windows 95 in a Day
Learn Microsoft Works 3.0 for Windows in a Day
Learn Peach Tree Accounting
Learn P-CAD Master Designer
Learn Red Hat Linux Server
Learn Red Hat Linux OS Tips
Learn ShapeSheet Programming for the Visio 2000 Masters
Learn Visio 5.0
Learn Visio 5.0 for the Advanced User 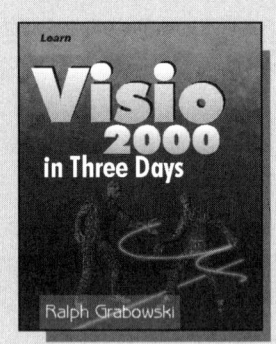
Learn Visio 2000
Learn Visio 2000 for the Advanced User
Learn Visio 2000 for the Masters
Learn Visio 2000 in Three Days
Learn Windows 95 in a Day
Learn WordPerfect 5.2 for Windows in a Day
Learn WordPerfect 6.0 for Windows in a Day
Visio 4 for Everyone
Windows NT Server 4.0/2000: Testing and Troubleshooting
Advanced 3-D Game Programming with DirectX 7.0
Collaborative Computing with Delphi 3
CORBA Developer's Guide with XML
Data Warehousing with MS SQL 7.0
Delphi Developer's Guide to OpenGL

Programming

Delphi Graphics and Game Programming Exposed! with DirectX 7.0
Developer's Guide to Computer Game Design
Developer's Guide to Delphi Troubleshooting
Developer's Guide to HP Printers
Developer's Guide to Lotus Notes and Domino 5.0

Visit our web site at **www.wordware.com**

Programming

Developer's Guide to Oracle Tools
Developer's Workshop to COM and ATL 3.0
Developer's Workshop to COM+
Developer's Workshop to COM and Visual Basic 6.0
Developing Enterprise Applications with PowerBuilder 6.0
Developing Utilities in Visual Basic 4.0
The HTML Example Book 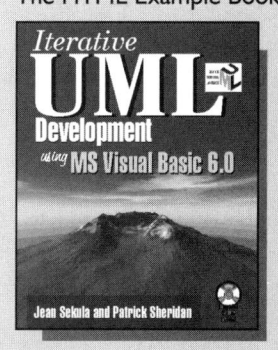
Iterative UML Development using Visual Basic 5.0
Iterative UML Development using Visual Basic 6.0
Iterative UML Development using Visual C++ 6.0
Learn ActiveX Development using Visual Basic 5.0
Learn ActiveX Development using Visual C++ 6.0
Learn ActiveX Scripting with Microsoft Internet Explorer 4.0
Learn ActiveX Template Library Development with Visual C++ 5.0
Learn Advanced HTML 4.0 with DHTML
Learn Advanced JavaScript
Learn Advanced JavaScript Programming
Learn C in Three Days
Learn C++ in Three Days
Learn Encryption Techniques with BASIC and C++
Learn Graphics File Programming with Delphi 3
Learn Microsoft Active Desktop Programming using Windows 98
Learn Microsoft Transaction Server Development using Visual C++ 6.0
Learn Microsoft Visual Basic in Three Days
Learn the MFC C++ Classes
Learn Object Pascal
Learn OLE DB Development with Visual C++ 6.0
Learn Oracle 8i
Learn Pascal

Programming

Learn Pascal in Three Days
Learn Personal Oracle 8.0 with Power Objects 2.0 
Learn SQL
Learn Visual Basic 5.0 in Three Days
Lotus Notes Developer's Guide
Nathan Wallace's Delphi 3 Example Book
Practical Guide to SGML Filters
Practical Guide to SGML/XML Filters
Practical Guide to XML
Real-Time Strategy Game Programming using DirectX
Squirrel's Computer Game Programming in C
Tomes of Delphi: Algorithms and Data Structures
Tomes of Delphi: Win32 Database Developer's Guide
Tomes of Delphi: Win32 Graphic Programming
Tomes of Delphi: Win32 Multimedia API
Tomes of Delphi 3: Win32 Core API
Tomes of Delphi 3: Win32 Graphical API
The Visual Basic 4.0 Example Book
The WordBasic Example Book

Networking/Internet

CORBA Networking with Java
DCOM Networking with Visual J++
Learn Internet Publishing with Microsoft Publisher 97
Learn Internet Publishing with Microsoft Publisher 98
Learn Lotus Domino
Practical Guide to Intranet Client-Server Applications using the Web

Visit our web site at **www.wordware.com**

VISIO TOOLS FOR UML DIAGRAMMING AND MODELING

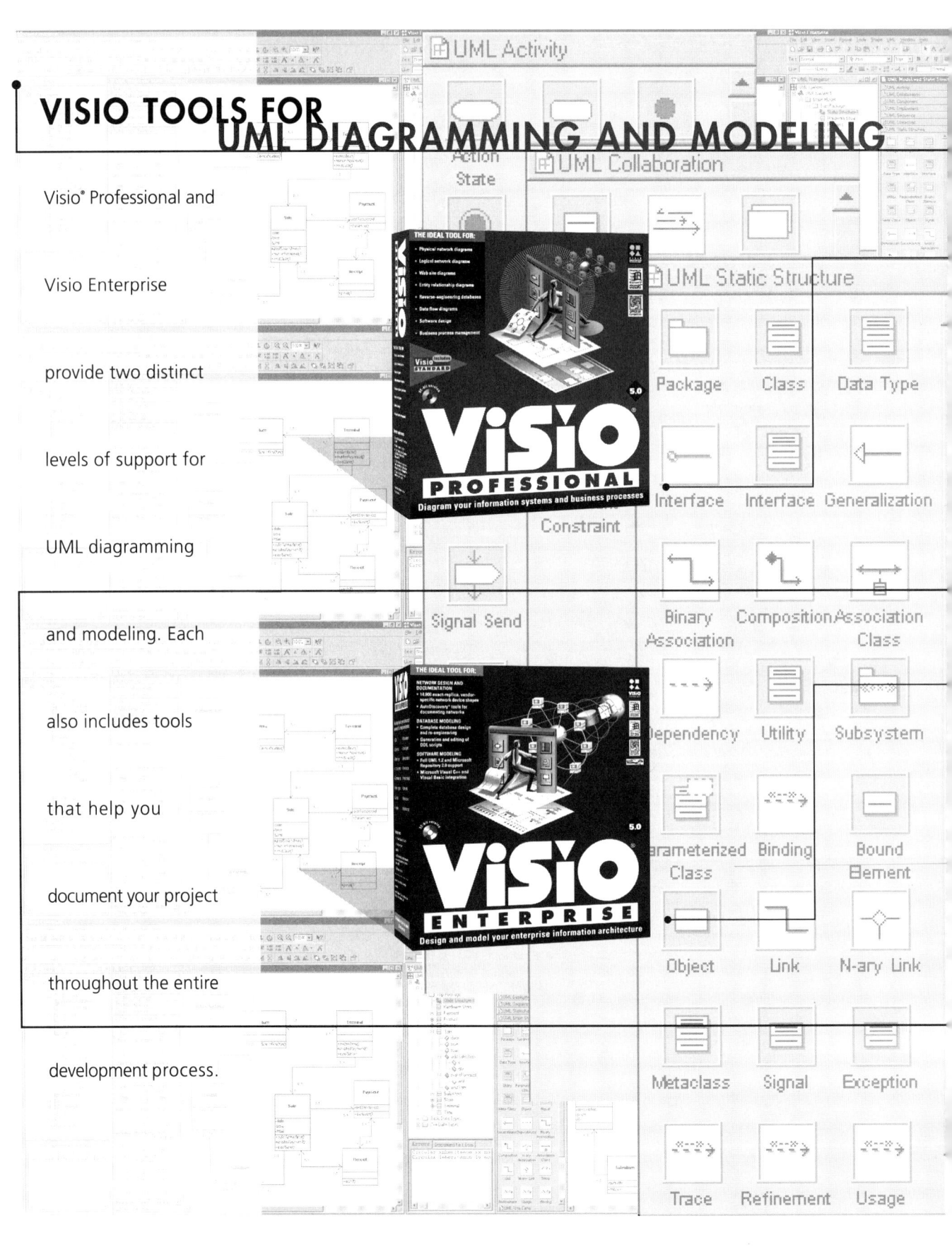

Visio® Professional and Visio Enterprise provide two distinct levels of support for UML diagramming and modeling. Each also includes tools that help you document your project throughout the entire development process.

Check out the free 60-day test drive of Visio Professional and Visio Enterprise included with this title!

Visio Professional 5.0 is ideal for quickly diagramming and documenting software applications using UML static structure diagrams.

Visio Professional 5.0 features:
- UML 1.0 support
- Basic error checking
- UML Help
- Microsoft Repository 1.0 integration

Visio Professional also includes tools for creating database documentation, project timelines, data flow diagrams, flowcharts, Web site diagrams, network documentation, and more. For more information about Visio Professional, visit *www.visio.com/products/professional*.

Visio Enterprise 5.0 includes all of the features of Visio Professional, plus enhanced UML notation support and integration with Microsoft Visual Studio.

Visio Enterprise 5.0 features:
- Support for all UML 1.2 diagram types
- UML Navigator
- Dynamic error checking
- Reverse engineering of Microsoft Visual Basic and Visual C++ code
- Microsoft Repository 2.0 integration

Visio Enterprise also includes tools for database design, generation, and synchronization; network AutoDiscovery™ technology; and a complete library of networking shapes. For more information about Visio Enterprise, visit *www.visio.com/products/enterprise*.

Join the **Visio Registered Developer Network** free of charge, and gain access to special resources on the site, such as tools and samples with commented code, online seminars, and developer training sessions. The **Visio Registered Developer Network** includes information about Visio development tools and the Visio platform to help you build custom Visio solutions. Check it out at **www.visio.com/vdn**.

©1999 Visio Corporation. All rights reserved. Visio, AutoDiscovery, and the VRDN logo are trademarks or registered trademarks of Visio Corporation in the United States and/or other countries.

CD-ROM Contents

The accompanying CD-ROM includes:

1. Case Study Source code (requires Microsoft Visual C++ 6.0) for all the examples discussed in the book. The main workspace is named TicketTakerApp.dsw; in addition, there is one workspace (.DSW) file for each of the service layers—TicketTaker.dsw (user layer), TicketTakerBusLayer.dsw (business layer), and TicketTakerDataLayer.dsw (data layer). The user layer forms the executable, while the other two are dynamic-link libraries. To view the source code, open the main workspace. Alternatively, you may open each .DSW project in a separate Visual C++ 6.0 session.

2. Microsoft Project 98 Template Project Plan of the phases, activities, and tasks within the approach. To use, open sample.mpp from the MS Project Plan folder using Microsoft Project 98.

3. 60-day test drives of Visio® Professional and Visio® Enterprise, version 5.0. Visio provides drawing support for all UML diagrams, source code reverse engineering, and a model syntax checker. It has the complete UML Specification online as well.

To use the Visio files on this CD, you must be running Windows 95, 98, or NT 4.0. A web page should automatically open when the CD is loaded. If it does not, choose Start|Run. Enter *d:\home.html*, where *d* is your CD-ROM drive. Click OK to bring up the web page.

To use the Source Code or MS Project Plan files, exit the web page and use Explorer to open the appropriate folder.

Notice: Opening the CD-ROM package makes this book non-returnable.